THE COMPLETE BOOK OF

PREGNANCY

& BABYCARE

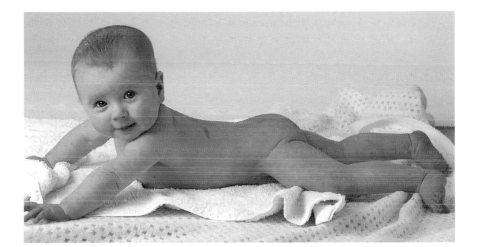

THE COMPLETE BOOK OF
PREGNANCY
& BABYCARE

ALISON MACKONOCHIE

LORENZ BOOKS
LONDON • NEW YORK • SYDNEY • BATH

A very special thank you to Robin for his unfailing support, to Lucy and Kate, without whom
we would not have had Christmas, and to Dominic for just being himself.

First published in 1996 by Lorenz Books

Lorenz Books is an imprint of
Anness Publishing Limited
Boundary Row Studios
1 Boundary Row
London SE1 8HP

© Anness Publishing Limited 1996

This edition distributed in Canada by
Book Express, an imprint of
Raincoast Book Distribution Limited

A CIP catalogue record for this book is available from the
British Library.

ISBN 1-85967-089-X

Publisher: Joanna Lorenz
Project Editors: Casey Horton, Nicky Thompson
Editor: Elizabeth Longley
Designer: Bobbie Colgate Stone
Special Photography: Alistair Hughes
Additional Photography: Carin Simon
Illustrations: Ian Sidaway
Hair and Make-up: Bettina Graham

Printed and bound in Hong Kong

ACKNOWLEDGEMENTS

The author and publisher would like to thank the many individuals
who helped in the creation of this book. In particular thanks are due
to Bobbie Brown, Elsa Jacobi, Pauline Richardson, Mary Lambert and
Jane Barret. Many thanks also go to everyone who modelled for special
photography: Yvonne Adams and Martin; Ruth Auber and Bethany;
Jo Bates and Lois; Amanda Bennet-Jones; Kim, Neil and Andrew
Brown; Christine Clarke; Jacqueline Clarke and Cassia; Jocelyn
Cusack and Beth; Sam Dyas and Colt; Patricia Gannon and Matthew;
Nici Giles and Fergus; Yiota Gillis and Cameron; Sandra Hadfield and
Annie; Louise Henriques and Joshua; Lynette Jones and Hugh and
Rhys; Karen, Mark, Megan and Robert Lambert; Claire Lehain and
Harriet; Lavinia Mainds and Polly; Pippa Milton and Oliver; Philippa
Madden and Inca; Jackie Norbury; Jess Presland; Katey Steiner;
Saatchi Spracklen and Niamh; Sophie Trotter and Archie; Josephine
Whitfield and Lily May; Lucinda Whitrow and Hector. Thanks also to
companies who loaned items and photographs: Blooming Marvellous
Ltd (pages 38-39), Boots Children's Wear and Toys, Fisher-Price,
Littlewoods Home Shopping, Maclaren Ltd and Mattel UK Ltd.

Picture acknowledgements: **Bubbles** 76; /Jacquie Farrow, 66, 211;
/Julie Fisher 7, /Nikki Gibbs 14 b, 78, /Paul Howard 73 t, /Julia
Martin 19 b, 83 (all 3), /S.Price 182 b; /Loisjoy Thurston 1, 27 b, 45 t
and r 50, 62, 79, 172, 182 t, 202, 203; /Ian West 75 b, 207 br; /J.
Woodcock 27 t, 76; /Richard Yard 67; **Lupe Cunha** 16, 17, 19 t and
b, 21, 24, 25 b, 31 t and b, 37 t, 50, 51 t, 59 bl and t, 59 r, 71 t, 80,
81 r and tr, 84, 85, 170 r; **PR Communications** 52 (box); **Science
Photo Library**/BSIP Bajande 87 b; /Mark Clarke 58, 59 t, 70, 71 b,
72, 73 b, 77 r, 86 t and b, 87 t and b, 179; /Custom Medical Stock 59
t, 87 t; /Simon Fraser 45, 71 b, 179 b; /Will & Deni McIntyre 22 t,
23 b; /Joseph Mettis 70; /Petit Format/Nestle 14 t; /Chris Priest 34;
37; /Richard G Rawlins 13 tl, 22 t, 23 b, 33, 34; /Pascale
Roche/Petit Format 86 t and b; /James Stevenson 18 br, 33 b, 45 bl;
/Ron Sutherland 77 r; /Sheila Terry 19 t, 63, 81 bl; /Jonathan Watts
58; **Carin Simon** 78 r. (**Key**: b – bottom, bl – bottom left, br – bottom right, r – right, t – top, tl – top left, tr – top right).
The publishers have tried to credit all agencies and photographers
whose pictures appear in this book and apologize for any omissions.

CONTENTS

INTRODUCTION

BEING A PARENT is the most important and responsible role you will ever have. And it begins long before the birth of your child. By making sure that you and your partner are both healthy before conception, you will be giving your baby the best possible start in life. Once you have conceived, and your pregnancy is confirmed, you will want to do everything you can to ensure that you are doing the best for your developing baby.

Understanding what is happening during your pregnancy and how your baby is developing will help you to cope with both the physical and emotional changes that you are likely to experience. Part One of this book guides you through your pregnancy. To keep things simple, a new topic is discussed for each week of your pregnancy. Do remember, though, that every pregnancy is different, and many of the topics mentioned will be relevant throughout the baby's development and not just for the week in question.

Thankfully the days when you had to give birth lying in bed, on your back, are gone. Today, you and your partner can usually choose where and how you give birth. Although this is good news, you may find it difficult to know what would be best for you. Once you know about the available options you can then make informed decisions.

As the end of the nine months draws near, it is natural to be concerned about the approaching birth. Sometimes fear about how you will cope can overshadow what is the most miraculous event you are likely ever to encounter. By preparing yourself for labour and understanding what will happen, both you and your partner will be able to make the most of this unique experience.

Once your baby is born, your role as a parent begins in earnest. You are now responsible for the care and well-being of this person. This can seem rather daunting at first as your baby will expect you to be on call whenever he wakes. Coping with tiredness, a completely new routine and the demands of a new baby can be overwhelming so it is most important that you look after yourself.

As time goes by, you will develop a routine that suits you both but at first you may need some help. Part Two guides you through the necessary daily babycare routines. So, whether you are concerned about feeding, bathing or nappy changing, you'll find help and practical advice in this section. Having a baby isn't all hard work and, if you use the time you spend each day on babycare to play and get to know your baby, you'll find that even the chores will be a pleasure!

Your baby's health and development are extremely important and as a parent you will be concerned about what to do if your child is ill or injured in any way. The chapters on first aid and illnesses are designed to be a quick and easy reference guide to help you to cope with emergencies and know when you should call the doctor. When your baby celebrates his first birthday you will look back and marvel at how much he has learned in this first year. Part Three explains, month by month, how your baby will progress during the first twelve months. Do remember that this is only a guide and that every child develops at his own rate.

So that you will be able to help and encourage your child, the final chapters look in more detail at the development of your child's senses and explain how he learns to talk and walk. Play and social behaviour are also an integral part of your child's development.

As a mother of three children I know that, more than anything else, during my pregnancies and their babyhood, I wanted to be reassured that I was doing everything "right". I hope that you will get this reassurance from my book and that you will find it a helpful companion during your pregnancy and your child's first year.

Alison Mackonochie

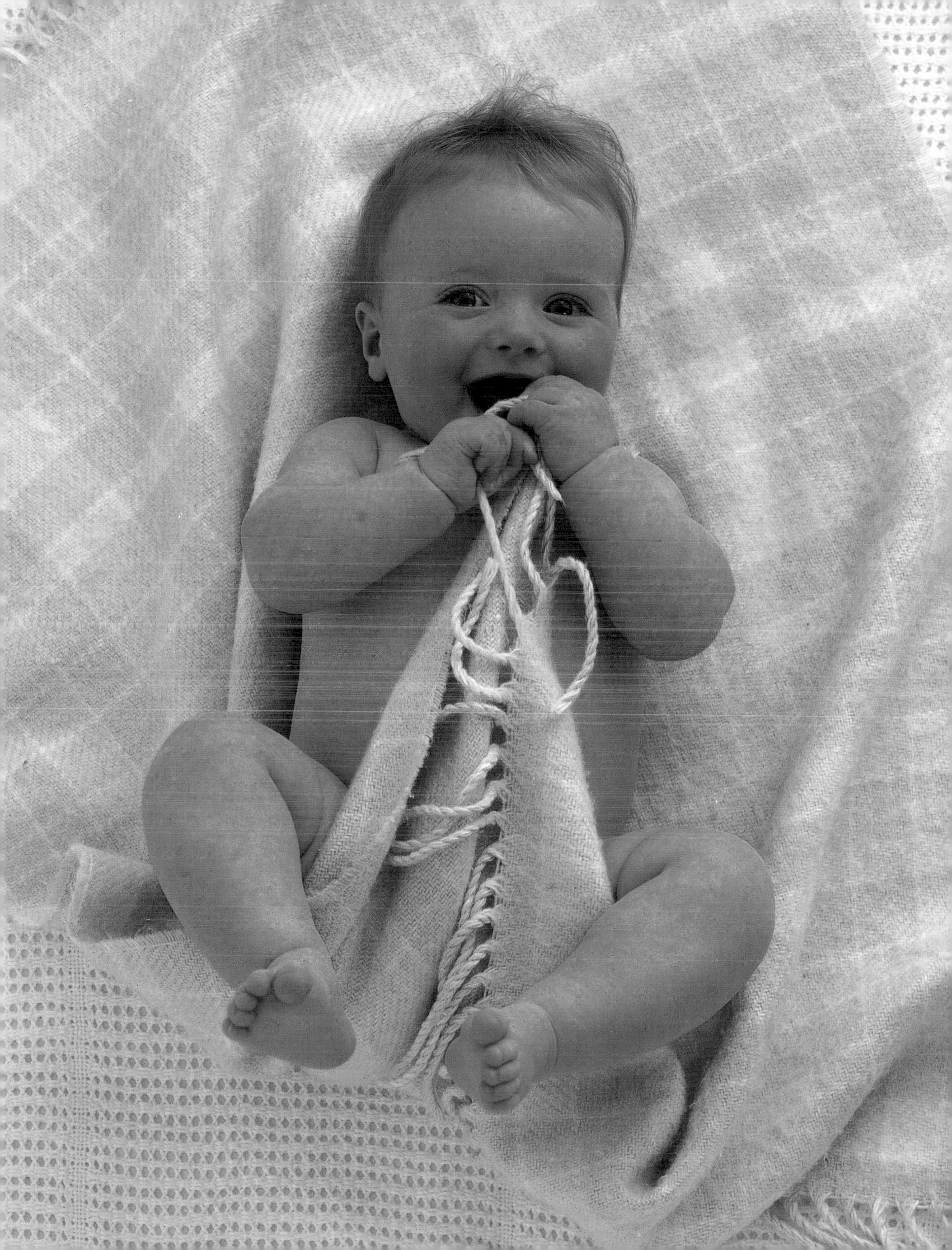

PART ONE

PREGNANCY

Pregnancy is a very special time for both you and your partner. Knowing what is happening to you and your growing baby during the weeks ahead will help you both to enjoy this exciting period in your lives. Starting with pre-conceptual care, this section explains how conception takes place and then looks at pregnancy and your baby's development week by week. Many of the issues raised will be relevant throughout your pregnancy and not just during the week in which they are first mentioned, so do read it all.

It is normal to experience some minor discomforts during pregnancy and you will want to know how to cope with them. More serious problems can occasionally occur, and it is important to recognize the symptoms so that you will know when immediate medical treatment is required. The birth is something you may feel anxious about and it will help you if you understand the choices available in both ante-natal care and childbirth. By being informed you will be able to choose the type of care and birth that is right for you.

As your body adapts to the changes that pregnancy brings, you will begin to prepare yourself physically, emotionally and practically for parenthood. A well-balanced, healthy diet is essential for both your well-being and that of your baby. Exercise has an important part to play too, not just in keeping you fit but also in preparing your body for the birth. Looking good will help you to feel good, so you should take care of your physical appearance throughout your pregnancy. Knowing how to select the right clothes to suit your changing shape and how to use make-up to emphasize your best features will help you to feel confident and make your pregnancy an even more enjoyable experience.

PREPARING FOR PREGNANCY

Once you have decided that you want to have a baby, you and your partner should concentrate on getting yourselves fit and healthy before you try to conceive. Ideally, you should begin preparing for pregnancy at least three months before conception so that you can be sure that your child will get the best possible start in life. If your pregnancy is unplanned, then start taking extra care of yourself as soon as you suspect that you might be pregnant. This may involve some basic changes in your lifestyle.

There is evidence that suggests that smoking by either partner can delay conception, so if you or your partner smoke you should stop now. In addition, smoking during pregnancy will put the baby at risk and can also affect your well-being; giving up before conception will benefit you and your child.

Alcohol can inhibit fertility, so both you and your partner should avoid drinking alcohol while trying to conceive. Once you are pregnant alcohol can restrict fetal development and could even cause malformation. Since there is no safe limit for alcohol during pregnancy it is better to give it up altogether.

MEDICATION

Fertilization and the early development of a baby are controlled by delicately balanced chemical processes in the body. Additional chemicals entering your body as medication can upset this development, so if possible you should avoid taking any medicines before conception and during pregnancy. If you are on long-term medication, you will need to talk to your doctor about alternatives. Medicines that are available over the counter, natural remedies, and vitamin supplements should also be avoided, unless they have been recommended by your doctor.

Oral contraceptives rely on chemically-produced hormones to control fertility. If you are taking the pill, change to a barrier method, such as the condom or diaphragm, for three months before trying to conceive. This allows your body to clear itself of synthetic hormones and to re-establish its own cycle.

IMMUNIZATIONS

An unborn baby exposed to rubella (German measles) during its early development can be born severely handicapped. Don't assume that because you were vaccinated in your teens, or you have had the infection, that you are automatically immune. Ask your doctor to give you a blood

Before trying for a baby, both partners should try to get fit by walking and other exercise.

Salmon is ideal as part of a balanced diet, because it is low in fat but full of vitamins.

By doing regular stretching exercises at home, or at an organized class, you will strengthen yourself for pregnancy.

test to check. If you are not immune you can be vaccinated, but you should not get pregnant until the vaccine virus has cleared from your blood, which takes about three months. If you have been given vaccines for tropical diseases, you should also wait for three months before getting pregnant.

NUTRITION AND EXERCISE
A well-balanced, healthy diet that contains reasonable daily amounts of carbohydrate, protein, fat, minerals, and vitamins is essential for both your well-being and that of your baby. Everything you eat will also become your unborn child's nourishment, and what you store before pregnancy is important for early fetal development when all the major organs are formed.

One of the B vitamins, folic acid, helps prevent neural tube defects (NTD), such as spina bifida, in unborn babies. It is recommended that all women planning a pregnancy should increase their average daily intake to 0.6 mg by taking a 0.4 mg supplement before attempting conception, and during the first 12 weeks of pregnancy. This is the time when your baby's organs and body systems are forming.

Regular exercise, such as brisk walking or swimming, is important if you are to maintain a healthy lifestyle. Exercise will help you get fit before conception and, as your pregnancy progresses, it will strengthen muscles in your lower back, stomach, and legs, which will help your body cope better with the demands of pregnancy.

As your legs have to carry more weight during pregnancy, try to do regular daily exercises such as running on the spot to build them up.

THE FIRST TRIMESTER

WEEKS 1–4: CONCEPTION

During the first half of the menstrual cycle two chemical substances called hormones are released from special glands into the bloodstream. One hormone stimulates the process that results in the production of an ovum, or ripe egg. The other hormone stimulates the endometrium, or lining of the uterus (womb), to thicken in readiness to receive a fertilized ovum. About two weeks from the end of your menstrual cycle the work of the first hormone is completed and you ovulate; that is, a ripe ovum is released from one of your ovaries. Conception occurs if your partner's sperm fertilizes this ovum. This usually takes place in the Fallopian tube that connects the ovary to the uterus. The fertilized ovum completes its journey to the uterus, where it implants into the thickened uterine lining. Once this process occurs the cervix increases slightly in width and becomes softer, and a thick mucous plug seals off the uterus to protect it from infection. After two weeks, if there has been no conception, the thickened uterine lining is shed and menstruation takes place.

AFTER FERTILIZATION
The fertilized single-cell egg multiplies into two, then four cells, and it carries on multiplying so that by about day seven, when it reaches the uterus, it has grown into a ball of over 100 cells with a fluid-filled cavity. This ball, called a blastocyst, has two layers: the outer one becomes the placenta, while the inner one forms the embryo, which develops into your baby.

The embryo is made up of three layers of tissue, each of which forms separately. The outer layer develops into the nerves and skin; the middle layer forms the bones, cartilage, muscles, circulatory system, kidneys, and sex organs; and the inner layer

You and your body
You won't be aware of the changes that are happening inside your body during these early weeks, although it is possible that you may experience very slight bleeding at the time when your next period would have been due. Usually the first indication that you are pregnant will be a missed period.

becomes the respiratory and digestive systems.

The placenta is the unborn baby's life-support system. It is attached to the lining of the uterus and separates the developing baby's circulation

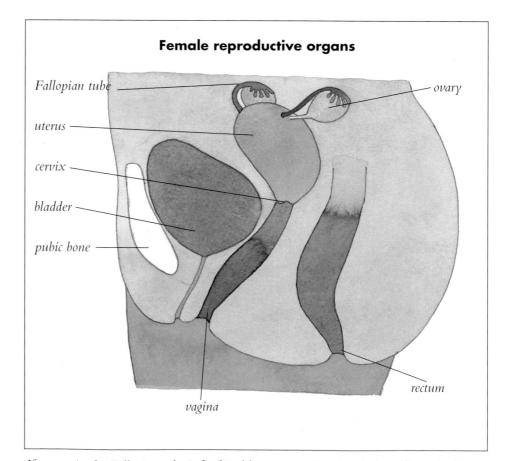

Female reproductive organs

Fallopian tube

ovary

uterus

cervix

bladder

pubic bone

rectum

vagina

If an egg in the Fallopian tube is fertilized by a sperm, it will embed itself into the lining of the uterus. If not, it is shed down through the cervix and out through the vagina.

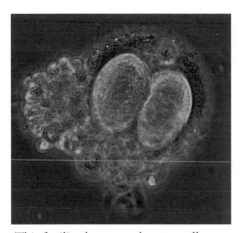

This fertilized egg now has two cells called blastomeres and is the primitive embryo. It will multiply to over 100 cells.

An enlarged sperm and ovum

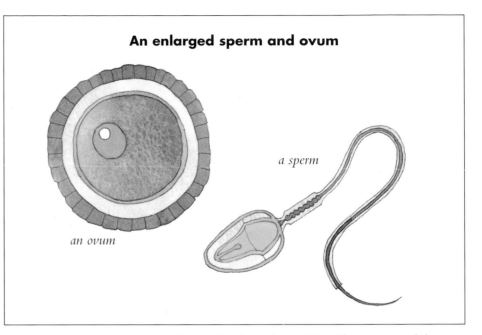

a sperm

an ovum

A sperm and an ovum are tiny. A man ejaculates about 500 million sperm, while a woman usually produces one ovum half-way through her menstrual cycle.

from its mother's. It allows oxygen and food, as well as protective antibodies, to pass from the mother along the umbilical cord to the baby. The placenta isn't fully formed until the end of the 12th week of pregnancy when it is able to take over the production of the pregnancy hormones, oestrogen and progesterone, from the ovaries.

Within the uterus, the embryo is contained in the amniotic sac. This is filled with fluid in which the developing child will float until birth. The amniotic fluid offers protection from any external pressures.

THE BABY'S SEX

A child's sex is determined by the father's sperm at the time of conception. Sperm carry either an X or Y chromosome while the egg has only an X chromosome. If a Y-chromosome sperm fertilizes the egg, the baby will be a boy. If the sperm carries an X chromosome, the baby will be a girl.

Male reproductive organs

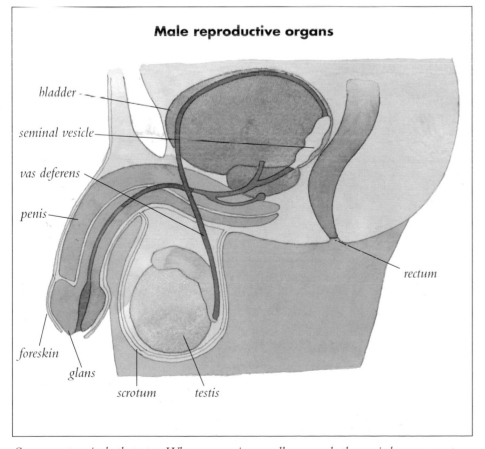

bladder

seminal vesicle

vas deferens

penis

rectum

foreskin

glans

scrotum   testis

Sperm mature in both testes. When a man is sexually aroused, the penis becomes erect and the outlet from the bladder into the ejaculatory duct is closed leaving it free for sperm.

Trimesters

Pregnancy lasts approximately 40 weeks and is calculated from the first day of your last period, although conception will probably not have taken place until around two weeks after this. Pregnancy is divided into three parts known as trimesters. The first covers weeks 1–13, the second trimester weeks 14–26, and the third trimester week 27 until birth.

WEEK 5: CONFIRMING PREGNANCY

Your growing baby
Although the embryo is only just visible to the naked eye, the spinal column and brain have already begun to grow and a blood vessel has developed which will become the heart. The embryo is 4 mm/⅛ in long.

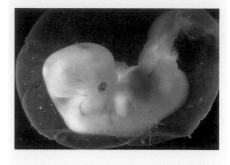

Pregnancy can be confirmed by means of a simple test that measures the levels of the pregnancy hormone, human chorionic gonadotrophin (HCG), that are present in your urine. The test can be carried out as soon as you reach the day that your next period should have started. Your doctor or Family Planning Clinic will do the test free, or you may prefer to carry out a home test yourself using one of the kits available from the pharmacist. Ensure that you choose a kit that will give an accurate result this early. Although many modern home-testing kits state that you can test your urine at any time, you may wish to use an early morning sample because this urine will contain the highest concentration of HCG.

If the result is positive, you must make an appointment to see your doctor so that he or she can make arrangements for your ante-natal care and the birth.

EARLY SYMPTOMS
Some women experience all the early symptoms of pregnancy, while others sail through the first weeks without any feelings of discomfort.
• Your body is having to work hard to adapt to the demands of pregnancy, so you may feel overwhelmingly tired. Try to get as much rest as possible. You will find that sitting with your feet up for even half an hour will help.
• Your breasts may tingle or feel tender, rather as they do before a period; your nipples will appear darker and more prominent and the veins will be more noticeable. You should wear a good support bra from now until after your baby is born.
• You may experience a strange metallic taste in the mouth, which

You and your body
This is the first week that you will be able to confirm that you are pregnant.

If you're lucky, you'll experience no nausea in pregnancy and continue exercising as normal.

To confirm a pregnancy, you can do a test with a kit from a pharmacist, but ensure you choose one that is suitable to use for a test at five weeks.

can be accompanied by going off certain foods and tea and coffee.
• A feeling of nausea, or even actual physical sickness in the morning or at any time during the day, is quite usual. It is often worse when your stomach is empty, so have a plain biscuit and a cup of tea before you get up in the morning. During the day try eating six high-carbohydrate meals, such as pasta, potato, and bread. Avoid rich or fatty foods.
• Finally, as the enlarging uterus presses on your bladder you may need to urinate more frequently.

DATING THE BIRTH

Once your pregnancy is confirmed, you will want to know your baby's likely date of birth. You can calculate an estimated date of delivery (EDD) by counting 40 weeks from the first day of your last period. But you should remember that since you don't know the exact date of ovulation this EDD is approximate. At about 10 weeks you may be offered an ultrasound scan to confirm the EDD.

Estimated date of delivery

JANUARY	1 2 3 4 5 6 7 8 9 10 11 12 13 14 15 16 17 18 19 20 21 22 23 24 25 26 27 28 29 30 31	JANUARY
OCTOBER	8 9 10 11 12 13 14 15 16 17 18 19 20 21 22 23 24 25 26 27 28 29 30 31 1 2 3 4 5 6 7	NOVEMBER
FEBRUARY	1 2 3 4 5 6 7 8 9 10 11 12 13 14 15 16 17 18 19 20 21 22 23 24 25 26 27 28	FEBRUARY
NOVEMBER	8 9 10 11 12 13 14 15 16 17 18 19 20 21 22 23 24 25 26 27 28 29 30 1 2 3 4 5	DECEMBER
MARCH	1 2 3 4 5 6 7 8 9 10 11 12 13 14 15 16 17 18 19 20 21 22 23 24 25 26 27 28 29 30 31	MARCH
DECEMBER	6 7 8 9 10 11 12 13 14 15 16 17 18 19 20 21 22 23 24 25 26 27 28 29 30 31 1 2 3 4 5	JANUARY
APRIL	1 2 3 4 5 6 7 8 9 10 11 12 13 14 15 16 17 18 19 20 21 22 23 24 25 26 27 28 29 30	APRIL
JANUARY	6 7 8 9 10 11 12 13 14 15 16 17 18 19 20 21 22 23 24 25 26 27 28 29 30 31 1 2 3 4	FEBRUARY
MAY	1 2 3 4 5 6 7 8 9 10 11 12 13 14 15 16 17 18 19 20 21 22 23 24 25 26 27 28 29 30 31	MAY
FEBRUARY	5 6 7 8 9 10 11 12 13 14 15 16 17 18 19 20 21 22 23 24 25 26 27 28 1 2 3 4 5 6 7	MARCH
JUNE	1 2 3 4 5 6 7 8 9 10 11 12 13 14 15 16 17 18 19 20 21 22 23 24 25 26 27 28 29 30	JUNE
MARCH	8 9 10 11 12 13 14 15 16 17 18 19 20 21 22 23 24 25 26 27 28 29 30 31 1 2 3 4 5 6	APRIL
JULY	1 2 3 4 5 6 7 8 9 10 11 12 13 14 15 16 17 18 19 20 21 22 23 24 25 26 27 28 29 30 31	JULY
APRIL	7 8 9 10 11 12 13 14 15 16 17 18 19 20 21 22 23 24 25 26 27 28 29 30 1 2 3 4 5 6 7	MAY
AUGUST	1 2 3 4 5 6 7 8 9 10 11 12 13 14 15 16 17 18 19 20 21 22 23 24 25 26 27 28 29 30 31	AUGUST
MAY	8 9 10 11 12 13 14 15 16 17 18 19 20 21 22 23 24 25 26 27 28 29 30 31 1 2 3 4 5 6 7	JUNE
SEPTEMBER	1 2 3 4 5 6 7 8 9 10 11 12 13 14 15 16 17 18 19 20 21 22 23 24 25 26 27 28 29 30	SEPTEMBER
JUNE	8 9 10 11 12 13 14 15 16 17 18 19 20 21 22 23 24 25 26 27 28 29 30 1 2 3 4 5 6 7	JULY
OCTOBER	1 2 3 4 5 6 7 8 9 10 11 12 13 14 15 16 17 18 19 20 21 22 23 24 25 26 27 28 29 30 31	OCTOBER
JULY	8 9 10 11 12 13 14 15 16 17 18 19 20 21 22 23 24 25 26 27 28 29 30 31 1 2 3 4 5 6 7	AUGUST
NOVEMBER	1 2 3 4 5 6 7 8 9 10 11 12 13 14 15 16 17 18 19 20 21 22 23 24 25 26 27 28 29 30	NOVEMBER
AUGUST	8 9 10 11 12 13 14 15 16 17 18 19 20 21 22 23 24 25 26 27 28 29 30 31 1 2 3 4 5 6	SEPTEMBER
DECEMBER	1 2 3 4 5 6 7 8 9 10 11 12 13 14 15 16 17 18 19 20 21 22 23 24 25 26 27 28 29 30 31	DECEMBER
SEPTEMBER	7 8 9 10 11 12 13 14 15 16 17 18 19 20 21 22 23 24 25 26 27 28 29 30 1 2 3 4 5 6 7	OCTOBER

Find the first day of your last period on the white bands; the date on the tint band below is your EDD.

WEEK 6: ANTE-NATAL CHOICES

Who looks after you, and where your ante-natal care takes place, will depend a lot on the type of birth you want to have. If you decide on a home birth, the care will be carried out at home by a midwife and at your doctor's surgery. If you want a hospital birth your care will probably be shared between a midwife, your doctor and the hospital.

If you are not registered with a doctor, or you want a home birth but your particular doctor doesn't want to assist in the delivery, or you would rather be seen by a woman doctor and your doctor is a man, you can go to see a different doctor just for your maternity care.

The actual care you get will be similar wherever you receive it, because all ante-natal care is designed to ensure that you and your unborn baby remain healthy during pregnancy.

These days, the best pattern of ante-natal care for a healthy woman is considered to be no more than nine ante-natal appointments. If you have any concerns between these appointments, you can telephone your midwife or doctor for advice.

HOME BIRTH

A home birth means you give birth in the familiar surroundings of your own home under the supervision of a midwife. If you want to deliver your baby in this way, you will need to talk to your doctor to see whether there are any medical reasons why this isn't advisable. It is also a good idea to contact the director of maternity services (or local supervisor of midwives) at your hospital in order to arrange for a midwife to

You and your body

If you are suffering from morning sickness, you may find that the smell of certain things, such as tobacco smoke or frying food, brings on the sickness or makes it worse. The texture of your skin may become dry and flaky, or you may get spots. Now is the time to start thinking about your ante-natal care, and the type of birth you want.

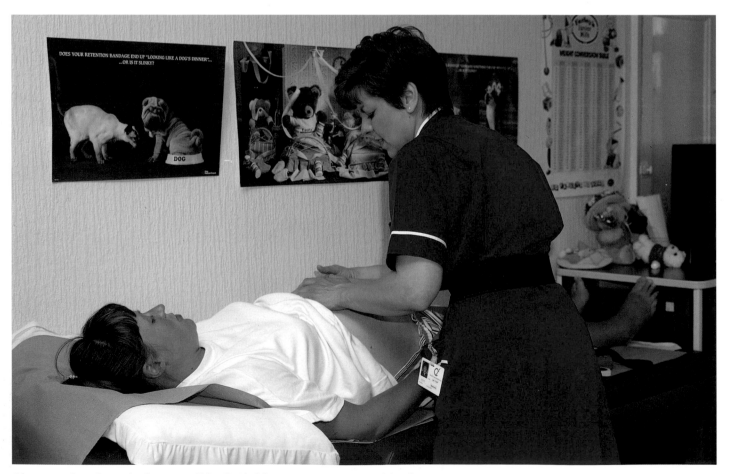

If you opt for a home birth, care will be divided between your home and local surgery.

come and visit you and discuss a home delivery in detail.

HOSPITAL BIRTH

Some women prefer a hospital birth because they feel safer knowing that there will be experts on hand to help if there are any complications. Also, if the baby needs special care this will be available almost immediately. Although hospitals are no longer the dictatorial places they used to be, and most try to cater for parents' wishes, not all of them are able to offer every type of birth. You will need to find out what facilities your local hospital offers. Before making your final decision talk to other mothers who have had their babies there recently. If you have any worries, discuss these with your doctor.

There are a number of hospital birth schemes that involve your doctor and midwife to varying degrees:
Midwife unit This is usually based at the hospital and is run entirely by midwives who undertake ante-natal care, delivery and post natal care. You can choose to have your baby at home or in the unit. These units are not widely available throughout the country, so this may not be an option that is open to you.
Domino scheme The Domino scheme (Domiciliary Midwife In and Out) means that your doctor and community midwife look after you throughout your pregnancy. Once you are in labour the midwife comes to your home and stays with you until you are ready to go into hospital. She then accompanies you to the hospital you are booked into, where she delivers the baby. You can usually return home around six hours after the birth. The midwife then continues to look after you at your home. Many women like the

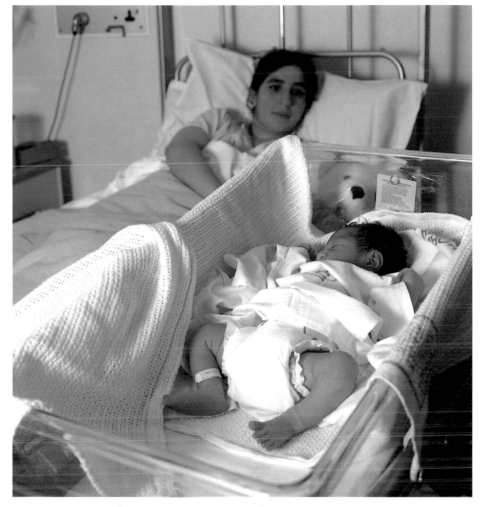

You can spend from between six hours to three days in hospital when you give birth, depending on your delivery. After the birth you may keep your baby beside you.

continuity this scheme gives them, but unfortunately it is not available in all areas at the present time.
Shared care Your ante-natal care will be shared between your doctor and the hospital where your baby is going to be born. The birth will take place in the maternity unit of this hospital and your doctor and midwife will look after you jointly on your return home with your young baby.

PRIVATE CARE

If you can afford it, you may like to consider having a home birth with a private, or independent, midwife taking care of you. She will provide all your ante-natal and post-natal care and will also deliver your baby.

Alternatively, you can decide to have your baby in a private hospital or maternity home.

Your growing baby

The heart has now formed in the chest cavity and is beginning to beat. By the end of this week the stalk connecting the embryo to the placenta will have begun to grow into the umbilical cord and blood vessels will have started to form. The embryo is now about the size of your little fingernail and its movements can be picked up by ultrasound scan. The head has the beginning of the eyes, ears, and mouth and there are tiny buds which will become arms and legs.

WEEK 7: POSSIBLE PROBLEMS

Although the majority of pregnancies go without a hitch, sometimes serious problems do occur and special care is needed. Complications can usually be resolved with monitoring, but occasionally the pregnancy comes to an end. Although the following conditions are not likely to affect you, you should be aware of their symptoms:

Pre-eclampsia This is a high blood pressure condition that can occur during pregnancy. If pre-eclampsia is left untreated it causes the blood vessels of the placenta to spasm, which reduces the oxygen flow to the fetus and puts it at risk; the fetal growth rate may also be affected. Symptoms include oedema, which is fluid retention causing swelling of the hands, feet, and ankles, protein in the urine and a sudden increase in weight. You will be tested for signs of pre-eclampsia at each ante-natal check. In the early stages pre-eclampsia is treated with complete bed-rest under medical supervision. Later in the pregnancy, if the condition is severe, it may become necessary to induce the birth as early as it is safe to do so. The mother's blood pressure will soon return to normal. If the condition is left completely untreated it can develop into eclampsia, which can be fatal for both mother and child. Today, this condition is extremely rare.

Bleeding in early pregnancy Bleeding or spotting from the vagina is known as a threatened miscarriage. It is possible to bleed quite heavily and not miscarry or do any harm to the baby. All bleeding in pregnancy must be taken seriously, however,

and you should report it to your doctor immediately. Your doctor is likely to carry out an internal pelvic examination and arrange for you to have an ultrasound scan to see whether the baby is developing normally. Providing everything is all right you will probably be told to rest until the bleeding stops.

Ectopic pregnancy This occurs when the fertilized egg implants itself in one of the Fallopian tubes rather than in the uterus. If it is undetected, the growing baby eventually ruptures the tube, which causes

You and your body

You may feel dizzy or even faint if you stand for too long or you are in a crowd. Overwhelming tiredness can also be a problem now, so make sure you get plenty of rest. If you don't feel like making love at the moment don't worry; this is quite normal and you may find that your sex life is better then ever in the second trimester.

Your growing baby

The unborn baby is now known as a fetus and is about 1.3 cm/½ in long. The nostrils, lips, tongue, and teeth are beginning to form and the arms and legs are growing. Lungs are beginning to develop and the intestines, spine, and brain are almost fully developed.

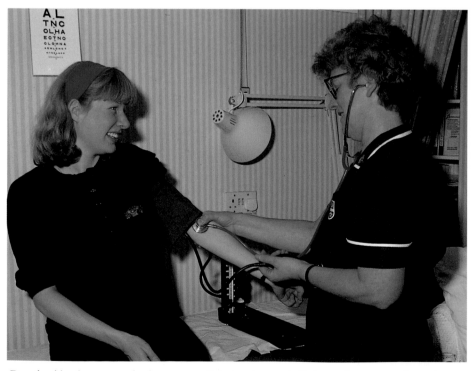

Regular blood pressure checks are essential at ante-natal clinics to detect pre-eclampsia.

Immediate surgery is required to terminate the pregnancy, and this often means losing the Fallopian tube as well. In extreme cases the ovary may also have to be removed. If the other ovary and Fallopian tube are healthy, there is no reason why another successful pregnancy should not take place. If the ectopic pregnancy is discovered early enough, a drug can be given that causes the embryo to be reabsorbed by the body; this prevents the Fallopian tube from bursting. Symptoms of an ectopic pregnancy include pain in the side of the abdomen, vaginal bleeding, and fainting.

Miscarriage The most common time for miscarriage is during the first three months of pregnancy, although losing a baby at any time before the 24th week is described as a miscarriage. Some miscarriages occur for no known reason. Known causes of miscarriage include hormonal problems, disease or infection, abnormalities of the uterus, or an incompetent cervix. If this last con-

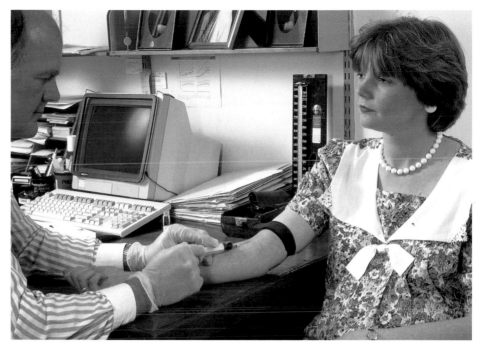

You will have a number of blood tests throughout your pregnancy but these are no cause for alarm. The tests are simply a means for your doctor to make sure that you are progressing normally and not experiencing any problems.

dition is known to exist, it can be dealt with by a simple surgical suture that will be removed shortly before the EDD.

Although it is unlikely that sexual intercourse will cause miscarriage, women who have experienced bleeding early in their pregnancy or who are known to have a tendency to miscarry are usually advised by doctors not to have intercourse for the first 12 weeks, until their pregnancy is well established.

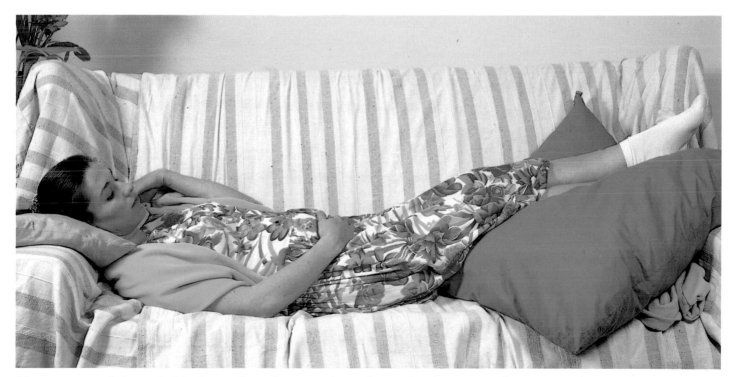

You may start to feel very tired in these early weeks, so get plenty of rest and make sure your feet are propped up.

WEEK 8: BOOKING-IN/ROUTINE TESTS

Your first ante-natal check-up will take place between eight and 12 weeks, either at your doctor's surgery or at the hospital where you plan to give birth. This first visit is usually referred to as the booking-in clinic. You will be asked a lot of personal questions about your health, family medical history, and possibly even about your and your partner's jobs and living accommodation. All this information is required to build up a picture of you and your pregnancy so that any potential risks can be spotted and help can be offered where needed.

If you have any questions or worries, this is a good time to discuss them. It's easy to forget to ask something important when there is so much to take in at one time, so it may help to write down things that you want to know about before you attend the clinic.

ROUTINE TESTS

Certain tests are carried out during pregnancy to ensure that both you and the fetus are progressing well. Some of these will be repeated at each ante-natal visit; others are only carried out at the booking-in clinic.

Blood pressure This will be taken at each visit. Increased blood pressure could develop into pre-eclampsia, which could endanger both you and the fetus.

Urine You will be asked to bring a sample of urine with you to each ante-natal visit. This will be tested for any infections that may require some treatment, as well as for sugar, protein, or the chemical substances known as ketones. Sugar in the urine could be a sign of diabetes; protein may indicate the onset of pre-eclampsia; and ketones may indicate that your kidneys are being adversely affected by your pregnancy.

You and your body

The changes to your body are becoming more noticeable as your breasts and nipples enlarge and become sensitive. Your vagina changes from light to dark pink, and you may notice an increased vaginal discharge.

It is time for regular monitoring of your pregnancy.

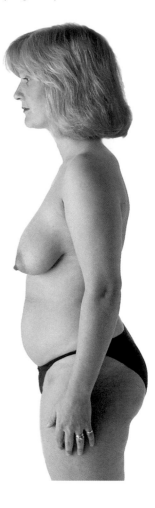

Weight Your weight may be monitored regularly to see how the baby is growing, although not all doctors do this. You can expect to gain anything from 6 kg to 19 kg/20 lb to 40 lb during your pregnancy, with most of this extra weight going on after the 20th week. A sudden increase in weight could be an indication of pre-eclampsia.

Height You will be measured at your first appointment because

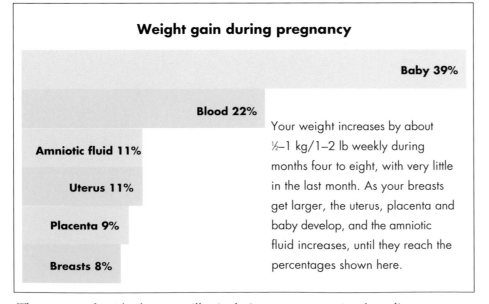

Weight gain during pregnancy

Baby 39%

Blood 22%

Amniotic fluid 11%

Uterus 11%

Placenta 9%

Breasts 8%

Your weight increases by about ½–1 kg/1–2 lb weekly during months four to eight, with very little in the last month. As your breasts get larger, the uterus, placenta and baby develop, and the amniotic fluid increases, until they reach the percentages shown here.

The amount of weight that you will gain during pregnancy varies, depending on your height and size, but can be as much as 19 kg/40 lb.

At your first ante-natal check-up, a blood sample will be taken to find out your blood group and type, and to make sure you're not anaemic or carrying a virus such as hepatitis B. You will have blood tests regularly through your pregnancy.

your height gives a rough guide to the size of your pelvis. If your pelvis is too small to accommodate your baby's head at the birth, then a Caesarean delivery may be indicated. It is worth noting, however, that most babies are in proportion to the mothers who carry them.

Blood tests At your first appointment you will be asked to give a blood sample to confirm your blood group and to find out if you are rhesus negative or positive.

Your blood will also be checked to see if you are anaemic and if you are immune to rubella (German measles). Other tests are also carried out to detect any serious conditions that could affect your baby, such as syphilis and hepatitis B. If you are of Afro-Caribbean descent, they will test your blood for sickle-cell disease; if you are of a Mediterranean ethnic group they will test for thalassaemia.

Sometimes your blood will also be tested anonymously to see if the HIV or AIDS virus is present.

Internal examination You may have an internal examination at your booking-in clinic. This is to check for any abnormalities of the vagina, cervix, or uterus. If you haven't had a cervical smear test during the last three to five years you may well be given one.

Wrists and ankles These will be checked at each visit for swelling, or oedema, caused by fluid retention, since these signs could possibly indicate pre-eclampsia.

Palpation The doctor or midwife will palpate, that is press, your abdomen to feel the top of the uterus (fundus). He or she will then feel down towards the pelvis to check the size of the fetus and the way it is lying.

Your growing baby

The fetus is now about 2.5 cm/ 1 in long, which is 10,000 times bigger than at conception. All the major organs are present, although still developing. The ears and eyes have formed and the skin covering the eyes will eventually split to form the eyelids. The middle ear, which controls balance as well as hearing, is also developing. The heart is now pumping with a regular beat, and blood vessels can be seen. As the arms and legs grow longer, the fetus begins to move around and starts to kick, although it is still too small at this stage for you to be able to feel it.

WEEK 9: SPECIAL TESTS

Your growing baby
The face is now developing and the mouth and nose are clearly visible. The limbs continue to grow rapidly and the fetus now measures about 3 cm/1¼ in.

Your blood will have been tested at your booking-in appointment to determine your blood group and to establish its rhesus (Rh) status. The rhesus status of your blood depends on whether or not it possesses the rhesus factor. If the factor is present, your blood is Rh-positive, if it is absent, your blood is Rh-negative. Most people's blood is Rh-positive.

If both you and the baby's father are Rh-negative, there is not a problem. Complications only occur when the father's blood is Rh-positive and yours is Rh-negative. The unborn baby may acquire the rhesus factor from its father, which can result in its blood being incompatible with yours. This can lead to a serious or even fatal illness for the baby before, or after the birth. Fortunately, this rarely affects a first pregnancy and it can be prevented in subsequent pregnancies by injections of anti-D gamma globulin, an antibody that may be given during pregnancy and again within 72 hours of a baby being delivered.

SPECIAL TESTS
There are a number of ante-natal tests that are used in special circumstances and usually only when there is some fear of genetic abnormality. They include:

Amniocentesis If you have a family history of genetic abnormalities such as Down's syndrome, cystic fibrosis, or spina bifida, or your blood shows a high or exceptionally low AFP (alpha-fetoprotein) level, you will be offered an amniocentesis usually at around 16–18 weeks. This test is also offered to all women over

In an amniocentesis test the fetus's position is checked by ultrasound, before amniotic fluid is taken by a needle from the uterus.

35 years of age because they have a higher risk of having a Down's syndrome baby. Guided by ultrasound scan, a long hollow needle is inserted through the wall of the abdomen and the uterus to draw out a sample of amniotic fluid. This is then tested

You and your body
You will start putting on weight now so it is a good idea to keep a record of any weight gain yourself if your antenatal care doesn't include regular weight checks. Your gums are becoming softer and thicker because of hormone changes so you will need to pay special attention to oral hygiene.

You should now familiarize yourself with some of the other ante-natal procedures and tests.

for abnormalities. You will get the results in about four weeks. The test carries a small risk of miscarriage.

Triple/double test The triple test is carried out at 16 weeks to measure the levels of three substances produced by the mother and the placenta. The levels change during pregnancy and a higher level could indicate that the baby may have Down's syndrome or spina bifida. The test cannot confirm that the baby is affected but it does indicate whether further tests, such as amniocentesis, are required. Not all areas use the triple test; some offer the double test, where two substances are measured; other hospitals don't offer the test at all, but you can have it done privately.

Chorionic villus sampling (CVS) CVS is done at around 11 weeks to test for Down's syndrome or other genetic or chromosomal abnormali-

Brush your teeth and gums regularly.

ties. A fine tube is passed into the uterus to remove some of the cells from the tissue that surrounds the baby. The cells are then tested, and the results are usually known within one to two weeks. The advantage of CVS is that if the baby is found to have a problem and you want a termination it can be done early in pregnancy. However, there is a slightly higher risk of miscarriage with CVS than with amniocentesis.

Cordocentesis This test is normally done to confirm diagnosis of chromosomal abnormalities and other handicaps, plus diseases such as rubella and toxoplasmosis. A hollow needle is inserted through the abdomen into the umbilical vein, close to the placenta, and a sample of the baby's blood is withdrawn. It is only performed after 18 weeks when the blood vessels are large enough. Results are usually known within about 48 hours.

GENETIC COUNSELLING
If you are worried about the possibility of your children inheriting a disease or handicap, you can talk to the genetic counsellor who is specially trained to help people with a family history of genetic disorders. Counselling is usually based on details of any genetic diseases that run in the family. A chromosome analysis from a blood sample may also be used. The counsellor will be able to explain the likelihood of future children being affected by the genetic disorder and also about any tests that can be carried out. It is a good idea to have this discussion before attempting to get pregnant so that you know what is involved. Otherwise, tell your doctor that you want to see a genetic counsellor when your pregnancy is confirmed.

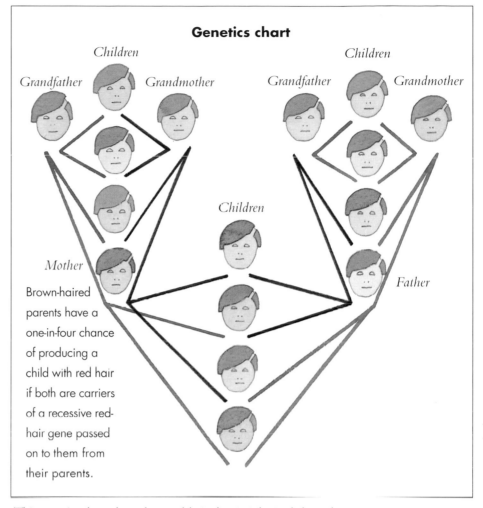

Genetics chart

Brown-haired parents have a one-in-four chance of producing a child with red hair if both are carriers of a recessive red-hair gene passed on to them from their parents.

This genetics chart shows how red hair that is inherited through a recessive gene can miss a generation, but has a high chance of re-appearing in the third generation. This can also apply to some inherited diseases.

If your family has a history of a genetic disorder, you can talk to a genetic counsellor who will discuss with you and your partner the likelihood of your baby having a problem.

WEEK 10: HORMONES/ MATERNITY RECORD

Hormones play an important part during pregnancy and labour. The prime source of the hormones related to pregnancy are the ovaries during the early stages, and then the placenta once it is established at around 12 weeks. These hormones dictate how fast the fetus grows and are responsible for the changes in your breasts and body. They also ensure that your labour occurs at the right time.

High levels of the hormone called human chorionic gonadotrophin (HCG) circulate in your body during the first 12 weeks of pregnancy. They are responsible for any emotional changes, feeling tired, nausea, and vomiting.

HORMONES AND YOUR EMOTIONS
Pregnancy can produce a number of conflicting emotions, ranging from feelings of pure joy to bouts of black depression. It is quite natural to feel like this as you adjust to your changing role and come to terms with the fact that your life will never be quite the same again. You may find that

you start worrying about whether you are ready for motherhood, or the effect that a new baby may have on your established relationship with your partner.

You may also find that mood swings, often brought on by the hormonal changes going on in your body, cause petty arguments between you. So it is most important

You and your body

There is an increase in the amount of blood that is circulating in your body, which may cause you to feel warmer than usual. Your uterus is now the size of a large orange and your changing shape may mean that you are more comfortable in loose-fitting clothes that do not restrict you.

Other changes are also taking place in your body. Although these are not always physically obvious, they are in fact the result of shifts in your body's chemistry.

Your growing baby

The external ears are now visible on the head, which is growing fast to make room for the brain. The fetal body is elongating and its fingers and toes are clearly defined but are still joined with webs of skin. At this stage of your pregnancy the fetus is now about 4.5 cm/1¾ in long and weighs around 5 g/¼ oz.

As you experience hormonal changes in your body you may find you become irritable and anxious. Discuss any of your worries with your partner who can talk things through with you and reassure you.

As your emotions are probably mixed up at the moment, don't brood over rows with your partner, but apologize and make up.

If you find you're getting very tense, try practising relaxation techniques on your own, or some deep breathing exercises.

Terms and abbreviations

The following terms and abbreviations may appear on your maternity record.

AFP: Alpha-fetoprotein.

BP: Blood pressure.

Cephalic: Fetal head is nearest the cervix.

Cx: Cervix.

EDD: Estimated date of delivery.

FHH: Fetal heart heard.

FMF: Fetal movement felt.

Height Fundus: The distance from the pelvis to the top of the uterus is known as the fundus.

LMP: Last menstrual period. This is the date of the first day of your last period before pregnancy.

NAD: No abnormality detected.

Oedema: Swelling of hands and feet because of fluid retention.

Relation of PP to Brim: The position of the fetus's presenting part (PP), that is the part ready to be born first, in relation to the brim of the pelvis.

Transverse: Transverse lie. The fetus is lying across the uterus.

Urine Alb Sugar: Indicates the results of urine tests for protein and sugar.

to make time to talk to each other so that you can both voice your feelings and share any worries or anxieties.

MATERNITY RECORD

You will be given your maternity record card at your booking-in clinic. It is used to record the results of all the tests and examinations that are carried out during your pregnancy. You should keep it with you at all times, so that if you ever need medical attention when you are away from home all the information about your pregnancy is readily available to the medical staff.

WEEK 11: COMMON DISCOMFORTS

As your body prepares itself for birth, you may experience some physical effects. These are perfectly normal, can usually be dealt with easily, and should not leave any long-lasting effects, but knowing the reason for a complaint can often help in dealing with it.

Backache This can occur at any time, but usually happens when you try to compensate for your baby's weight by leaning backwards which puts a strain on the lower back's muscles and joints. Try to avoid lifting heavy objects, bend with your knees bent, wear flat shoes, and always

Your back is now more vulnerable, so support it with a cushion when you sit down.

sit with your back well supported.
Bleeding gums Hormonal changes can cause a build-up of plaque on your teeth, which can

lead to bleeding gums. It is important to pay special attention to oral hygiene and to avoid snacking on sweets and sugary drinks. Dental treatment is free while you are pregnant so have at least two check-ups during this time.

Cramp You may have a sudden sharp pain in your legs and feet, often at night. Try pulling your toes upwards towards your ankles and rub the affected muscles. Regular gentle exercise will help prevent cramp.

Constipation Some of the extra hormones produced in pregnancy can cause the intestines to relax and become less efficient. Eating plenty of fruit, vegetables and fibre, and drinking water will help.

Fainting You may feel faint if you

You and your body

Any sickness should start to fade and you will begin to feel less tired. You should start to think seriously about ante-natal classes because private ones can get booked up quickly. Contact your hospital or the National Childbirth Trust, or ask at your doctor's surgery about local classes.

stand for too long or get up too quickly. This happens because not enough blood is getting to your brain; if the oxygen level gets too low you may actually faint. Try to rise slowly from either sitting or lying positions and, if you are standing, sit down and lower your head towards your knees.

Piles Technically known as haemorrhoids, these are a form of varicose vein that appear around the back passage (anus). They can be very uncomfortable as they are itchy

Eating a high-fibre diet can help prevent painful constipation in pregnancy.

Your growing baby

Most of the major organs are formed, so the most vulnerable time will be over by the end of this week. The fetus is now relatively safe from any congenital abnormalities and infections, excepting rubella.

The external genitals have formed, along with either ovaries or testicles. The heart is now pumping blood to all the major organs of the body. The fetus weighs around 10 g/½ oz and is now about 5.5 cm/2⅛ in long.

Although you may now be feeling less tired than in the early weeks, you should still rest as much as you can.

and may even bleed slightly. If left untreated they can become prolapsed, which means they protrude through the anus, causing a good deal of pain. Eating high-fibre foods will keep your stools soft so that you don't have to strain, which puts pressure on piles. An ice pack wrapped in a soft cloth, or a witch hazel compress, will bring relief, or you can buy a specially formulated haemorrhoid preparation from the pharmacist. Piles usually disappear within a couple of weeks of the birth.

Vaginal discharge An increase in vaginal discharge during pregnancy is quite normal as long as the discharge is clear and white. If it becomes coloured, smells, or makes you itchy, you may have developed an infection, such as thrush, which will need treatment.

Take some gentle, regular exercise with your partner as this will help to prevent cramps and keep you feeling fit.

WEEK 12: HEALTHY EATING

The fetus gets all the nourishment it needs to grow from what you eat, so it is important to maintain a good diet throughout pregnancy. To achieve a healthy balanced diet you need to eat foods containing reasonable amounts of starchy carbohydrate, protein, fat, minerals, and vitamins each day. Starchy carbohydrates are found in bread, cereals, pasta, rice, and potatoes; they provide energy, vitamins, minerals, and fibre. Meat, fish, eggs, nuts, beans, peas, and lentils supply protein and minerals. Milk and dairy products such as hard cheese and yogurt will give you protein, vitamins, and calcium. Fresh fruit and vegetables and well-washed salads are good sources of minerals and vitamins. Folic acid can be found, with other vitamins, in green leafy vegetables, fruit, nuts, bread, and rice.

If you are a vegetarian, you will need to increase your milk intake to at least 600 ml/1 pint a day of either pasteurized milk or fortified soya milk, or the equivalent in cheese, yogurt, and dairy products.

Vegans will need to discuss their diet with a qualified dietitian as they could be deficient in calcium, iron, and vitamin B_{12}, which is found in foods of animal origin. Try to avoid

You and your body

You can expect to put on about one-quarter of your pregnancy weight between now and week 20. You may be beginning to feel more energetic and generally better than during the past few weeks. You should consider telling your employer at this time that you are pregnant.

Meanwhile, look at your lifestyle and be sure that your diet includes a sensible range of foods – for you and the unborn baby.

eating sugary snacks and fizzy drinks and keep "junk" foods down to a minimum. Cut down on your caffeine intake from drinks like tea, coffee, chocolate and cola; try drinking bottled water and diluted fruit juices as alternatives.

Eat plenty of fruit when pregnant as it is a good source of minerals and vitamins.

Cut down on your caffeine levels and drink more diluted fruit juices.

A grain salad will give you plenty of fibre.

Vegetables are important in your pregnancy diet as they are low in fat and contain minerals, vitamins and folic acid in leafy varieties.

Use olive and sunflower oils for cooking.

YOUR WEIGHT

Although you need extra energy during pregnancy to meet the needs of the developing fetus, and to store fat ready for breast-feeding later, you are not likely to need special energy foods. If you were an acceptable weight for your build before pregnancy, the only extra calories you should need are during the last three months when you eat around 200 extra calories a day. However, if you were overweight or underweight your weight gain will need monitoring, and a special diet may be necessary. Ask a professional for advice.

Your growing baby

The fetus's heart is beating at between 110 and 160 times a minute and its chest is beginning to rise and fall as it practises future breathing movements. Features are becoming more clearly defined and fingers and toes are now fully formed, with tiny nails beginning to grow. The fetus can suck its thumb and it swallows amniotic fluid and passes it back as urine. The amniotic fluid is completely replaced every 24 hours. The fetus is now about 6.5 cm/2½ in long and weighs 20 g/¾ oz.

WEEK 13: THE HEALTH PROFESSIONALS

Now that you are at the end of the first trimester and your pregnancy is a visible state, you should start to familiarize yourself with some of the professionals with whom you will regularly be interacting.

During pregnancy, and after the birth, a number of different people will be involved in your care. How many you see will depend on where you are having your baby and the kind of ante-natal care that is being offered. The type of professionals involved in your ante-natal and post-natal care will be the same wherever you are having your baby.

Midwife Your midwife has been trained to be an expert in pregnancy and she will care for you from the time your pregnancy is confirmed until after the birth of your baby. She will be able to give you physical and psychological support and to help with any medical problems that arise during this time.

Building up a relationship with you and your family is an essential part of the midwife's job, so it is important for you to establish contact with her as soon after your pregnancy is confirmed as possible. Your midwife will usually be found at your local health centre or your doctor's surgery, although it may also be possible to contact her direct through the Supervisor of Midwives at your local maternity unit.

Your midwife will be able to help you make an informed choice about your right to have your baby where and how you wish. She will advise you on the most appropriate care for

your needs and, if specialist help is required, she will know the right person to contact. The midwife will continue to look after you and your family until she hands over your care to a health visitor at between 10 and 28 days after the birth.

Health visitor The health visitor is a fully-qualified nurse who has had extra training in caring for people in the community. Her role is to help families, especially those with very young children. Your health visitor will visit you at home sometime after your baby is 10 days old. She will give you information about feeding, as well as general health and safety, and can offer advice and give support if you have any worries about your baby or if you yourself have any problems.

You and your body
Your uterus is enlarging at a noticeable rate and you will be able to see the first signs of a visible bump. Your nipples have become darker and the blue veins in your breasts are a lot more obvious.

The health visitor will give you a telephone number where she can be contacted if you need help. You can arrange to see her at home, or at the child health clinic, health centre, or doctor's surgery.

General practitioner Your GP will probably have confirmed your pregnancy and will be able to help you plan your ante-natal care. He or she may be responsible for all or part of your ante-natal care and will work closely with your midwife. If you are having a home birth, your GP may be involved in your baby's delivery, together with your midwife. If you are going to have a hospital birth

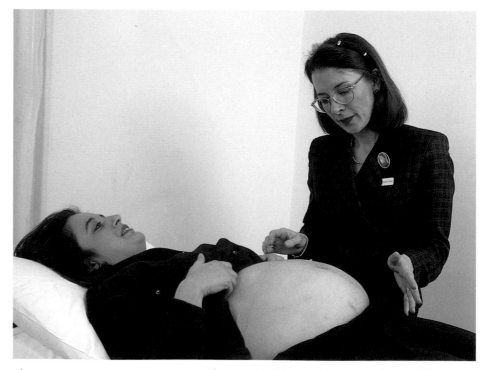

As your pregnancy progresses you may be examined by an obstetrician who specializes in birth and child care. She will advise on your baby's development and discuss any problems.

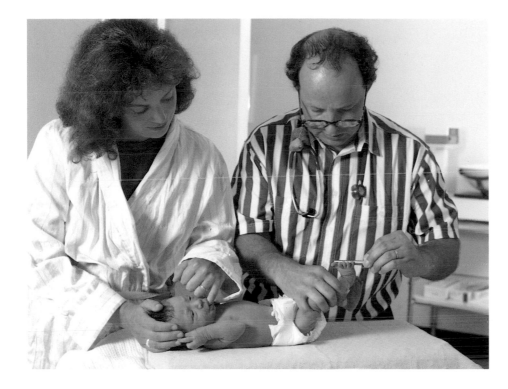

Your growing baby

The fetus is now 7.5 cm/3 in long and weighs 30 g/1½ oz. The bone marrow, liver, and spleen have now taken over production of blood cells. The bones are developing and the teeth are in place. The fetus may already be practising lip movements to develop the muscles needed for the sucking reflex after the birth.

The pediatrician will perform several checks on your baby after birth. Here he is checking that the newborn's foot reflex works correctly.

your GP should come and visit you and your baby soon after you get back home.

You need to register your baby with the GP as soon after the birth as possible. You can contact your GP at any time if either you or your baby are ill. Your doctor may have an arrangement where young babies are seen without making an appointment, possibly at the beginning or end of the surgery, or it may be possible to obtain some advice over the phone. Your GP may hold a clinic at the surgery, and will normally work closely with the health visitors in your area.

Obstetrician This is a doctor who specializes in the care of women throughout their pregnancy and subsequent childbirth. If you are having a delivery in a hospital, the consultant you are under will be an obstetrician who is part of a special medical team.

Pediatrician This is a doctor who specializes in caring for babies and children. Your baby will be checked by a pediatrician after the birth.

Your health visitor will visit you after your baby's birth and check that the navel is healing.

THE SECOND TRIMESTER

WEEK 14: SEX DURING PREGNANCY

To be able to enjoy sex it is important to know that making love cannot harm the developing fetus. It is well protected in the uterus by the amniotic fluid and membranes, and the uterus itself is sealed with a plug of mucus, which stays in place until just before the birth. Even deep penetration is safe, but it should of course be gentle so that it doesn't cause discomfort.

Many women find that the middle months of pregnancy are a sensual and even erotic time. Physical changes, such as the increase in the size of your breasts, can actually serve to heighten your interest in sex, which in turn leads to an increase in sexual pleasure. Your genitals may also appear bigger and the pressure from the growing baby can actually make them more responsive. Some women find that they experience orgasm for the first time during pregnancy, while others come to orgasm much more quickly.

Experiencing orgasm is perfectly safe, in fact it can be considered to be beneficial since the uterus often remains hard and firm for several minutes afterwards. This is similar in effect to the Braxton Hicks, or practice contractions you experience towards the end of your pregnancy that prepare the uterus for the birth of your baby.

You may of course find that you feel a lessening of desire during pregnancy, or even a complete loss of interest in sex. These feelings are not uncommon, but they can cause unnecessary stress between you and your partner if they are not brought out into the open and discussed.

You and your body

You are now beginning the second trimester when you should start experiencing what is known as mid-pregnancy bloom. You will be feeling better about everything; if your sex drive has diminished over the last few months it will probably return and sex may be better than ever.

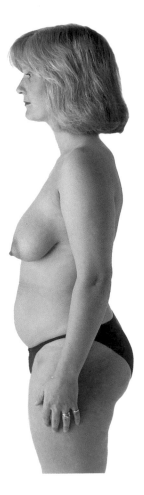

If you don't feel much like making love in early pregnancy, still cuddle your partner and show him lots of affection.

Your partner may feel that he is being rejected, so it is important to find alternative ways of giving each other love and reassurance.

DIFFERENT WAYS TO MAKE LOVE
It is important that you and your partner show each other physical affection during pregnancy, but this does not always have to involve sexual intercourse. You may find as your pregnancy progresses that you want lots of cuddles and other signs of affection from your partner without actually having sex. Men often find this hard to understand as they tend to link such physical contact with intercourse. Explain to your partner how you feel so that together you can find other ways of expressing your love for each other.

Try experimenting with different forms of sex play that don't necessarily end in penetration, so that you can still make love even if you don't feel like intercourse. Take time to

Often during the middle months of pregnancy, you can start to feel more sensual and show renewed interest in sex.

find out what you both enjoy and don't be afraid to tell your partner what you do and don't like.

Stroking, massage, mutual masturbation, and oral sex are some alternative ways of making love which you can both enjoy and which may at times be more appropriate than full intercourse.

As you grow larger you'll find some positions for lovemaking more comfortable than others. Experiment with positions which keep your partner's weight off you.

USING SEX TO INDUCE LABOUR
Sex can sometimes be a way of

inducing labour. Your partner's semen contains a hormone called prostaglandin, which will help to soften the cervix in preparation for birth. Lovemaking will also stimulate the cells in the cervix to secrete their own prostaglandins; this too may help bring labour on.

Breast stimulation in late pregnancy sometimes produces quite strong contractions which are thought to help prepare the way for labour by softening and drawing up the cervix. It has been discovered that stimulating nipples can reactivate a labour that has halted – something that your partner might like to remember.

Your growing baby
The fetus is beginning to look human as the chin, forehead, and nose become more clearly defined. It can now turn its head and even wrinkle its brow. The fetus may even respond to external stimulus by actually moving away when the doctor or midwife feels your abdomen. The fetus is now 9 cm/3½ in long and weighs about 60 g/2 oz.

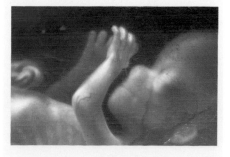

WEEK 15: HEALTH AND SAFETY

You may hear about risks during pregnancy. Some are valid, others are based on misinformation.

If you work with dangerous substances such as chemicals or in a job which requires you to do heavy lifting, you could be risking your health and the health of your child. Your employer must offer you an alternative job if yours is a recognized risk. If you are concerned about risks at work talk to your doctor, your employer, or union representative.

A common concern among working women is that sitting all day in front of a VDU screen such as a computer terminal or word processor will harm the developing fetus. The most recent research shows no evidence of this being a risk, but you may need to have your microwave checked out for any minor radiation leaks, although with modern equipment these are very unlikely.

You and your body

Your heart has enlarged to cope with the increased amount of blood circulating in your body and the fetus's need for oxygen, and has increased its output by 20 per cent. You will be feeling more energetic than before and now is a good time to have a holiday before the birth.

HEALTH HAZARDS

While you are pregnant you should avoid eating unpasteurized milk and products made with unpasteurized milk; pâté made from meat, fish, or vegetables; soft and blue vein cheeses; soft-whip ice cream; pre-cooked poultry and cook-chill meals; and prepared salads (unless washed thoroughly) because of the risk of listeria.

Listeria monocytogenes is the bacterium which causes listeriosis in humans and animals. Animals that carry the bacterium are likely to infect the milk they produce and the meat that is produced from them. The bacterium is usually destroyed during the pasteurization of milk and milk products. However, if food is contaminated and then refrigerated the bacteria will continue to multiply. Listeriosis can also be spread through direct contact with animals that are infected.

Toxoplasmosis is a disease that occurs in both humans and animals. It can be extremely dangerous if it is contracted during pregnancy because it may cause miscarriage or severe fetal abnormality. The disease is spread to humans by eating undercooked or raw meat and through coming into contact with cat faeces. The infection can also be caught from sheep at lambing time. As it is

Recent evidence has shown that there is no risk to the growing fetus for women who regularly use computer terminals. However, move around often to minimize backache.

Your growing baby

The fetal skeleton is developing and its legs are now longer than its arms. The hair on its head is becoming thicker and it has eyelashes as well as eyebrows. The fetus can probably hear now and the amniotic fluid makes an excellent sound conductor, so it will be able to hear your stomach rumbling and your heart beating as well as the sound of your voice. The fetus is 12 cm/4¾ in long and now weighs 100 g/3½ oz.

quite possible to have the disease without knowing it, you should have a blood test to find out whether or not you have immunity. If you are immune, you definitely cannot infect your baby.

If you find that you are not immune, you should take a number of precautions during pregnancy. Avoid any meat that has not been cooked thoroughly and wash your hands, cooking utensils, and surfaces after preparing raw meat. Wash fruit and vegetables to remove all traces of soil. Avoid unpasteurized goats' milk and goats' milk products. Finally, wear rubber gloves when gardening and wash your hands afterwards. Cover your children's sand boxes in the garden to prevent any cats from using them as litter trays. Always wear rubber gloves when handling cat litter, and wash your hands and the gloves afterwards.

Above: Hard cheeses are safe to eat in pregnancy. However, make sure you only eat hard-boiled eggs and drink pasteurized milk to avoid Listeria monocytogenes. Right: Always wear some gloves when gardening during pregnancy as toxoplasmosis can be caught from cat faeces.

Food safety

Avoid putting yourself at risk during pregnancy by taking the following precautions with food.

● Wash all fruit, vegetables, and salads, including any pre-packed salads, thoroughly.

● Don't eat raw or undercooked meat.

● Eggs must be well cooked and all dairy products should be pasteurized.

● Avoid eating any soft, imported cheeses such as Brie and Camembert, blue-vein cheeses, and those that are made from goats' and sheep's milk because of the risk of listeria.

● Don't eat liver and liver products, such as pâté and liver sausage. They contain high levels of vitamin A, which is toxic in excess amounts.

● Avoid cook-chill meals and shellfish.

● Keep your fridge below 5°C/41°F and don't refreeze any previously frozen foods.

● Pay special attention to hygiene in the kitchen.

● Don't eat food that is past its "sell by" or "best before" date.

WEEK 16: SCANS/TWINS

You and your body

You may feel your baby's first movements around this time. These early movements are like a fluttering, bubbling sensation. You may notice the beginning of *Linea nigra*, a dark line which appears down the centre of your abdomen. This will disappear after the birth.

At around 16 weeks you will probably be offered an ultrasound scan so that you can see your baby for the first time. A scan can be carried out at any stage of pregnancy, but is usually offered between 16 and 20 weeks (although a dating scan may be offered as early as ten weeks).

The procedure is completely painless. High-density sound waves are used to create a picture of your baby in the uterus, and you will be able to see this on a screen. The best pictures are obtained when you have a full bladder so you will be asked to drink a lot of fluid beforehand. You lie on a couch and your stomach is lubricated so that the person performing the scan can pull the scanner smoothly across it. The picture that appears on the screen may not be clear, so ask the radiographer to explain the images to you, if you are unsure of what you are seeing.

The fetus's age can be determined from a scan; it also shows up most abnormalities of the head and spine that may have occurred and will detect the presence of twins. The exact position of the placenta and the fetus can be seen, so if there are any problems, for example when the placenta is situated very low down, extra care will be taken throughout your pregnancy.

TWINS

There is about a one in 80 chance that you and your partner will conceive twins. However, you are more likely to give birth to twins if you have a history of them in your, or your partner's, family.

Identical twins come from one egg which, once fertilized, then splits into two separate cells. Each of the cells then grows into a separate fetus, but they usually share the same placenta. Because identical twins originally came from the same cells they are always the same sex and look like each other.

Non-identical twins, also known as fraternal twins, are the result of two eggs being fertilized by two different sperm at the same time. Each fetus has its own placenta and the sexes of the babies may differ.

Fraternal twins usually don't look any more alike than brothers and sisters who are born years apart.

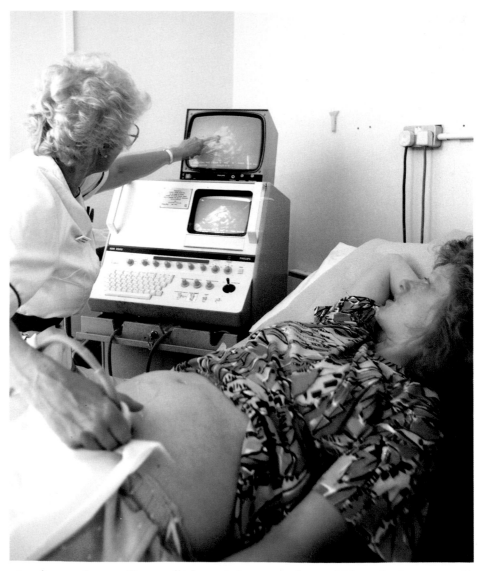

An ultrasound scan will normally be carried out around your 16th week of pregnancy. It will show up any abnormalities in your baby and also indicate the presence of twins.

The arrival of twins can come as rather a shock. Get your partner to help as much as he can and you will soon find that you both start bonding with them.

Your growing baby

The fetus will be moving around frequently now, although you may have only just started to feel these movements. The body will become covered in a fine downy hair called lanugo, which is thought to maintain the right body temperature. It is possible to tell a baby's sex now through an ultrasound scan. The fetus is 16 cm/6¼ in long and weighs 135 g/5 oz.

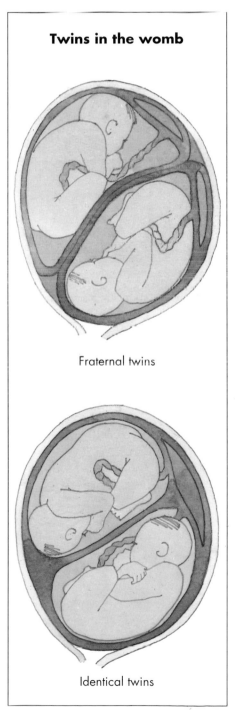

Twins in the womb

Fraternal twins

Identical twins

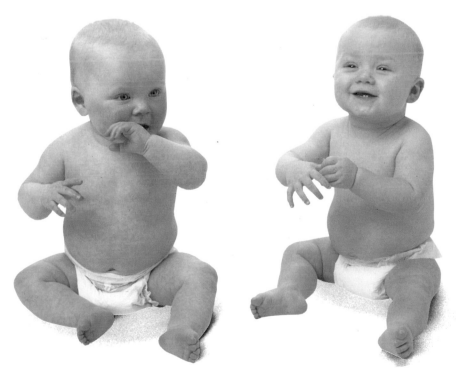

The joy of having twins is that as they grow up they will learn to play with each other.

WEEK 17: YOUR PREGNANCY WARDROBE

You will find that loose ordinary clothes, in a bigger size if necessary, will see you through most of your pregnancy. A few basic garments that are interchangeable will help you achieve a variety of looks. Buy skirts and trousers with elasticated waists, baggy shirts, and big T-shirts in natural fibres such as cotton. Choose underwear with some cotton content for softness and absorbency and maternity tights or stockings to give your legs support. As your breasts are likely to increase in size rapidly during the early months of pregnancy, it makes sense to buy a well-fitting support bra early. This will prevent your breasts sagging which will help them to return to their normal shape once the baby is born.

You and your body

Your waistline will have completely disappeared and you may have begun to develop stretch marks. Bleeding gums may be a problem, so if you haven't had a dental check-up now is the time to go. If you work, you should start thinking about when you intend to leave and whether you will want to return.

Your growing baby

All your baby's limbs are now fully formed as well as the skin and muscle. Its taste buds are beginning to develop so that it will be able to distinguish sweet from non-sweetened fluid. The fetus is now about 18 cm/7 in long and weighs around 185 g/6½ oz.

Maternity rights and benefits

Once your pregnancy is confirmed, you should make enquiries about your maternity rights and benefits. You will probably be entitled to some financial and/or medical benefits from the government. If you work you may qualify for statutory maternity pay from your employer. This may be in the form of a weekly allowance which is paid by your employer. You are entitled to take time off work to attend ante-natal clinics and parentcraft classes, so you will need to let your employer know that you are pregnant before your booking-in visit. Your midwife or health visitor will be able to give you help or advice if you are unsure of what to do.

A baggy cardigan worn over a skirt with an elasticated waist helps conceal your bump.

A loose-fitting trouser suit with a long jacket can look and feel good in pregnancy.

Front-opening dresses won't be restricting, and can be useful for breast-feeding.

If your feet ache take off your shoes inside your home, but take care on polished surfaces.

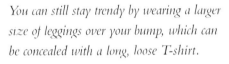

You can still stay trendy by wearing a larger size of leggings over your bump, which can be concealed with a long, loose T-shirt.

Front-opening dungarees are comfortable to wear in both early and late pregnancy, as they expand with you.

WEEK 18: LOOKING YOUR BEST

You may find that your hair behaves in a rather unpredictable way while you are pregnant. Hormone changes mean that your hair may appear thicker than usual, or in some women the opposite happens and the hair loss increases so that the hair looks thinner. Dry hair may become even drier and oily hair more greasy. Whichever condition applies to you, just wash your hair using a mild shampoo. If your hair tends to be very dry, use a good conditioner after every wash and, if possible, allow it to dry naturally rather than using a hair dryer.

Try using hypoallergenic skin-cleansing products on your skin as it will be particularly sensitive at this time.

Dry hair will need extra conditioning during your pregnancy because it becomes drier as your hormones change.

Pregnancy hormones can affect the colour and texture of your skin. Uneven patches appear and dark-skinned people may even get a but-terfly-shaped patch of pigmentation across the face which is known as "the mask of pregnancy" Concealing foundation will help hide these marks and a UVA sun screen will prevent any further increase in pigmentation. Pregnancy "bloom", which is caused by an increase in the tiny blood vessels under the surface of the skin, can be toned down with green cream or powder. It is a good idea to use hypoallergenic skin-care products as your skin may be particularly sensitive at this time.

FLUID RETENTION

Your body retains more water than usual during pregnancy, so your hands and feet may become slightly swollen and you may find that your eyes get puffy and your face looks fuller. The best solution is to get as much rest as possible, sitting with your feet higher than your heart, as this will help reduce the swelling in your feet and ankles. While you are resting, place some cottonwool pads soaked in witch hazel, or slices of cucumber, on your eyes. This will soothe them and reduce any puffiness. You can disguise a fuller face by applying blusher below the cheekbones and blending a darker shade of foundation along your jawline. Alternatively, you can draw attention away from your face by wearing a colourful scarf or a chunky necklace round your neck.

Try not to be too critical of your looks; many other people will consider that this new, softer look to your appearance makes you seem younger and healthier.

You and your body

You should be able to feel the fetal movements quite clearly now. Your nose may become blocked as pregnancy causes the membranes inside the nasal passages to swell. You may also notice an increase in vaginal discharge. You will find that there are several physical changes besides the predictable weight gain.

Your growing baby

The skin is still wrinkled because the fetus hasn't started to gain body fat and is very active. It is becoming aware of sounds outside the uterus and you may be able to feel it jumping at unexpected noises. The fetus is now around 21 cm/8½ in long and weighs about 235 g/8 oz.

With extra care you can transform your face from looking tired and pale in pregnancy (left) to attractive and striking (right). A concealing foundation masks any pigmentation marks, mascara and soft eye shadows can highlight your eyes, and a stunning lipstick can emphasize your mouth.

WEEK 19: EXERCISE

Regular, gentle exercise has an important part to play in keeping you fit during pregnancy and will help you get back into shape after the birth. Remember, if you ever feel faint, light-headed or breathless while you are exercising you must stop immediately. If you haven't been taking exercise, start swimming, or take up yoga or walking as

they can all be done at a gentle, rhythmical pace which can be adapted to suit each stage of your pregnancy. If you find it easier to follow an exercise routine you can do at home, never include sit-ups or exercises that involve raising the legs when you are lying down as these could damage the abdominal muscles. It is important to stop and relax

You and your body

You have started to put weight on your bottom, hips, and thighs as well as your abdomen. Tiny veins may start appearing on your face. These are very small broken blood vessels which are caused by circulation changes. They will disappear after the birth.

between exercises and to make sure that your breathing always remains at a controlled rate.

Toning your breasts

1 *Hold arms at breast level with hands loosely clasping opposite arm. Tighten grip and hold briefly, then relax.*

2 *Still keeping your hands clasped, raise them to eye level and tighten your grip and hold, then relax.*

3 *Lower your arms down to your waist, tighten and hold, then relax. Repeat this sequence several times.*

Feet exercises

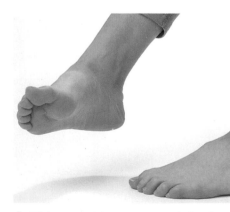 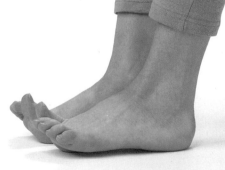 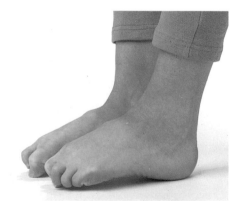

1 *To loosen ankles, sit down with feet flat on the ground. Lift one foot at a time and circle ankle five times in both directions.*

2 *To tone the feet, place your feet flat on the floor. Now lift your toes up as far as you can and hold briefly, then relax.*

3 *Now clench your toes hard, hold for a few seconds, then relax again. Repeat this technique, and Step 2, 10 times.*

Taylor sitting and squatting exercises

1 *To loosen the groin and hips and stretch the inner thighs, sit with the soles of your feet together. Holding ankles, bring your pelvis and feet together by moving your hips towards your feet.*

2 *This is a good position for labour. Squat down keeping a straight back; try to put your heels down placing your weight evenly. Press your elbows against your thighs stretching the inner groin and thighs.*

Tummy toning exercises

1 *Put a folded towel or pillow under your head and lie with your knees bent and your feet flat on the floor. Press the small of your back down on the floor.*

2 *Slowly extend both your legs in front of you until they are both completely straight, but still keep your back pressed well down onto the floor.*

3 *Draw one knee up and then the other, without lifting your back off the floor. Relax your legs until straight; repeat five times.*

Your growing baby

The fetus is starting to put on weight and its rapid rate of growth has begun to slow down. The milk teeth have developed in the gums and the buds for the permanent teeth are beginning to form. The fetus is around 23 cm/9 in long and weighs about 285 g/10 oz.

WEEK 20: SKIN CARE/CRAVINGS

Your breasts are likely to increase by as much as two bra sizes during pregnancy, so you will need to make sure that they are well supported so that they do not sag and become uncomfortable. Small bumps may appear in the skin around your nipples. These are sebaceous glands which secrete sebum, a fatty lubricant. As your pregnancy progresses, your nipples grow softer and gentle massage will help make them supple and ready for breast-feeding. Your breasts may leak a yellow fluid called colostrum, which will form a crust on the nipples. You will need to wash and dry them gently and thoroughly at least twice a day.

Your nails are made of protein and are affected by the hormonal

changes taking place in your body. Usually they grow longer and stronger during pregnancy, but occasionally pregnancy will cause them to split and break. If this happens, keep them short and protect them by wearing gloves when you are doing rough jobs or when you immerse your hands in water.

If the elasticity of your skin becomes overstretched as you put on

Your nails may be brittle during pregnancy so keep them short to stop them splitting.

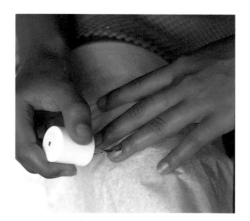

Paint on a nail strengthener to keep your nails strong at this time.

Check your bra size by measuring around your ribcage. For cup size measure around your bust at its fullest.

You and your body

Your uterus is enlarging quite rapidly now so that you look pregnant. Your navel may be flattened or pushed out and it will stay this way until after the birth. Heartburn may start to become a problem because the uterus is starting to push against your stomach.

weight, you may develop stretch marks. These usually appear on the breasts, stomach, and the tops of the thighs as thin, reddish lines. There is little you can do to avoid them, but keeping your skin well moisturized, and being careful not to put on too much extra weight, will help minimize them. Stretch marks fade to thin silvery lines after the birth.

Varicose veins can be caused by pregnancy hormones or, later in pregnancy, by the uterus pressing down and obstructing the flow of blood from the legs to the heart. Although not serious, they can lead to aching or sore legs. Try to avoid standing for long periods and put your feet up whenever possible to ease any discomfort. Walking will help the blood flow; put on support tights or stockings when you get out of bed in the morning to give your legs more support. Varicose veins usually disappear soon after the birth.

CRAVINGS

No one is sure why some pregnant women have cravings while others don't. Doctors disagree about them; some are sympathetic while others doubt that they actually exist. If you desire a certain food there is no reason why you shouldn't indulge yourself within reason, but make sure that you don't exclude other more nourishing foods as a result.

Above: Your legs may ache more with the increased weight you're carrying, so try massaging them with a pleasant body lotion. Right: You can't prevent stretch marks appearing on your stomach, but rubbing in lotion regularly helps to reduce them.

Your growing baby

Vernix, a white greasy substance, is starting to form over the fetus's skin to protect it from the amniotic fluid. This usually wears off before the birth, but sometimes traces of it can be seen. At this stage in your pregnancy the fetus weighs around 340 g/12 oz and measures about 25.5 cm/10 in.

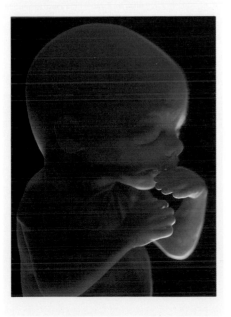

WEEK 21: MINOR COMPLAINTS

You and your body

You should be able to see your abdomen ripple as the fetus moves. You may be feeling slightly breathless as your expanding ribcage pushes upwards, giving your lungs less room. You will probably be feeling energetic so now is the time to tackle things such as planning the nursery.

By now you may be experiencing some of the minor problems that occur later in pregnancy. These include:

Heartburn This is a strong burning feeling in your chest which often happens during the last few months of pregnancy. It is usually worse when lying down. Hormones cause the valve at the top of your stomach to relax, which allows stomach acid to pass back into the gullet (oesophagus), causing a burning sensation. Avoid eating spicy and fatty foods. Eating small, but frequent meals will help reduce heartburn. Sleeping propped up at night and drinking a glass of milk before you go to bed will also help ease the discomfort.

If you are suffering from heartburn, try drinking a glass of milk before you go to sleep at night.

Your doctor may prescribe an antacid if the problem keeps you awake at night. If you buy an over-the-counter remedy always tell the

pharmacist that you are pregnant because some of the remedies available are not suitable for use during pregnancy or breast-feeding.

Insomnia Sleeplessness often

Insomnia can be a problem in later pregnancy. If you can't sleep, try supporting your tummy on pillows to make yourself more comfortable.

becomes a problem as your pregnancy progresses because you find it difficult to get comfortable, and you have to make frequent trips to the toilet. Vivid dreams can also be a problem at this time. A bath followed by a warm drink at bedtime will help you relax. It is important to find restful sleeping positions, so use lots of pillows to support your abdomen when you lie on your side. You could also try practising some relaxation techniques.

Itching This often occurs on the

areas of skin around the bump and is sometimes accompanied by a rash. Calamine lotion should help relieve the itching and since it is usually caused by sweating, wearing loose clothes made of natural fibres can help prevent it. Severe itching during the last three months of pregnancy could be a warning of pregnancy cholestasis – a rare but potentially dangerous liver disorder – and you should consult your doctor.

Oedema (swelling) This occurs in the feet and ankles and sometimes

Your growing baby

The fetus is very active now and you will probably be able to feel it kicking quite easily. If this disturbs you at night, stroke your tummy and talk to the fetus because it will be soothed by the sound of your voice. The fetus is now around 28 cm/11 in long and weighs about 390 g/14 oz.

the hands because your body is holding more fluid than normal. By the end of the day this fluid tends to gather in your feet, especially if the weather has been hot or you have been doing a lot of standing. Try to sit or lie with your feet up whenever you can, as this will help reduce the swelling. Wear support tights and comfortable shoes during the day and avoid standing for long periods. You should always tell your midwife or doctor about any swelling that you experience as it could be a sign of pre-eclampsia.

Tiredness The extra weight you carry during late pregnancy can make you feel more tired than usual. It is important to build some regular rest periods into your day when you

can sit down with your feet up. If the tiredness you are experiencing feels excessive, you may be suffering from anaemia. Make sure you are getting plenty of iron in your diet by eating lean red meat, whole grains, dark green leafy vegetables, nuts, and pulses. If the feeling still persists then consult your midwife or doctor.

Above: You may well be feeling more energetic than usual at this stage in your pregnancy, but don't forget to give yourself time to sit down and rest.
Below: If your ankles start to swell when you have been on your feet for a while, lie down on the floor with your head supported by a pillow and your feet propped up on several pillows.

WEEK 22: RELAXATION AND MASSAGE

It is important to be able to relax, both mentally and physically, during pregnancy because this will help you to rest. Knowing how to make your body relax during labour will allow you to work with the contractions rather than against them.

Physical relaxation
Start by getting comfortable and make sure that every part of your body is supported. Then concentrate on tensing and relaxing individual parts of your body. Start at your toes and work gradually upwards to your head and then back down to your toes again. By the time you have finished this exercise you should be feeling nice and floppy.

Mental relaxation This requires deep concentration so you need to be completely comfortable and in a quiet place where no one will disturb you. Empty your mind and concentrate on your breathing. Breathe in deeply and hold your breath for a few seconds before letting it out slowly. Once you have established a steady pattern of breathing you should make sure that all your muscles are relaxed, then allow your mind to float away. One way to do this is to imagine that you are floating gently on calm water under a clear blue sky, in tranquil surroundings.

You and your body
Your lower ribs are starting to cause you pain as they get pushed outwards by your growing baby and your expanding uterus. Your ribcage rises by a small amount as it is pushed upward. To minimize the discomfort, try sitting up as straight as you can or lifting your arms above your head. This is an ideal time to investigate the different methods that you can use to ease discomfort now and during labour and birth.

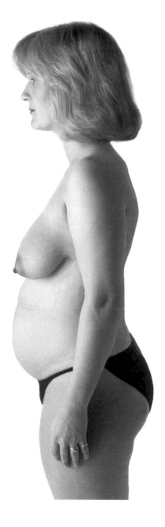

OTHER TECHNIQUES

Massage is an excellent way of relieving tension. It is best done on bare skin, but if you find your skin is particularly sensitive, it can be carried out through a thin cotton nightdress. Massage strokes should be firm, smooth, and rhythmical.

Aromatherapy massage uses essential oils which are added to a carrier oil before being applied to your skin. Certain essential oils can be dangerous during pregnancy because they may trigger uterine contractions, so you must always get qualified professional advice. Many aromatherapists will not treat a pregnant woman at all. Most of those who will treat expectant mothers will do so only after the sixth month of pregnancy. One effective blend is mandarin oil well diluted (i.e. a maximum solution of one per cent: no more than 10 drops of oil to 50 ml carrier oil) in a sweet almond carrier oil. A well-diluted solution of true lavender, jasmine, and rose in sweet almond oil is also thought to be beneficial during labour and birth.

In acupuncture tiny needles are

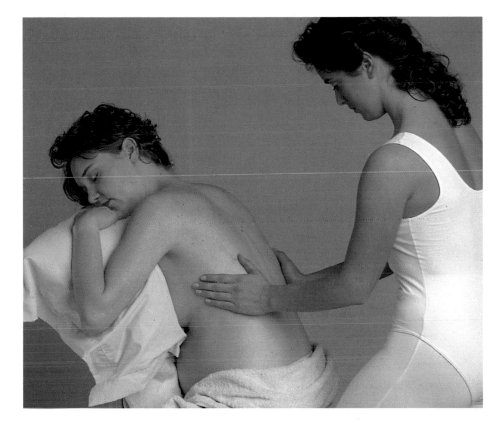

used to stimulate meridian points situated on the body's energy lines with the aim of rebalancing the energy flow. The treatment can help backache, but some points on the body are thought to stimulate uterine contractions, so it is important to visit a qualified practitioner and let him or her know that you are pregnant.

Above: If you are suffering regularly from backache, having a soothing massage from a qualified practitioner can help. With an aromatherapy massage, make sure she chooses oils that will not affect the baby.

Below: Regular massage on your legs will help to relieve any aches and pains that you are experiencing.

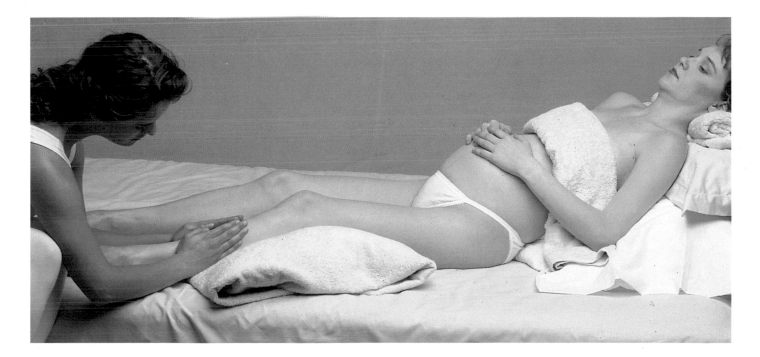

WEEK 23: PREPARING THE NURSERY

This is a good time to think of practical things like planning the baby's nursery. Whether you have a spare room which you are going to turn into a nursery, or you intend to make a nursery corner in your own bedroom, you should start getting it ready now while you have the energy.

Before you begin you will need to take into consideration the shape and size of the area so you can work out how much furniture and baby equipment will comfortably fit into it. You should also check whether there are enough electrical sockets; that there is sufficient heating and that the ceiling or wall lights are where you want them. Major

changes such as rewiring or putting in another radiator are better done before you start to decorate or carpet the nursery.

Babies enjoy looking at bright, primary colours and big, bold patterns so choose a colourful paint and paper; washable materials will make it easier to keep the walls looking bright and fresh. Transfers, borders, pictures, and mobiles can be used very effectively to brighten up a plain background if you are reluctant to commit yourself to a colour scheme until you know your baby's sex.

Rugs and polished floors look nice but are unsuitable because of the risk of you slipping on them

You and your body

The baby can be felt through your abdominal wall and the midwife or doctor will palpate your abdomen to see how the baby is lying. You may occasionally feel a pain rather like a stitch down the side of your stomach. This is the uterine muscle stretching and it will go away after you have had a rest.

while holding the baby. Any flooring needs to be warm underfoot and non-slip. Sealed cork tiles are ideal because they are warm and any spills can be wiped up without damage to the floor. Fitted carpets and carpet tiles are suitable alternatives, but don't buy expensive carpet because it will probably need replacing after a relatively short time.

An overhead light with a dimmer switch or a specially designed nursery light is very useful for night feeds as it gives out a soft comforting glow which won't startle either of you too much in the middle of the night. A plug or cot light will provide enough illumination for you to check on your sleeping baby, but you will need a brighter light for nappy changing and general care. Avoid any lamps with trailing flexes that you could trip over, and fit all unused electrical sockets with a safety cover.

FINISHING TOUCHES
The room where the baby sleeps must be draught-proof so cover any windows with thick, lined curtains. These will not only keep out any draughts but will also keep the morning light from waking your baby during the summer. Windows need to be fitted with childproof

Planning the nursery for your baby can be enjoyable. You can start to buy some outfits in advance, but remember that you will often be given baby clothes when your baby is born.

locks and the curtains should be out of reach of the cot. Never place the cot or crib under a window or near radiators. Young babies cannot regulate their own temperature so they need to be kept in a comfortably warm environment at around a constant 18°C/65°F. A special nursery thermometer or a thermostat fitted to the radiator will help ensure that you maintain the room temperature.

Babies actually require very little in the way of furniture. Somewhere to sleep, a cupboard or chest to keep clothes in, and somewhere for changing and storing toiletries and nappies, as well as a chair for you to sit in while you are feeding or rocking the baby, is all that you really need for the first few months. All nursery furniture should be sturdy enough that it can't be pulled over when babies are older and using it for support as they begin to pull

themselves up on to their feet.

If you buy secondhand furniture, you will need to make sure that any paint or varnish is non-toxic and lead-free. If you are in any doubt, rub down the furniture well and repaint with safe materials. Also check that there are no broken bits that could harm your baby.

Your growing baby

The fetus is beginning to look as it will at birth, with the head more in proportion to the body. In a boy, the scrotum is now well developed and in a girl the ovaries already contain several million eggs. (These will reduce to around two million at birth and will carry on decreasing until puberty.) The fetus is around 31 cm/12¼ in long and weighs approximately 440 g/ 15½ oz.

When decorating your baby's nursery, bear in mind that babies like bright, primary colours. They also love pretty mobiles.

A Moses basket can by kept by or near your bed, and your baby can sleep in it for up to three months.

WEEK 24: BABY CLOTHES AND EQUIPMENT

Start planning what you need to buy for your baby so that by the birth you will at least have purchased the major items. If you leave everything until the end of the pregnancy, you may be too tired to enjoy shopping for your baby.

Only buy a few basic first size or newborn garments as your baby will probably rapidly outgrow these. Also, most baby clothes are sized by the approximate age and height of the child and you won't know the size of your child until she is born.

Choose some well-designed baby clothes, which will make your life easier and allow you to dress and undress your baby with the minimum of time and fuss. Clothes with envelope necks or a shoulder fastening will let you slip clothes over the

baby's head easily, and poppers up the inside of legs of rompers or all-in-one suits will help to ease the regular nappy changing.

Your new baby will probably get through as many as three changes of clothes a day, so it is a good idea to check the washing instructions on any garment before you buy. These instructions will tell you how best to care for each garment so that you

You and your body

You will noticeably be putting on weight, perhaps as much as 0.5 kg/1 lb per week. Your feet and legs may start to feel the strain of carrying this extra weight, so make sure that you wear comfortable shoes and that you get plenty of rest.

can see whether it is easy-care, or if it will require a lot of attention.

BABY'S TRANSPORT

Before you decide on a pram, buggy, or combination, you need to consider your lifestyle and the various methods of transport you will be

A baby's layette: a bonnet, vest, an all-in-one, mits, bootees, nappy and a cardigan.

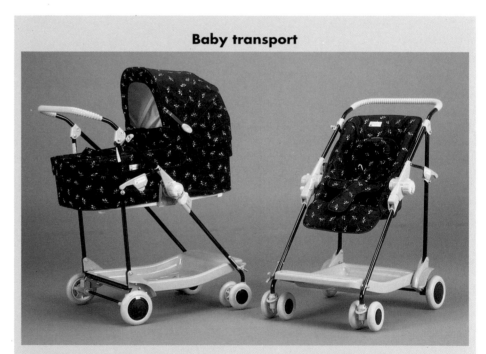

Baby transport

The frame of a combination pram (left) will also take a fold-flat buggy (right).

A traditional pram is sturdy with plenty of space for shopping, and it will take a toddler seat. It is probably the best option if you walk everywhere and you are planning to have another child fairly quickly. Generally, prams are unsuitable for cars unless they have a detachable body.

A fold-flat buggy with a reclining seat can be used from babyhood through to toddler stage. Choose one that is light enough to carry on and off public transport.

A 3-in-1 combination converts from pram to push-chair and has a separate baby carrier or carry cot.

A fold-flat buggy with a parcel shelf can be very useful when you go shopping with your baby.

using regularly. You also need to think about where it will be stored when not in use. Once you have selected the type most suitable to your needs, ask the shop you order it from to keep it for you until after the baby is born.

If you need a car seat, you can choose between an infant carrier, which is suitable from birth to six months, or a combination seat, which is suitable from birth to around four years. Both types are held securely in place using the existing car seat belts.

EQUIPMENT

Whether you buy a cot, Moses basket, or carrycot will probably depend on where your baby is going to sleep and how much space you have. If the baby is going to sleep in your room at first and you haven't much space, think about buying a cot later.

However, when you do purchase a cot make sure that the new mat-

Your growing baby

Vigorous movements followed by periods of quiet will start to occur as the fetus develops its own waking and resting periods. The pattern that develops now may well continue after the birth so it's a good idea to monitor it for a few days to see how it compares with the sleep pattern once the baby is born. The heartbeat can be heard with an ordinary stethoscope and the fetus can hear you clearly when you speak. It is now around 33 cm/13 in long and weighs about 0.5 kg/1 lb.

tress you get to go in it is firm. It should also fit snugly into the base of the cot.

You need to have at least six sheets and several lightweight blankets for the cot and another six sheets and at least three more blankets for your chosen pram. You may want to include a cot bumper and throwover as well.

A two-level high chair can be used in the higher position when your baby is young (left) and in the lower position (above) when he is older. Always make sure you fix him in securely.

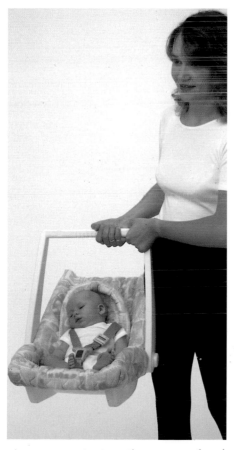

A car seat carrier is easily transported and can be bought in different sizes to suit the age of your baby.

WEEK 25: FEEDING CHOICES

Now is the time to start thinking about how you are going to feed your baby. Whether to breast- or bottle-feed is a personal and emotional decision and one that you need to feel completely happy about. Before you make up your mind talk it over with your partner and your midwife, and get some first-hand experiences from other mothers.

BREAST-FEEDING

Breast milk is the best possible food for your baby because it contains everything he or she needs in the right proportions, and it changes as the baby grows. It contains antibodies which will help protect the baby and it is easily digestible so less likely to cause stomach upsets. Breast-fed babies are also less likely to develop conditions such as eczema and asthma and are less prone to some infections, such as glue ear.

Breast-feeding has advantages for you as well. Not only is breast milk free and always on "tap", at the correct temperature, it also releases hormones that encourage the uterus to shrink back to its original size more quickly. It uses up calories too, so it will help you get your figure back.

During pregnancy the skin around your nipples will appear darker and raised sebaceous glands will appear as little bumps in the areola, the dark area surrounding the nipple. As your pregnancy progresses the nipples will grow softer. You can help make them more supple by gently massaging them. Take extra care washing and drying your breasts towards the end of pregnancy when they may leak a little, and avoid using soaps that have a drying effect on the skin. You may find that you need to use breast pads to prevent your clothes becoming stained.

You and your body

You should be looking rosy-cheeked and healthy because of the increase in blood circulation under the skin. Pressure from the growing uterus on the bladder means that you need to make frequent trips to the lavatory. Cramp, heartburn, and backache are often problems now.

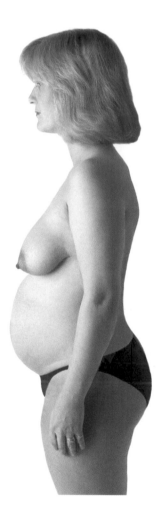

Breast milk is free so the only additional cost involved at first is for nursing bras and breast pads. Choose cotton, front-opening nursing bras, with adjustable straps and fastenings because the size of your breasts will change. Wait until after your 30th week of pregnancy before buying a nursing bra – one that fits you then should fit you after the baby is born.

If you want to be able to express

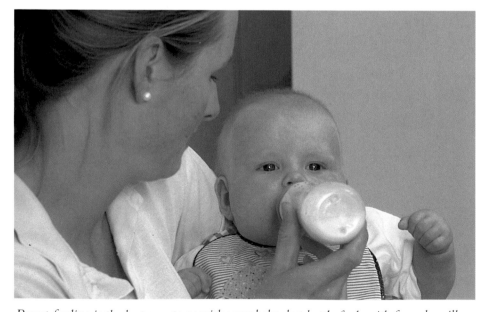

Breast-feeding is the best way to nourish your baby, but bottle feeds with formula milk can be gradually introduced as he gets older, and can be given by both partners.

milk you will also need a couple of bottles and teats, sterilizing equipment, and possibly a breast pump.

BOTTLE-FEEDING

Formula milk has been specially produced for bottle-fed babies. It contains the right balance of vitamins and minerals that a baby needs to thrive. Formula milk has more protein than breast milk, which means that it takes longer to digest. There are a number of brands to choose from and most are based on cows' milk, although alternatives are available which are designed for children who require special diets for medical reasons. It is very important to follow the instructions when making up formula milk because too much or too little can be harmful. The baby will gradually settle into a routine but until then you will need to respond to his or her hunger just as you would if you were breast-feeding.

One of the main advantages of bottle-feeding is that you and your partner can share the feeds between you, so that you can both use the time when you are feeding to get to know your baby.

Hygiene is very important when you bottle-feed because your baby is not getting protection from the antibodies that he or she would have from breast milk. You will need to take particular care over washing and sterilizing bottles and teats. There are several ways of sterilizing feeding equipment and it is important to choose the method which best suits your needs.

As well as formula milk you will need at least six bottles and teats, with caps, a sterilizing unit or container, a bottle brush, and you may also find a bottle warmer is useful for the night feeds.

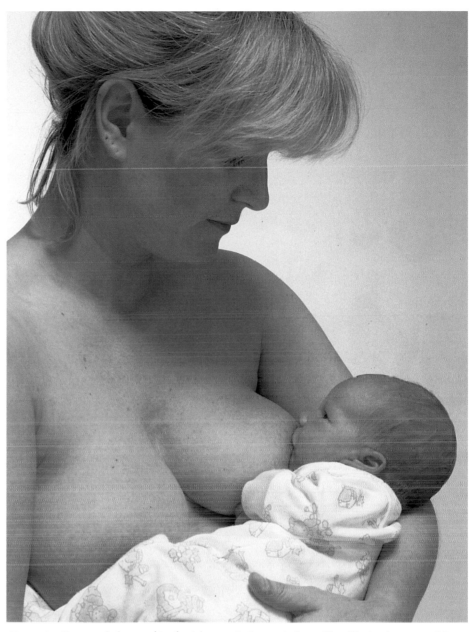

Breast-feeding can help you bond with your baby, and the milk will give her everything she needs, including protection against infection.

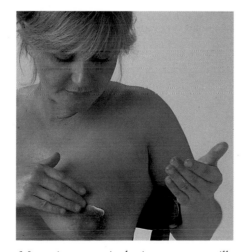

Massaging your nipples in pregnancy will make them more supple for breast-feeding.

Your growing baby

The fetal brain cells continue to develop and become more sophisticated and the bone centres are beginning to harden. The fetus actively practises breathing, inhaling and exhaling amniotic fluid, as more air sacs develop in the lungs. When too much amniotic fluid is swallowed, you may feel a hiccup. The fetus is about 34 cm/13½ in long and weighs around 0.6 kg/1¼ lb.

WEEK 26: PARENTCRAFT CLASSES

You and your body

If you are working you need to decide when you are going to stop. Remember that you should notify your employer in writing three weeks before you intend to leave. If you think you may qualify for maternity allowance from the DSS, now is the time to apply for it. If you haven't started taking regular exercise you should now, because this will help prepare your body for the rigours of labour.

You should be about to start parent-craft classes. You may choose one or more of these. Parentcraft classes show you practical techniques such as relaxation, breathing, and postures for labour and birth. The teacher can answer any questions you may have during the last few months of your pregnancy and will be able to give you information on the birth. Your partner will be welcome at some classes and you will find that they are a good way of meeting other pregnant women and sharing mutual anxieties. The hospital and locally run classes are free, but classes such as National Childbirth Trust and Active Birth charge a fee.

HOSPITAL CLASSES

These are run by the hospital where you plan to give birth and usually take place over six to eight weeks, starting around the 28th week. You need to attend the course that is nearest to your expected date of delivery. Some hospitals have a par-entcraft teacher, who co-ordinates ante-natal education. You will be taken on a hospital tour so that you can see the labour ward, post-natal ward, and the special care baby unit.

LOCAL CLASSES

These are usually run by a midwife or a health visitor attached to your doctor's surgery or health centre and take place over six to eight weeks.

Active birth classes

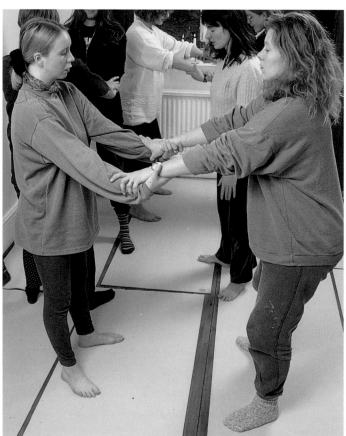

NATIONAL CHILDBIRTH TRUST (NCT)
NCT classes are privately run, usually by mothers who have been trained by the NCT. They need to be booked early because they are deliberately kept small and they become fully booked very quickly. Although everything covered on the hospital and local parentcraft courses is included on the NCT course, the classes are more discussion-based and there are no rigid relaxation and breathing techniques. You are taught a variety of skills for dealing with labour and the birth, from which you can choose when the time comes.

ACTIVE BIRTH CLASSES
These are privately run weekly classes that concentrate on the physical preparation for labour and birth. You are taught a range of yoga-based stretching exercises as well as breathing and relaxation techniques. These classes are mainly for women, with a special session for fathers, and you can join them at any time during your pregnancy.

BREATHING TECHNIQUES
Controlled breathing is important during labour and you need to practise the breathing exercises you will be taught at your classes. Breathing needs to be slow and smooth with deep breaths, inhaled through your nose and exhaled through your mouth. A long slow breath at the beginning of each contraction will help oxygenate your blood and this may help relieve any pain caused by lack of oxygen to the muscles of your uterus. Oxygen is also carried in the blood flowing through the placenta into the umbilical cord, so if you do not get enough, your baby will suffer a shortage too.

During contractions you will be concentrating on each outward breath as this will help you to relax your muscles. It will be important not to over-breathe during the second stage of labour, because this may make you feel dizzy and light-headed. If you do find yourself needing to breathe more quickly then you should concentrate on making each breath as light as possible.

Your growing baby
Although still appearing rather scrawny, the fetus is beginning to lay down fat under the skin. This fat will help regulate body temperature now and after the birth. The fetus is around 35 cm/13¾ in long and weighs approximately 0.7 kg/1½ lb.

Gentle yoga-based exercises are ideal preparation for labour and help you to get ready physically and emotionally, so that you are in tune with the demands on your body. They should always be done under qualified supervision. Exercises include going down into a squatting position (far left and left) in anticipation of labour; massage, which particularly helps if you've got sciatica (below left), and stretching to ease pressure at the base of the spine (below right).

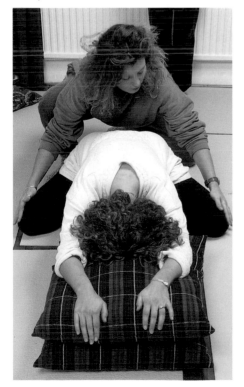

THE THIRD TRIMESTER

WEEK 27: CHOICES IN CHILDBIRTH

Now that you have entered the third trimester you should start planning the kind of birth that you want. If you are having a hospital birth, you will need to discover what facilities are on offer and then try to plan the birth around them. Although nowadays hospitals do try to accommodate a mother's wishes, not all are able to offer every type of birth. If you want an active or water birth, you will have to find out whether it is possible at your hospital. If you are having a home birth then having an active birth or a water birth in a hired pool is easier to arrange. However, you need to remember that if complications occur during labour any decisions you make now may have to be changed.

You and your body

You will be getting noticeably larger and will have put on weight around your chest as well as your breasts. Make sure that you are wearing the correct size of maternity bra. Avoid lying on your back too much because this may make you feel faint, as the enlarged uterus presses directly against blood vessels.

NATURAL BIRTH

This is when you go through labour and birth without any of the medical procedures that often alter the natural rhythm of labour. Natural childbirth involves the use of breathing and relaxation techniques and sometimes homeopathic remedies.

WATER BIRTH

You spend part of your time in a birth pool, which is filled with warm water, and give birth either outside the pool or in the water. The warm water eases contractions, making them less painful, and helps you to relax. Although there is no evidence to prove that there is an increased risk of complications if you actually have your baby in the water, you should still talk to your midwife or doctor before planning to do this.

ACTIVE BIRTH

This means that you are free to move and walk about during labour. Keeping mobile allows the contractions to be more effective. Being in an upright position helps the baby's circulation and encourages the baby to rotate into the best position for

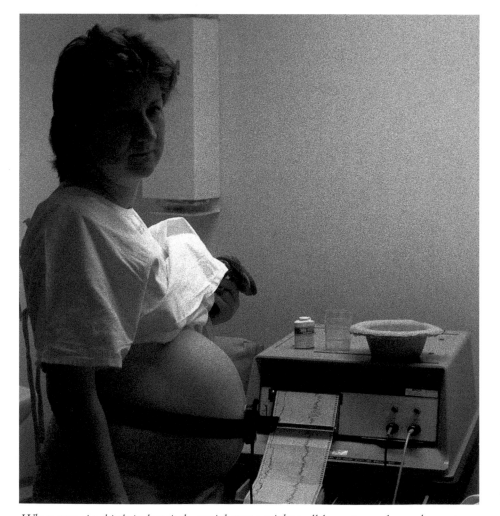

When you give birth in hospital, special straps might well be put round your bump to attach you to a monitor that checks the strength of your baby's heartbeat.

In a natural birth you go through labour without painkillers, using only relaxation methods and maybe homeopathic treatments.

delivery. Gravity aids the baby's descent, and giving birth in a squatting or kneeling position increases the size of the pelvic outlet.

HIGH-TECH BIRTH
Labour is controlled by medical methods such as induction, where labour is started artificially using chemical substances, or the waters are broken manually. Painkilling

drugs are used and an episiotomy (a surgical incision in the perineum to allow passage of the fetal head when there is some fear that the perineum will otherwise be torn) may be done to enlarge the birth canal.

CAESAREAN BIRTH
This is when the baby is delivered through an incision that is made through the wall of the abdomen

into the uterus. It is done under a general anaesthetic, or sometimes with an epidural (an injection that deadens pain only in the lower spine). If an epidural is used you will be awake during the delivery, although a screen is placed across your body so that you don't actually see what is happening. You will be given your baby to hold as soon as it is born. After the birth, the incisions are stitched and you will be kept in hospital for about five days. A Caesarean may be chosen if the reasons that make it necessary are evident before labour begins. This is known as an elective Caesarean. If it is decided on after labour has started, it is known as an emergency Caesarean. Reasons for a Caesarean include abnormal presentation of the baby (that is, not head-first towards the cervix), fetal distress where the baby suffers from lack of oxygen, and high blood pressure in the mother.

When you hold your newborn baby in your arms all the hard work of labour will seem worthwhile.

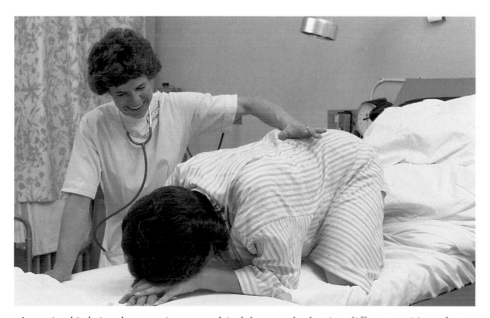

An active birth involves moving around in labour and adapting different positions that will help your baby's descent.

Your growing baby
The fetus's eyes are open and it will be able to see light through the skin of your abdomen. It will have started to practise sucking and may even be able to suck its thumb or fist. The fetus is now about 36 cm/14¼ in long and weighs about 0.8 kg/1¾ lb.

WEEK 28: THE BIRTHPLAN

Some hospitals include a special form with your notes, on which you can make a written plan of the way you would like your labour and birth to be managed. If you haven't received one of these, talk to your midwife about drawing up your own plan. Even if there are still things concerning labour or the birth about which you are undecided, writing out a plan will help you focus on the type of birth you want. It will also give you the opportunity to discuss the birth in detail with your partner.

When drawing up your birthplan it is important to remember that there is no right or wrong way to give birth. Your plan should reflect what you feel is right for you, while taking into account your medical history as well as the facilities available at the place where you are going to have your baby.

A birthplan is a guide to how you would like things to be, but in the event of a problem this ideal may become totally impractical so you will need to be flexible. Once you have finalized your birthplan ask for a copy to be kept with your notes so that the doctor and midwife who attend you during labour have it to

You and your body

Your breasts are producing colostrum, the fluid which precedes breast milk. If your breasts are leaking put breast pads or folded tissues inside your bra. If you have an ante-natal appointment you will probably have a second blood test to check for anaemia. If you are anaemic, iron supplements may be offered.

hand. Keep a copy for yourself so that your birth partner can refer to it if necessary.

BIRTH PARTNER

Although your partner will be encouraged to be with you during labour, you may prefer to have another woman as your actual birth partner, especially if your partner is

Write a birthplan with your choices.

Birthplan checklist

The following questions will help you prepare your own birthplan.

- Whom do you wish to have with you during labour – your partner, your mother, a friend? You can choose more than one birth partner.
- Can your birth partner remain with you if you have to have a Caesarean or forceps delivery?
- Are there special facilities such as a birthing pool or bean bags available to you?
- Do you want to be free to move around during labour, or would you rather be constantly monitored while staying in bed?
- Is there any special position you want to use for the birth?
- Do you wish to wear your own clothes during labour and the birth?
- Would you like music, soft lighting, massage or other therapies to help you cope with getting through labour?
- How do you feel about pain relief? If you want to manage without any, you will need to make sure that everyone knows. If you want pain relief which sort do you want?
- Are you prepared to have an episiotomy if it is required, or would you rather tear naturally?
- Do you want your baby placed straight onto your abdomen or do you want him or her cleaned up first?
- Are you going to breast-feed? If so, do you want to put your baby to the breast immediately?
- Do you want an injection to help deliver the placenta or would you prefer to wait for it to be delivered naturally after the birth?
- How soon after the birth would you like to go home, assuming that there are no complications?

Once you've made your birthplan and put your feelings on your baby's birth in writing, you will feel happier

worried that he may not be able to cope with seeing you in pain. Whatever you decide, make sure you talk about it together so that there are no misunderstandings and you don't get upset about the final choice.

Your growing baby

Now fully formed, the fetus would be viable if it were born at 28 weeks, although the body systems are still very immature. The heart is beating at a rate of around 150 beats a minute. The fetus weighs around 0.9 kg/2 lb.

If your partner is worried about being with you during a long or painful labour, talk it through with him and make your feelings known if you're counting on his support.

WEEK 29: SPECIAL CARE

If you suffer from a medical condition or blood disorder your pregnancy
will require careful managing. Your
doctor will need to monitor your
progress and you may have to have
special ante-natal checks. If there is a
possible problem, you will be offered
another scan during the last
trimester, which will clearly show
the fetus's breathing movements,
how it is lying, and the position of
the placenta.

Anaemia is caused by an abnormally low level of red corpuscles in the
blood and is treated with iron supplements. You can build up your
body's store of iron by eating a diet

which includes red meat, whole
grains, dark green leafy vegetables,
nuts, and pulses. Liver is not recommended because of the high levels of
vitamin A, which could be toxic. A
second blood test is done in late
pregnancy to check for anaemia.

Kidney infection is usually caused
by bacterial infection and you should
contact your doctor if you think you
have a kidney infection. Symptoms
are pain, frequent urination accompanied by a burning sensation, and
occasionally blood in the urine.
Other symptoms you may experience include back pain, high fever,
chills, nausea, and vomiting.

You and your body

You will probably be able to feel the
fetus's bottom and feet as it moves
around. The fetus will be putting pressure on your stomach and diaphragm
now and you will need to sit down
and rest more often.

Placenta praevia is a rare condition
which usually occurs when a woman
has had more than one child. The
placenta is situated low in the uterus
so that it blocks, or partially blocks,
the cervix. The pressure of the fetus
on the placenta may cause painless
bleeding any time after 28 weeks. If
this happens, you may have to stay in
hospital until after your baby is born.
If the obstruction is particularly
severe, your baby may need to be
delivered by Caesarean.

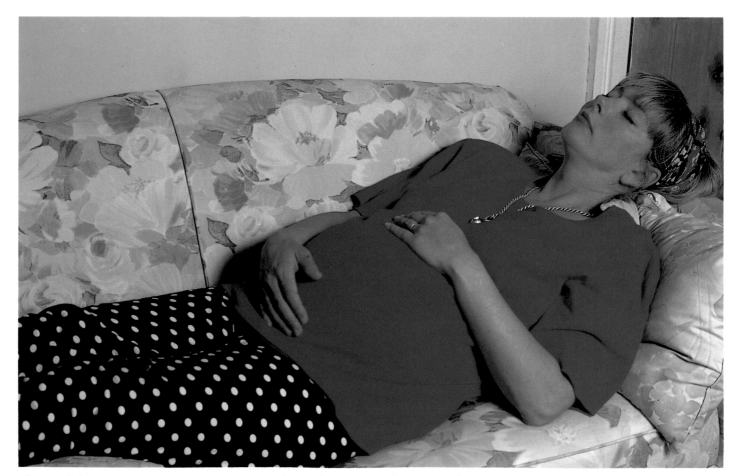

As your baby starts to put pressure on your stomach, you'll need to lie down more often to rest.

If the weather is pleasant, you might well prefer to take your regular rests in the garden, but remember to support your legs.

Abruptio placentae is when part of the placenta comes away from the wall of the uterus causing some abdominal pain and bleeding. You should call the doctor immediately. The fetus could be at risk if a large part of the placenta has come away, because it will be deprived of necessary oxygen and nutrients. Sometimes a blood transfusion is necessary and in late pregnancy the baby may be delivered by Caesarean. If only a small part of the placenta has come away, you will need to have complete bedrest until the bleeding stops.

Placental insufficiency occurs when the placenta doesn't function efficiently and the fetus grows more slowly than normal because of lack of nourishment. If this happens, you will be told to rest so that the blood flow from the placenta to the fetus can improve. A urine test will also be taken to see whether the health of the fetus is being affected and whether induction is going to be necessary for the birth.

Your growing baby

The fetus is filling almost all the space in your uterus and its head is now more or less in proportion with the rest of the body. The eyebrows and eyelashes are fully grown and the fetus has quite a lot of hair which is still growing. The eyes, which can now open and close, are beginning to focus. The fetus weighs around 1 kg/2¼ lb and is about 38 cm/ 15 in long.

WEEK 30: TRAVEL/BACKACHE

There is no reason why you shouldn't travel during pregnancy, but during the later stages you should check with your doctor if you are going abroad. Airlines may not be willing to take you once you are past 28 weeks because of the risk of a premature labour occurring.

If you want to fly you will need to check with the airline before you book a ticket; the airline may insist on a medical certificate stating that it is safe for you to travel. If you wish to visit a country where immunization is required, you will have to get medical advice because some vaccines should be avoided completely in pregnancy.

You will probably want to avoid long car journeys towards the end of pregnancy because you may find them uncomfortable. When travelling by car it is important to wear your seat belt so that it fits neatly across your thighs and above your abdomen, but not across the middle. If the belt was worn across your body it could possibly cause damage to your baby if you were involved in a car accident.

BACKACHE

This can be particularly troublesome during the last months of pregnancy. Hormones have softened your ligaments and the additional weight you are carrying inevitably puts a strain on your stomach muscles, which in turn puts strain on your back muscles. If the backache you are suffering is particularly severe, always check it out with your doctor because it can indicate the presence of a kidney infection.

You and your body

You will feel larger and clumsier now and your movements will be slower. It is important to try to maintain good posture to prevent backache. You may have problems sleeping and become a bit breathless if you walk too fast or climb stairs.

Ease upper backache by lying flat on a firm surface with pillows under your head and knees. Lower backache can be helped by kneeling on all fours, with your back straight and your hands and knees well apart, then dropping your head and arching your back. Repeat this exercise several times.

You can help to avoid backache by wearing low-heeled shoes and trying not to hollow your back when you are standing. When you sit down, put a cushion in the small of your back; when you get out of a chair, push yourself right to the edge before attempting to stand up.

A firm mattress will help when you are lying down; when you get up from the lying position, roll over onto your side and then push yourself slowly up. If you have to bend down, always bend your body from the knees and then squat down to pick up anything from the floor.

Your growing baby

The fetus is beginning to move about less vigorously now because it has less space to move around in the uterus. To get comfortable it is likely to adopt a curled-up position with arms and legs crossed. The fetus is now about 39 cm/15½ in long and weighs around 1.1 kg/2½ lb.

Don't fasten your seat belt over your bump as your baby could be damaged in a accident.

Fasten your seat belt under your bump and across your thighs to protect your baby.

Bending in pregnancy

1 *In later pregnancy particularly, bend your knees, not from the waist, and pick up the object when you are squatting.*

2 *As you get up from the squatting position, keep your back straight and lift up the object at arm's length.*

3 *As you gradually become upright, straighten your bent knees without making any jerky movements.*

How to relieve backache

1 *To relieve painful aches in your lower back in pregnancy, try this exercise. Kneel down on the floor on all fours with your back straight, your head facing down, and your hands and knees spaced well apart.*

2 *Drop your head right down and arch your back to stretch out the painful muscles, hold for several seconds, then release, raising your head up again. Repeat the exercise several times for the best relief.*

WEEK 31: DEALING WITH DISCOMFORT

The fetus is getting quite big and will be putting pressure on your diaphragm, which may mean that you are now finding it more difficult to breathe. This breathlessness should pass once the fetus's head drops into the pelvis and becomes engaged in a few weeks' time. Try sitting and standing as straight as possible, and put some extra pillows behind your shoulders when you are in bed.

You are likely to need a larger size of bra towards the end of pregnancy and the one that you buy now should fit you after the baby is born. If you are intending to breast-feed, buy a front-opening nursing bra that will be suitable both now and after the birth.

Choose a bra with wide adjustable straps and fastenings and which has a broad supportive band under the cups. Make sure that the cups fit comfortably and do not gape under the arms. Buy one made from cotton or a cotton mixture that will be more comfortable to wear, and allow your skin to breathe properly, particularly in hot weather.

BRAXTON HICKS CONTRACTIONS
During pregnancy you will experience contractions which may be uncomfortable but are not usually painful. These are known as Braxton Hicks contractions, which tighten the muscles of the uterus about every 20 minutes throughout pregnancy, although you have probably not been aware of them during the early months. In the last weeks of

pregnancy these contractions become more noticeable as they begin to prepare the uterus for labour by drawing up the cervix and making it thinner. When you have

You and your body

Breathlessness may be more of a problem now, especially if you overdo things. Try to get as much rest as possible and slow down any exercise regime to a pace that suits you. If your breasts feel uncomfortable when you go to bed, wear a maternity or specially designed sleep bra at night.

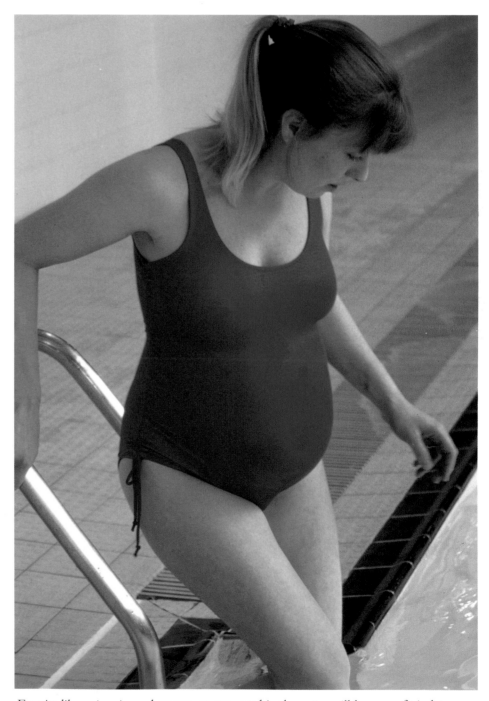

Exercise like swimming, where you are supported in the water, will keep you fit in late pregnancy. It will also relieve backache as the swimming motion will stretch the back muscles.

these contractions, practise your breathing techniques for labour.

KICK COUNTS

You can check on your baby's well-being by keeping a count of the fetal movements. If there is any concern about the fetus's development you may be asked to keep a kick chart recording the first 10 movements each day. For your own peace of mind you should be aware of these movements so that if for any reason they become less frequent, or even stop altogether, you will notice immediately. If you are ever concerned about lack of movement, seek some medical advice immediately because it could indicate some trouble with the fetus.

As your pregnancy progresses and the fetus gets bigger it has less room to manoeuvre, so movements will be more noticeable, but less frequent. By the end of your pregnancy the fetus will probably move between 10 and 12 times in a 12-hour period.

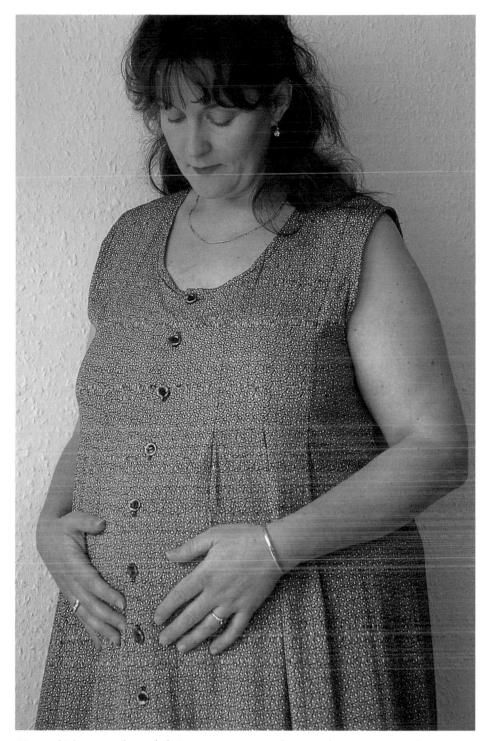

Keep a kick count of your baby's movements on a chart, so that you can monitor any noticeable changes and seek medical help if you feel it is necessary.

Try sitting in a yoga position with your back straight to alleviate the pressure your baby is putting on your diaphragm.

Your growing baby

The organs are almost completely developed, apart from the lungs which are still not fully mature. The brain is still growing and the nerve cells and connections are now working. A protective sheath is developing around the nerve fibres so that messages travel faster, enabling the fetus to learn more. It can feel pain, will move if prodded and you can feel it jump at loud noises. The fetus is around 40 cm/15¾ in long and weighs about 1.4 kg/3 lb.

WEEK 32: POSITIONS FOR LABOUR

It is a good idea to practise some of the positions that will help you through the different stages of labour. During the first stage you should try to stay upright and keep active. Being upright will make your contractions stronger and more efficient. It will also allow gravity to keep the baby's head pressed down, which will help your cervix to dilate faster so that labour is speeded up. Remaining active will give you more control over labour so that you should feel less pain. If you are lying down, your uterus presses on the large blood vessels running down your back and this can reduce the blood flow through the placenta to and from the baby. If you feel you want to lie down during labour, try to position yourself on your side rather than on your back.

COPING WITH CONTRACTIONS

You should aim to give the fetus as much room as possible in your pelvis and the best way to achieve this is by keeping your knees well apart and leaning forward so that the uterus tilts away from your spine. During the first-stage contractions it may help to lean against your partner, or if you prefer you can kneel down resting your arms and head on a cushion on the seat of a chair. If you find being upright tiring, try kneeling on all fours. This allows you to keep the weight of the fetus off your lower back. By the time your contractions are coming every few minutes you may want to adopt a squatting position, or you could try kneeling forward onto a pile of cushions or a bean bag with your legs wide apart. It may help if your

You and your body

If you work, you may have left by now or will have a date when you are going to leave. Enjoy the last weeks of your pregnancy and spend time singing and talking to your baby. You may find the fetal movements uncomfortable now that it is so much bigger. Occasionally, you may feel its feet getting stuck under your ribs.

partner massages your back while you are in this position.

When you reach the second stage you'll want to find a comfortable position for the birth. If you lie on your back you will literally have to push the baby uphill. If you remain upright your abdominal muscles will work more efficiently as you bear down, and gravity will help the baby out. Try squatting, supported on both sides, or with your partner supporting you from behind, so that your pelvis is at its widest and you have control over the pelvic floor

Labour positions

1 *Relax on all fours by flopping forward onto a pile of cushions or a bean bag to give the fetus as much room as possible in the pelvis. Your partner can help by massaging your back.*

2 *Take the weight of the baby off your spine by kneeling on the floor on all fours with your arms and legs wide apart. Keep the small of your back flat and not hollowed.*

Your growing baby

The fetus is now very energetic and it will have periods of extreme activity, and you will feel it twisting and turning. As it continues to grow it will have less and less room to move in, so it will soon settle, probably in the head-down position, ready for birth. The fetus is about 40.5 cm/16 in long and weighs about 1.6 kg/3½ lb.

which you will need to relax. Kneeling with your legs wide apart and supported on both sides is another good position for pushing.

Once you have tried these positions, experiment with others which you feel may be right for you during labour. Try them on the floor, on the bed, leaning on or against furniture, or using your partner for support. This way, when you are in labour, you will already know how to get into positions that are comfortable for you and that will help you cope with contractions.

Partner support

1 *Practise using your partner for support during labour by leaning back against him, allowing him to take your weight.*

2 *Stand with feet well apart and lean on your partner, putting your head on your arms to ease pressure on your uterus.*

3 *Kneel on all fours with your forearms on the floor and your knees spread wide so that your abdomen is hanging between them. It can help to rock backwards and forwards in this position.*

4 *In this squatting position, your pelvis is wide open and the baby's head is pressed down. You may find that it helps to place your hands on the floor to give yourself some support.*

WEEK 33: EMOTIONS IN LATE PREGNANCY

It is not just your body that is going through great changes while you are pregnant. Your whole way of life is changing and this can lead to conflicting emotions, especially during the last few months. You may wonder how you are going to cope with all the new responsibilities and be concerned about your baby – whether it will be born perfect in every way. Vivid dreams are common at this time and can be worrying, especially if they are about the birth or babies. You may even feel occasionally that the whole thing has been a ghastly mistake and that you want to go back to the way things were before you became pregnant. Don't worry, all these feelings are quite normal.

It helps to talk about your fears and concerns, either to your partner or to a close friend who has had similar feelings. Parentcraft classes are also a good place to discuss these worries, especially as you will be with other women who are experiencing the same emotions. If you find that talking about it doesn't help and that anxiety is taking over your life, discuss how you feel with your midwife or doctor.

YOUR PARTNER

It is easy to forget that an expectant father is also going through emotional changes as he comes to terms with impending parenthood. He doesn't have any outward sign of the change that is about to occur in his life, but that doesn't mean he isn't feeling the same concerns as you. He also has additional worries about you and how you will cope during labour; he may even secretly fear for your safety during the birth. If he is now solely responsible for providing financially for you and the baby he

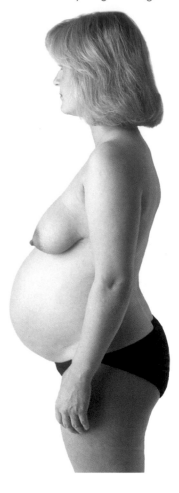

You and your body

Your weight gain should have slowed down. If it hasn't and you are still gaining more than 1 kg/2¼ lb a week, you should check with your doctor that everything is all right.

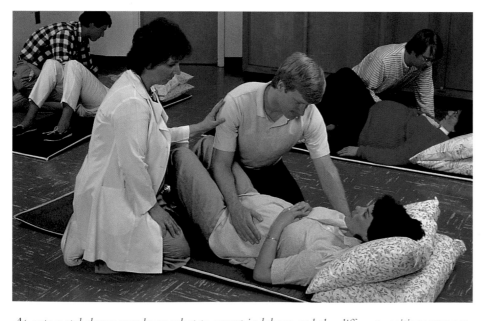

At ante-natal classes you learn what to expect in labour and the different positions you can adopt. Your partner is usually welcome to come with you and find out how he can help.

may be feeling considerable stress.

Make time to talk to each other about your feelings and try to ensure that these last weeks before the birth are special for you both. Share the preparation for the birth so that each of you is involved in what is going to happen. Plan some treats where you can be alone together, such as a special dinner at a favourite restaurant, a trip to the theatre, or a weekend away at a hotel. By making time for yourselves you are less likely to have misunderstandings which could lead to hurt and disappointment.

Your growing baby

The fingernails are fully formed although the toenails are not quite so advanced. The vernix covering the skin has become thicker. The lungs are almost fully developed and the fetus will be practising breathing in preparation for the birth. It measures around 41.5 cm/16½ in and weighs about 1.8 kg/4 lb.

OTHER CHILDREN

If you have other children you may have told them about the new baby early on in your pregnancy. Very young children will need to have it explained to them over and over again, because the concept of a new baby is hard for them to grasp. Older children will probably be very excited and will enjoy being involved in any preparations you are making for their brother or sister.

How children react once the baby has arrived depends a lot on their age and personality, as well as their relationship with you. A pre-school child may react by being naughty for a period in an attempt to get your attention. A toddler, who has recently been potty-trained, may start wetting or dirtying him- or herself again. Both age groups may start waking at night. Use common sense and tact to minimize any problems. Talk to your children about the new baby, encourage their help and involvement when he or she is born but always make sure that they have time with you on their own.

When your doctor checks your baby's heartbeat, let any older children be present if they are interested.

Let an older child feel your bump, and talk to him or her about their new brother or sister, so they can get used to the idea of a new family member.

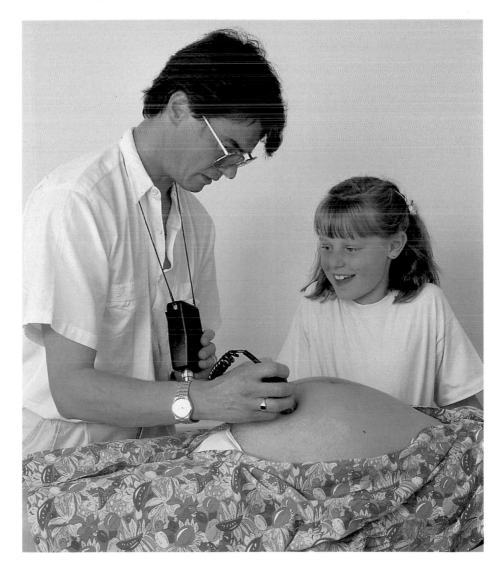

WEEK 34: OLDER FIRST-TIME MOTHERS

If you are 35 or over, you will have been offered an amniocentesis because of the higher risk of fetal abnormality. The amniotic fluid will have been screened for a number of chromosomal disorders, which include Down's syndrome and spina bifida. Of course, you don't have to have this test, but many mothers find it reassuring.

It is important that you attend all your ante-natal clinics so that a close check can be kept on you and the unborn baby all through pregnancy. Many older expectant mothers prefer to have the ante-natal care at a hospital where expert medical help is on hand. The risk to the baby during labour and birth increases with rising maternal age, but many factors affect labour, including the general health of the mother during pregnancy. Although nearly 70 per cent of women over 30 have normal deliveries, there is a greater risk of complications during labour for women who are over 35. This is usually because the baby is in distress through lack of oxygen because of placental deterioration. As a result of these complications older women tend to have more forceps and Caesarean deliveries.

BIRTH AND THE OLDER MOTHER
Most older women go full term, and if you are between 30 and 34 there is no reason why you shouldn't have a natural birth. If you are 35 or over, or if there is a suggestion that your baby may be small, you may have to have continuous monitoring. This

may also be necessary if there is a likelihood of a prolonged labour, or if the waters, when they break, show some sign of staining. This means that you will be unable to move around freely. But this is a small

You and your body

Your blood pressure may be slightly raised and you will probably be told to take things easy. Swelling of the hands and feet could also be a problem so try to get as much rest as possible, preferably with your feet up.

Seeing her baby on an ultrasound scan can be very reassuring for an older mother.

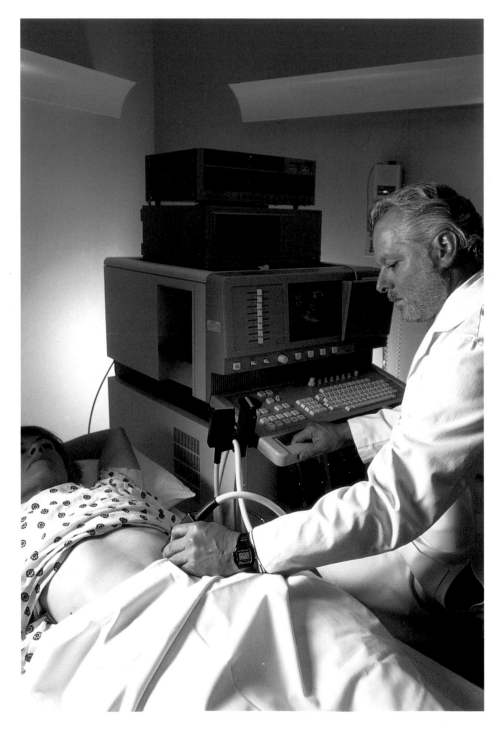

price to pay for a healthy baby.

Babies born to older mothers have a greater chance of being born preterm. This is often because of the failure of the placenta, which means the baby is no longer getting sufficient oxygen and nourishment. If this happens you will probably have to have a forceps delivery, or you may be offered a Caesarean.

Your growing baby

The weight gain continues to increase. The eyes respond to bright lights and the fetus will practise blinking; eyebrows and eyelashes are fully developed. A boy's testicles will have descended into the groin. The fetus is 43 cm/17 in long and weighs about 2 kg/4½ lb.

Below: The doctor will talk about your baby and give you a printout of your scan.

Right: As time progresses, you will find you need more rest with your back supported.

WEEK 35: FINAL PREPARATIONS

Even though your baby is not due for some weeks, you should be ready in case he or she decides to put in an early appearance. Check the nursery and make sure all the baby's sheets and blankets have been washed and aired. Sort out all the baby clothes and put the ones you will want immediately after the birth in your hospital case.

It's a good idea to stock up on non-perishable goods and to fill the freezer, if you have one. This will save you from having to do a lot of shopping over the next few weeks and will allow you more time with the baby when you first come home.

Make sure you know where your partner is going to be over the next few weeks; if he is out and about you may want to consider hiring a bleeper so that you can keep in constant touch. Keep your car filled with petrol and make sure that you both know the quickest route to the hospital. Have a list of emergency numbers, including a local taxi firm, beside the telephone.

THE HOSPITAL

Pack what you want to take to hospital several weeks before the delivery date; keep the bag where you can easily get it when the time comes. Remember that there are three separate aspects to consider: labour, your hospital stay, and going-home clothes for you and the baby.

You should bring any personal items that will make life more comfortable for you during labour. Include anything from a personal

You and your body

Discuss any worries you may have about labour and birth with your doctor or midwife. You will be feeling tired and even a little fed up, so try to get as much rest as you can. Pay special attention to your diet: you will be needing another 200 calories a day during these last weeks. Some practical planning now can save time and forestall anxiety at the time of labour and delivery.

stereo and your favourite music to a face cloth and massage oils. You may even want to take along a bean bag if you are planning an active labour and your hospital doesn't provide these. Leave some room for last-minute items such as an ice pack for backache and even a snack and drink for your partner. Don't forget to put your birthplan and maternity record right at the top so that you can give these to the midwife when you

It is a good idea to buy vegetables and other food that can be cooked and frozen in preparation for when you return from the hospital.

You might need to get to the hospital quickly, so have your bag packed and keep a local taxi number close to hand.

It is sensible to pack a small bag for your brief stay in hospital well in advance in case you have to leave in a rush. Don't forget some clothes for your new baby to wear.

arrive at the hospital. It is sensible to pack things for labour separately, since you will want to be able to get to them quickly.

How much you pack for the hospital depends on your planned length of stay after the birth. The hospital may issue a list of the items that you will need to bring with you. But if it doesn't, ask your midwife whether you need to take in baby clothes and nappies, or contact the maternity unit direct. If you are staying in for a few days and aren't too tired, you might want to write cards to your friends and relatives announcing your baby's arrival, so remember to include birth announcement cards, your address book, and stamps. You should also bring change in case you need to use hospital pay phones.

You will need clothes for you and the baby when it's time for you to return home. It is sensible to pack a small bag now with all the items you think you'll want for your return journey; you can either bring it with you or your partner can bring it later. Remember that although you will feel considerably slimmer than you were before the birth, it takes a while before you get your figure back, so your going-home outfit will still need to be loose.

Your growing baby

The fetus is putting on weight each day and now fills most of the uterus, so you may find it uncomfortable when it moves around. The fetus now does body rolls rather than the more energetic movements it made when it was smaller. It is now about 44.5 cm/ 17½ in long and weighs around 2.3 kg/5 lb.

WEEK 36: DISCOMFORTS IN LATE PREGNANCY

As you find getting around more difficult and everything generally more of an effort, you may become irritable over the smallest things. You will be impatient for your baby to arrive, and concern about the impending birth and worries about how you will cope with being a parent can make you short-tempered, especially with your partner. Tell him how you are feeling so that he understands why you are being so irritable and perhaps not paying him as much attention as usual.

Aches or pains around your pubic area, in your groin, or down the inside of your legs can be caused by your baby's head pressing on the nerves, or by your pelvic joints beginning to soften in preparation for labour. Pain under your ribs is caused by the expanding uterus pushing the ribs up. These aches and pains are not serious, but they can be quite uncomfortable. Sitting or standing as straight as you can, or stretching upwards, will help ease most of these discomforts, although

You and your body

You will be able to feel the top of your uterus just below your breastbone. This can make breathing uncomfortable and you may suffer from pain in your ribcage. Your ante-natal checks will be weekly from now on.

you may find lying down better for relief of pelvic pain. If you get severe pain in your abdomen, or if you suffer any abdominal pain that is also accompanied by vaginal bleeding, you must get in touch with your doctor at once.

It is quite common to suffer from heartburn and nausea towards the end of pregnancy. This is caused by the enlarged uterus pressing on your stomach. It often helps to eat small

Soaking in a warm bath can help to relieve any aches and pains you are suffering.

meals at frequent intervals, rather than two or three big meals a day.

ANTE-NATAL CHECK

An internal examination or a scan may be carried out to check the size of your pelvis. If there is any concern about the size of your pelvis in relation to your baby's size, or there is some other reason for the baby's delivery not being straightforward, a Caesarean may be discussed. If this is thought to be necessary, the doctor at the hospital where the delivery is to take place will explain the medical procedures that will be used.

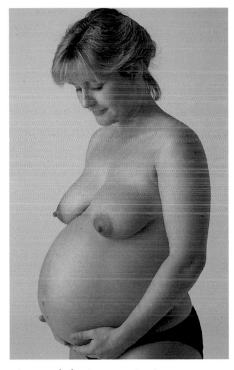

As your baby increases in size, you may begin to find breathing uncomfortable and get some pain in your ribcage.

Your growing baby

The nervous system is maturing and the fetus is getting ready for birth by starting to practise breathing movements, sucking, and swallowing. It is now about 46 cm/18¼ in long and weighs around 2.5 kg/5½ lb.

In this late stage of pregnancy you will probably be able to feel the top of your uterus which is now positioned just below your breastbone.

WEEK 37: AS BIRTH APPROACHES

Your growing baby

The lanugo, the fine hair that covers the fetus's body, is beginning to wear off. The fetus has started to produce a hormone called cortisone which will help the lungs to become fully matured so that they are ready to cope with breathing once it is born. The fetus will be practising breathing although there is no air in its lungs. The fetus is now about 47cm/18½ in long and weighs around 2.7 kg/6 lb.

Between weeks 36 and 38 the baby's head is likely to "engage". This is when it settles downwards, deep in your pelvis ready for the birth. You should feel some relief from the pressure in your abdomen when this happens which is why it is sometimes referred to as "lightening". You will start to feel less breathless now because the baby is no longer putting any pressure on your diaphragm and your lungs.

If this is not your first baby, but your second or third child, the head may not engage until you actually go into labour.

PREMATURE AND TWIN BIRTHS
If the baby is born before 37 weeks it will be described as being preterm or premature. Most premature babies are nursed in a special care baby unit (SCBU) or, if very sick or small, an intensive care baby unit (ICBU). Babies are given expert care and

This is probably the last time for a while that you will have time to yourself, so make the most of it and rest often.

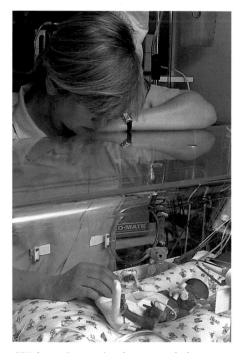

With modern technology even babies as young as 24 weeks normally survive in the special baby units.

attention in these facilities, so that even those who are born as young as 24 weeks have a reasonable chance of survival.

If you are giving birth to twins, the labour doesn't usually take any longer than if you are giving birth to a single baby (singleton). Because twins tend to be smaller babies, the labour and birth can often be easier and less painful. Once the birth canal has been stretched to allow one baby to be born, the second baby will usually be born quite quickly. If twins share the placenta, they will both be born before it is delivered. Even if they are fraternal twins and each have their own placenta they will usually be born first, although occasionally one baby is born, followed by its placenta, before the second baby arrives.

You and your body

Your baby could arrive at any time from now until the end of week 42, so check that you have everything organized. You will probably be able to visit the hospital about now and see where you are going to give birth. Don't be afraid to ask questions if there is anything you don't understand about hospital procedures.

Sometime between now and the birth, you may experience a sudden burst of energy, known as the nesting instinct. Don't overdo things and decide to spring-clean your whole house. Remember that you will shortly need all your energy reserves for the exhausting demands of labour.

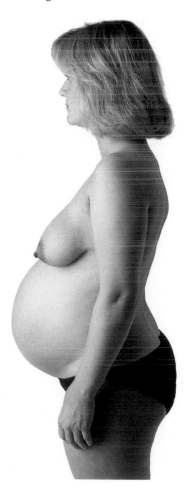

As the birth approaches, it is a good time for you and your partner to start making a list of names that you both like.

WEEK 38: INDUCTION/PAIN RELIEF IN LABOUR

Sometimes labour has to be started artificially because of a problem such as pre-eclampsia, bleeding, diabetes, or you are well past your due date and the placenta is no longer working efficiently. Induction involves several techniques.

Pessaries Prostaglandin pessaries, made from a naturally occurring hormone, may be inserted into the vagina to soften the cervix and to start the contractions.

Artificial rupture of the membranes (ARM) This involves puncturing the amniotic sac in which the baby is sealed so that the increased pressure on the cervix causes the contractions to become much stronger.

Syntocinon drip A hormone that stimulates contractions is put into a vein to help them remain constant and steady. This may lead to stronger contractions than you would otherwise have had.

PAIN RELIEF

You will have been told about the various forms of pain relief at parentcraft classes. If you want to have a completely natural birth make sure that this is marked clearly on your birthplan and inform the medical staff who will be attending you during labour.

Remember that you can always change your mind later if you find coping with the pain too difficult. If you have decided to opt for some form of pain relief, there are a number of options you can choose from:

Gas and air (Entonox) A mixture of oxygen and nitrous oxide which is breathed in through a mask and takes the edge off pain. This is the most controllable form of pain relief because you hold the mask and regulate the gas and air intake yourself. The gas is processed in your lungs so it doesn't affect the baby.

Injections Drugs like pethidine and meptid can be given during the first stage of labour. They will help you relax and relieve pain but they can affect the baby, making him sleepy at birth and afterwards.

Epidural A local anaesthetic is injected into the space between your spinal column and the spinal cord, numbing the nerves that serve the uterus. It may also numb your leg nerves, making it hard for you to move around. An epidural may also be used if a Caesarean delivery is performed because it allows the mother to stay awake while her baby is being delivered.

An anaesthetist is needed to give an epidural injection, which takes around 30 minutes to set up, and then usually requires topping up every hour and a half.

Transcutaneous electrical nerve stimulation (TENS) This is a technique which involves a weak electric current being used to block pain sensations in the brain and to

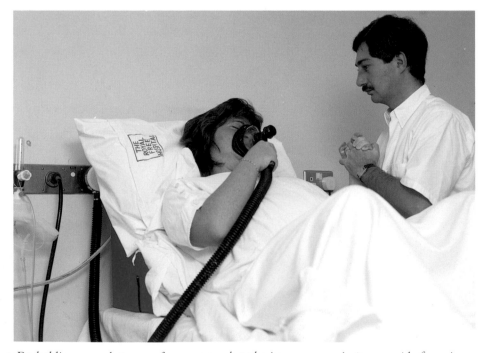

By holding a mask to your face, you can breathe in oxygen and nitrous oxide for pain relief during contractions.

stimulate the release of endorphins, the body's natural painkilling hormones. TENS is not available at all hospitals so you may need to hire a machine before you go into labour.

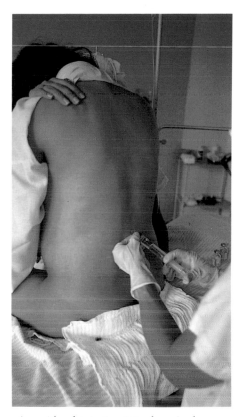

An epidural injection into the spinal area helps deaden the nerves around the uterus.

At the most painful times in your labour, lean on your partner for support and encouragement. He can also massage your back if it is really painful.

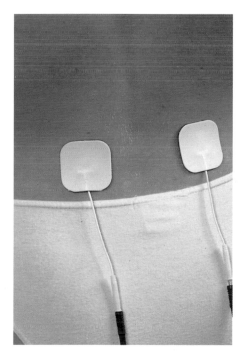

Pads from a TENS machine can be fitted to your back to ease pain in labour.

Your midwife should be able to give you all the necessary details.

Alternative pain relief Both acupuncture and hypnosis can be used to relieve pain during childbirth, but if you are having a hospital birth you will need permission to have a private practitioner with you during labour. Used correctly, massage, aromatherapy, and reflexology can all help to ease labour. You should get some expert advice before the birth if you intend to use any of these techniques.

Your growing baby

The fetus has put on fat so that it now appears rounded and its skin has a pinkish look. The hair may be as long as 5 cm/2 in and the nails already need cutting. The vernix, which has been protecting the skin of the growing fetus from the amniotic fluid, is beginning to dissolve. At this stage of your pregnancy, the fetus now measures about 48 cm/19 in and weighs around 2.9 kg/6½ lb.

WEEK 39: COMPLICATIONS DURING BIRTH

The ideal position for your baby to be born is with its head lying down with its back against your abdomen. This way it has less distance to rotate in the birth canal. Sometimes a baby is in an abnormal position which can make birth more complicated, but this does not necessarily mean that it can't be born in the normal way.

An occipito posterior position means that the baby is lying with its back towards your back and, if it fails to turn, will be delivered normally, but will be born face up. This way of lying often leads to a long, back-aching labour.

In a deep transverse arrest, the baby's head partially rotates in the birth canal and then becomes stuck with its face towards one side. The baby will need to be helped out. This can sometimes also happen if you push too hard by mistake in the second stage of labour.

Disproportion means that the baby's head is too big for your pelvis. A scan will be done to decide whether there is enough room for a normal delivery to take place. If there isn't, your baby will probably be born by Caesarean.

BREECH BIRTH
A small number of babies don't turn around in the last weeks of pregnancy. This means that their feet or bottom would come out first so the birth canal will not have been stretched enough when the head, the largest part of the baby's body, is ready to be born. Doctors have different opinions about the best way of delivering a breech baby; some insist that a Caesarean is the safest method, others believe that birth should take place under an epidural, and some think that if the mother remains mobile throughout the first stage of labour the baby will get itself into a good position for birth. It may then be helped out with forceps or by vacuum extraction.

You and your body
The waiting is nearly over and you will probably be feeling both excited and apprehensive. You may be having quite strong Braxton Hicks contractions as the cervix softens in readiness for the birth. Although you may be feeling heavy and weary, don't simply sit around waiting for something to happen. Keep up your social life and talk to other friends from your parent-craft classes who are at the same stage as you.

FORCEPS DELIVERY
In a forceps delivery, your legs will be put up in stirrups and then the forceps, which are like a pair of large, shallow metal spoons, will be inserted into the vagina and cupped around the baby's head. The doctor helps the baby out while you push.

VACUUM EXTRACTION
Vacuum extraction (ventouse) is sometimes used instead of the forceps method. With this technique the doctor places a suction cup on the baby's head and the baby is sucked out as you push down with each contraction.

If the birth canal is not going to be big enough for the baby's head and there is a risk that the perineum may tear, a small cut is made in this area under local anaesthetic. This

Your growing baby
The fetus is now able to function on its own, although it is still getting nourishment from the placenta. The fetus is in position for birth and is about 49 cm/ 19¼ in long and weighs around 3.1 kg/7 lb.

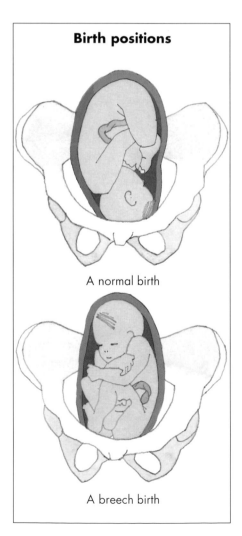

Birth positions

A normal birth

A breech birth

type of incision is called an episiotomy and is stitched after the birth, again under local anaesthetic.

FETAL MONITORING

This keeps a check on the unborn baby's heartbeat during labour and birth. Monitoring can be done the low-tech way by simply placing a stethoscope against the patient's abdomen, or through electronic fetal monitoring (EFM).

There are two types of EFM and they both give a continuous readout of the baby's heart and uterine contractions; if the EFM method is used then you are having a high-tech birth.

There are two different methods of fetal monitoring. The basic method is to listen to the fetal heartbeat using a fetal stethoscope (top right). The position of the baby will also be checked at the same time (right). Electronic fetal monitoring (EFM) (below) involves placing a belt around your bump which is attached to a monitor. This gives a continuous readout of the baby's heart.

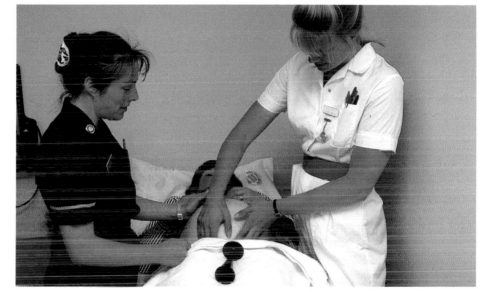

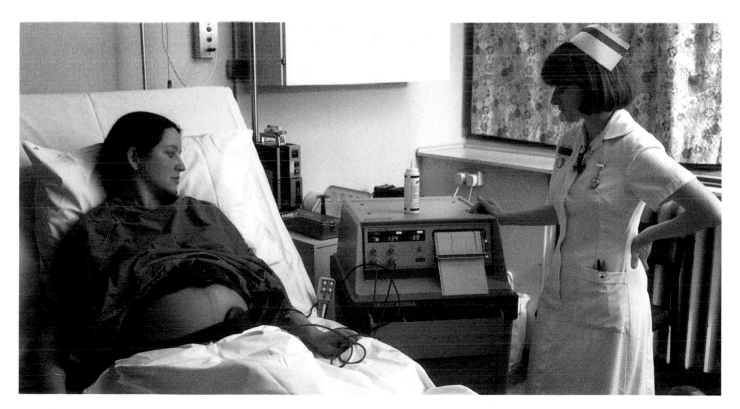

WEEK 40: LABOUR AND BIRTH

You and your body

You will probably be impatient for labour to start as you approach your EDD. If nothing has happened by your due date try not to be too disappointed; only around five per cent of babies actually arrive on the date they were expected. Keep yourself busy and make plans for each day so that you are not just sitting and waiting for something to happen. Once you are close to your EDD you may feel more confident wearing a sanitary towel just in case your waters break.

It is unlikely that you won't recognize the beginnings of labour as the signs, when they come, are generally unmistakable. There are three main indications that labour is about to start, or has started, and they can occur in any order. Once one or more of these has occurred you should let the hospital or midwife know immediately:

A show The protective plug, which sealed the cervix at the neck of the uterus, comes away and passes down the vagina. It usually appears as a small amount of bloodstained mucus. A show occurs before labour starts or during the first stage.

Waters breaking The membranes of the amniotic sac in which your baby has been floating break, causing either a trickle or a sudden gush of clear fluid from the vagina. If the fluid is yellow, greenish, or brown in colour you will need to go to the hospital straight away because the baby may be in distress. Your waters can break hours before labour starts or when it is well underway.

Contractions The regular tightening of the muscles of the uterus occurs throughout labour. During the first stage, the contractions thin out and dilate the cervix from closed to 10 cm/4 in open; in the second stage they help to push the baby down the vagina and after the birth they then deliver the placenta (afterbirth). For most women they feel rather like bad period pains. Contractions may also be accompanied by uncomfortable backache, sickness, and diarrhoea.

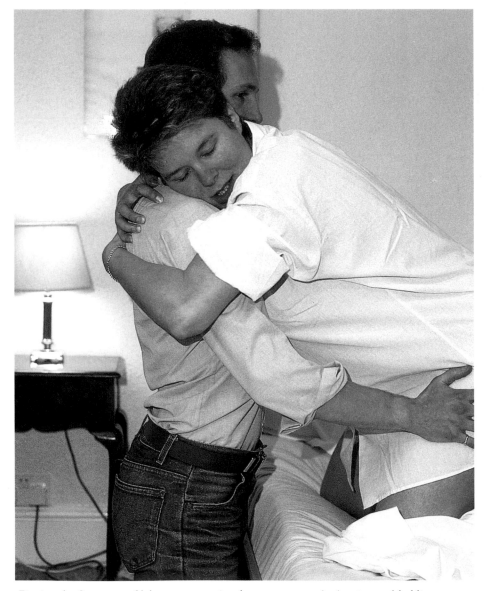

Your growing baby

Your baby is curled up, head down, in the fetal position with legs drawn up underneath and waiting to be born. He or she measures about 50 cm/19¾ in and weighs around 3.4 kg/7½ lb.

During the first stage of labour, you can involve your partner by leaning and holding onto him for comfort and also physical support.

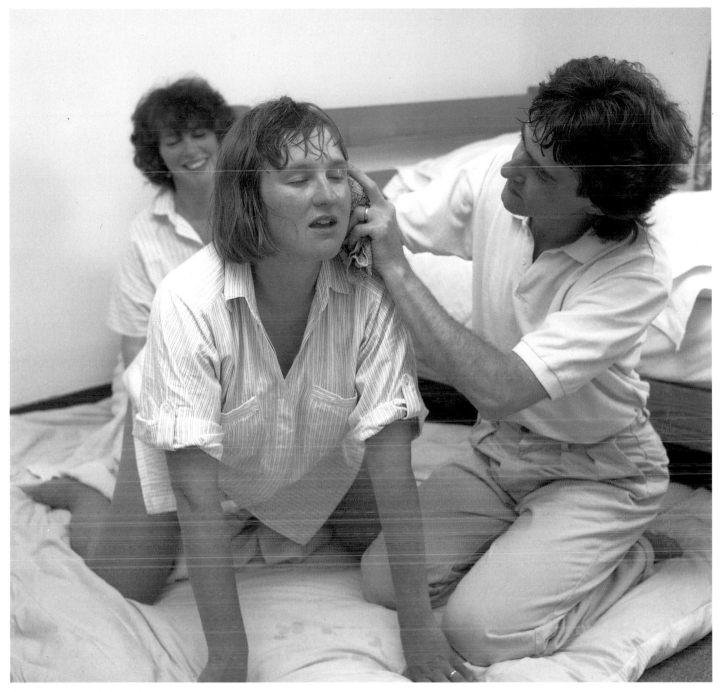

Your partner can help and encourage you when you're on all fours to keep the weight of the baby off your back in an active birth.

STAGES OF LABOUR

The first stage: There are three stages of labour and the first is usually the longest, lasting generally from 12 hours upwards for a first baby. Contractions, which may have started off as mild and infrequent will, by the end of the first stage, be very strong and coming close together. Once they are coming regularly

Tips for labour

- Keep active for as long as you can during the first stage of labour.
- Don't be on your own: get your partner, mother or a friend to stay with you once labour has started.
- If your waters break check that the fluid is clear: yellow, greenish, or brown fluid could mean that your baby is in distress and you should go to the hospital immediately.
- Try different positions to help you cope with the pain of contractions.
- Ask for pain relief if you need it.
- Get your birth partner to make sure your wishes are known to whoever is delivering your baby. You may be too busy coping with contractions to explain clearly what you want.
- Put your baby to the breast soon after the birth. This will stimulate your milk supply and help to speed up the delivery of the placenta.

every 10 minutes, or are each lasting for around 45 seconds, you should start getting ready to go to the hospital, or call the midwife if you are having your baby at home. When you get to the hospital, or the midwife attending you at home arrives, you will be examined to see how far your cervix has dilated and your blood pressure will be checked.

Although you will be able to carry on fairly normally for quite a lot of the first stage you should have someone with you. It is advisable to eat very little once labour has begun in case you need an emergency anaesthetic for any reason and to avoid being sick.

Towards the end of the first stage you will go into what is known as the transitional stage which can last for anything up to an hour. During this transitional period your baby moves down the birth canal and you will feel pressure on your back passage which may make you want to start pushing, even though the cervix is not fully dilated. By using the breathing techniques you have been taught you will be able to control this urge.

The second stage: Once the cervix is fully dilated and you start pushing the baby out you have entered the second stage. It can last for as little as half an hour or for as long as two hours or more. Once the baby's head is visible to the midwife she will tell you to start pushing. When the head reaches the vaginal opening you will be told to pant in short breaths so that the head can be delivered as slowly as possible. This allows the skin and muscle of the perineum to stretch so that the head can be born. If tearing seems likely an episiotomy, a small cut in the perineum, the area between the vagina and anus, may be given. Once the head is born your baby's body will follow quite quickly.

As soon as your baby is delivered it will be lifted onto your stomach for you to see it. The umbilical cord will be clamped and cut and the midwife will check the baby to make sure that it is all right and breathing properly. You may want to put your baby straight to the breast. You'll certainly wish to admire it with your partner and welcome your child into the world.

With a water birth, contractions can be eased by the warm water. Your baby can be delivered in the water or outside.

If you have your baby in the water, he will be given to you immediately after the birth for you and your partner to cuddle.

*Above: A doctor holding a newborn
baby boy, with the umbilical cord still
attached, at a home delivery.
Right: With a Caesarean the baby is delivered through an incision. It is performed
when there are risks from natural childbirth.*

The third stage: The final stage
of labour is the birth of the placenta,
which usually takes less than half an
hour. You may be given an injection
to speed up the delivery. The midwife will check to see that the placenta is whole and that nothing has
been left inside you. If you have had
an episiotomy it will be stitched up.

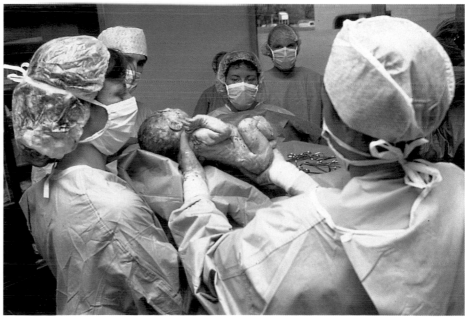

PART TWO

BABYCARE

A NEW BABY can seem rather overwhelming, especially if this is your first experience of motherhood. Suddenly you are responsible for the care and welfare of a very demanding little person who needs looking after almost 24 hours a day. If you have never fed, bathed or changed a baby you need to learn how to carry out these daily routines. This section looks at basic babycare and explains, in simple terms, everything that you are likely to need to know about caring for your baby during the first year of life.

It is important to take care of yourself too, especially in the days after the birth, so your post-natal care is described at the beginning of this section.

Feeding your baby should be a special time for you both, regardless of whether you are breast- or bottle-feeding in the early months. But when things go wrong, or your baby doesn't feed in the way you expect, it can be difficult to know what to do. Breast- and bottle-feeding are discussed here, along with the latest information on when and how to introduce first foods.

When your child seems unwell it is quite natural to be concerned. Knowing what to do and when you need to call the doctor comes with experience. In the meantime the section on common childhood ailments such as coughs, colds, teething and sickness tells you how to relieve discomfort and when you should seek medical help. There is also a comprehensive first aid section which explains exactly what you should do if your child has an accident.

Caring for your baby will take up a great deal of your time during the first year, so use the daily routines of bathing, feeding and changing as a time to get to know and enjoy each other.

POST-NATAL CARE

Although your new baby will probably give you intense emotional satisfaction, you may well be physically uncomfortable. Your body has gone through many changes during pregnancy and it will take a while for it to return to its pre-pregnancy state.

Six weeks after the birth your doctor will examine you to make sure that everything is returning to normal; this also gives you a chance to discuss any worries you may have. The doctor will take your blood pressure and check a sample of your urine. Your breasts and abdomen will be examined and the doctor will make sure that any stitches have healed properly. You will probably have an internal examination to check the size and position of your uterus and you may have a cervical smear test if one is due.

If your baby was born in hospital, a midwife or doctor will probably talk to you about contraception before you go home. Alternatively, you can discuss this at your six-week check. Don't take any risks; to avoid getting pregnant again you should

use contraception as soon as you resume intercourse. It is an old wives' tale that breast-feeding prevents conception.

If you were not immune to rubella (German measles) during your pregnancy, you will probably be offered the immunization before you leave hospital or at your six-week check-up. Ask your doctor if you are at all unsure about your immunity.

YOUR BODY

Immediately after the birth your breasts will produce colostrum, a high-protein liquid full of antibodies. Then, after the pregnancy hormones decline, your main milk supply should come in around the third or fourth day. At this time the breasts swell, feel hard, and can sometimes be painful. Bathing them with warm water is soothing, and letting the baby have frequent feeds will also help. This initial swelling subsides after a few days as both you and your baby get used to feeding. However, if you have decided to bottle-feed, your breasts will remain full for a

few days until they gradually stop producing milk. Your breasts will probably never be quite as firm as they were before pregnancy, but a well-fitting support bra and exercise will help greatly.

After delivery your abdomen will probably be quite flabby and wrinkled because of slack muscles and stretched skin. Gentle post-natal exercises will help tighten up your abdominal and vaginal muscles, so make time to do them every day. If you feel you're not disciplined enough to exercise on your own, join a local post-natal class.

Following the birth you will have a vaginal discharge which is known as lochia. This will be like a very heavy period for a few days, with the flow gradually getting lighter until it disappears within a few weeks. Use maternity pads or large sanitary towels to absorb the discharge because there is a risk of infection if you use tampons in the early weeks after the birth. Your uterus will take about six weeks to

Your newborn will find your physical presence very reassuring during the first days after the birth. She will also find your smell comfortingly familiar.

Post-natal exercises

Pelvic floor: Lie flat on the floor with your legs drawn up and slightly apart. Close the back passage by drawing it in, hold for the count of four, then relax. Do as often as possible.

Tummy toner: Sit up with knees bent and feet flat on the floor. Fold arms in front. Lean back until you feel the abdominal muscles tighten, hold, then sit up and relax. Repeat several times.

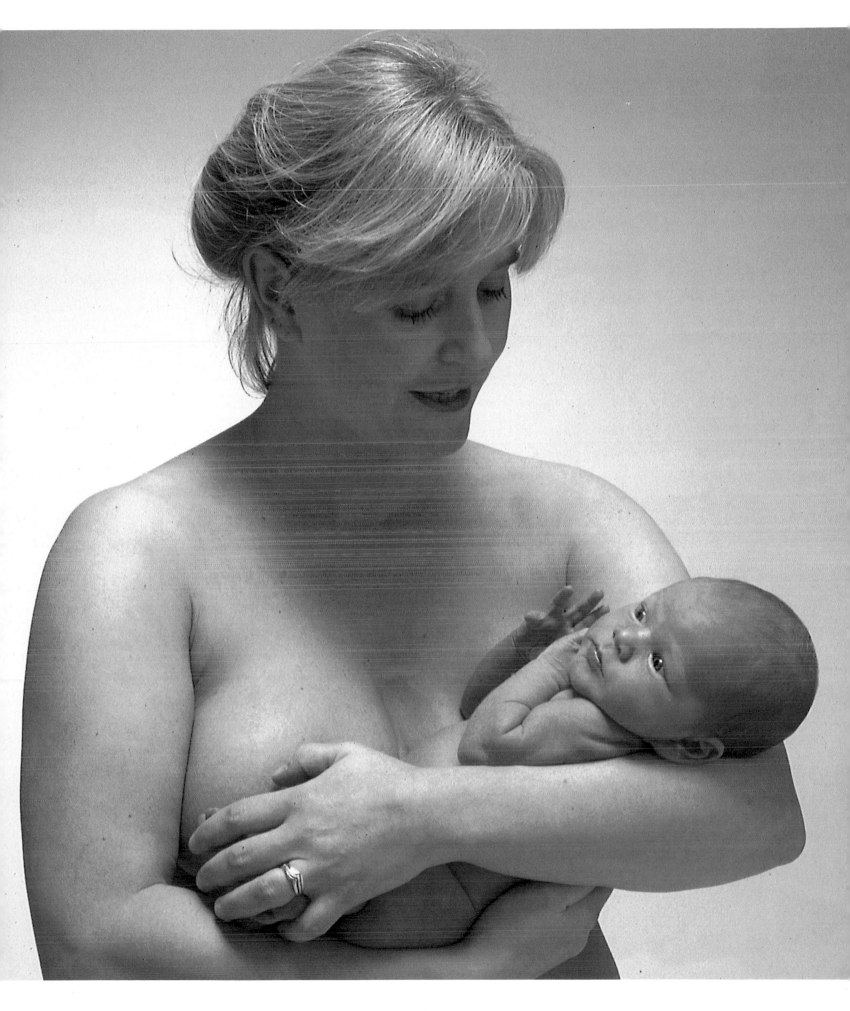

1 *Curl-ups: This exercise will help strengthen your vertical abdominal muscles. Lie on your back with a pillow under your head, your knees bent and your feet flat on the floor.*

2 *Pull in your abdominal muscles and, raising your head, stretch your arms towards your knees. Hold for the count of five and then relax slowly. Repeat several times.*

Leg slide: Lie with your head on a pillow with the small of your back pressed against the floor and your knees bent. Gently slide one leg away from your body until it is fully extended, keeping the small of your back pressed against the floor for as long as you can. Slowly draw the leg back towards your body and then repeat with the other leg. Do this several times.

return to its original size. If you are breast-feeding you may feel it contract as you feed the baby.

If your perineum (the skin between the vagina and anus) was bruised during labour, or if you had stitches, you will find that anything that puts pressure on the area painful. Soreness can be soothed with an ice pack (or ice cubes wrapped in a flannel) held against the perineum or by splashing with warm water. Try drying the area with a hand–held hair dryer, set on cool, rather than with a bath towel.

Do not put the dryer too close to your skin, or use it in the bathroom. Adding a cup of salt to the bath water will also help the stitches to heal.

GETTING BACK INTO SHAPE
Despite losing the combined weight of the baby, the placenta, and the amniotic fluid, you will still be heavier than you were before you became pregnant. You may even find that you have to continue to wear maternity clothes for a short while. As your uterus shrinks during the six weeks following the birth you will

lose more weight, but you will need to watch your diet to regain your pre-pregnancy shape. Try to eat regularly and healthily and don't be tempted, because you're short of time, to snack on foods containing empty calories such as sweets and fizzy drinks. If the weight isn't disappearing as fast as you'd like, ask your health visitor for advice. Do not attempt any diet now or while you are breast-feeding – this would simply increase stress as your body is struggling to regain its equilibrium. Doing exercises will help you get

1 *Waist trimmer: Lie on the floor with your arms away from your side, with your knees bent and feet flat. Pull in your abdominals and, with knees together, roll over to the right. Take your knees back to the middle and pause.*

2 *Rest briefly, then pull in your abdominals again and roll your knees to the left, then back to the middle and pause. Keep your shoulders flat on the floor as you roll from side to side. Repeat six times and work up to 20.*

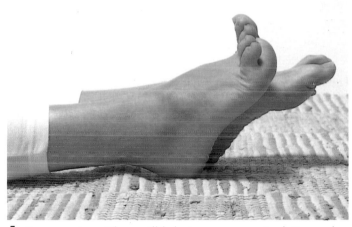

1 *Foot exercises: These will help improve your circulation and are especially important if you are confined to bed. Lie with your legs straight and knees together and bend and stretch your feet.*

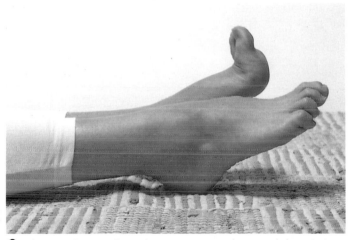

2 *Flex one foot, pulling the toes up towards you while pointing the other foot away from you. Repeat, alternating the feet. Do this exercise quite briskly for about 30 seconds.*

Post-natal depression

Two or three days after the birth you may suddenly feel very tearful and depressed. This is commonly called the "third day blues", or the milk blues, because it usually coincides with the milk coming into your breasts. These feelings are caused by all the hormonal changes that are going on in your body and should disappear after a few days. If they don't go away, however, you need to talk to your health visitor or doctor. You may be suffering from post-natal depression (PND) which, if left untreated, can go on for several months. Symptoms of PND include feeling unhappy and wretched as well as irritable and exhausted, yet unable to sleep. You may also lose all interest in food, or find yourself eating too much and then feeling guilty afterwards. PND is one of the most common illnesses following childbirth and it is likely that it is related to the huge hormonal changes that take place at the time of the birth, but it is still unclear as to why it affects some women so badly but not others. If you think you are suffering from PND, don't feel ashamed and don't ignore it. You need help and the sooner you ask for it the sooner you will begin to feel better and able to cope with life again. Post-natal depression is a common condition. Many women are affected by it, and it needs to be treated early on, not ignored in the hope that it will just go away on its own.

your figure back, get you moving again, and make you feel fitter. Those for strengthening the pelvic floor are among the most important post-natal exercises. The pelvic floor muscles support the bladder, uterus, and rectum, so it is vital that their tone is restored after being stretched during childbirth.

TIREDNESS AND RELAXATION
Tiredness goes hand in hand with being a new mother, but you need rest to help your body recover from

childbirth. It is tempting to use the baby's sleep times to catch up on chores, but do try to have a nap or proper rest at least once during the day. You and your child are more important than housework, so find ways to cut down the work. Accept offers of help and, if no one volunteers, don't be afraid to ask people.

Another way to cope with tiredness or stress is relaxation, so try using the ante-natal relaxation exercises to help you now. Also a long, lazy bath with a few drops of relaxing oil in the

water will work wonders. For a real treat, ask your partner to give you a massage using a specially formulated oil before you go to sleep.

HAIR AND NAILS
The condition of your hair is likely to change during this time. It may become more greasy, or the opposite may happen and it will become noticeably drier than before. You may also suffer an increase in hair loss or your hair may seem a lot thicker than it did before you

became pregnant. Whichever condition applies to you, wash your hair using a mild shampoo and avoid rubbing or brushing oily hair too much as this will only stimulate the sebaceous glands to produce more oil. Dry hair should be conditioned after every wash and, if possible, allowed to dry naturally.

Your nails are made of the same tissue as your hair, so if you are having problems with one you are likely to have problems with the other. These are due to fluctuating hormone levels and as soon as these settle your hair and nails will return to normal. Meanwhile, include enough protein and B vitamins in your diet because these will help improve the condition of both your hair and nails.

Left: A long, lazy bath with a few drops of oil, such as lavender, in the water will help you to relax.

Below: A stimulating rub with a loofah brush or mitt will help remove dead cells on the skin's surface, and will stimulate the circulation.

Below right: Try using some unscented soap or a soapless cleansing bar if your skin is very itchy.

Above: Eating regularly and healthily will help you to regain your pre-pregnancy shape.

CARING FOR YOUR NEWBORN

You may find the first weeks at home with your new baby quite difficult, especially if you are still feeling weak and emotionally down. Don't get upset if the house is a mess; it is much more important for you to spend time with your baby than to do housework. If you are still in your dressing gown at lunchtime don't worry; your baby will not care and it is how he or she feels that matters most at the moment.

Your newborn will seem fragile at first, but is actually quite tough. It is natural to be worried about how to pick your new baby up and hold him without hurting him in any way. Before you pick up your baby make sure that you have his head and neck supported with one hand, then slide the other hand underneath his back and bottom to support the lower part of his body before lifting. Hold your baby firmly against you, either cradled against your chest with one arm still supporting the head and the other holding the bottom and lower back, or cradled in your arms with your baby's head lying in the crook of one arm while your other arm supports his back and legs. Always keep any movements gentle so that you don't hurt or frighten your baby.

THE NEWBORN AT DELIVERY
As soon as the baby is born it will be assessed on the five points of the Apgar Score: heart rate, respiratory rate, colour, activity, and response to stimulation. The baby will be given a maximum of two points for each category, so if he is pink, active, and responsive the score is 10. The Apgar Score is usually done twice – one minute after birth and five minutes after birth – and it may be done again later if there are any problems.

Your baby will also be weighed and measured by the doctor and will probably receive the first of three doses of vitamin K, by mouth, to prevent a rare bleeding illness which occasionally affects newborn babies. A second dose is given at 10 days and a third at six weeks. Vitamin K is given by injection to very premature babies or those who have had a traumatic birth.

After the birth, the umbilical cord will be cut and a plastic clamp placed about 1-2 cm/½-1 in from the infant's body. Over the next few days

A newborn baby boy's genitals may appear rather big in proportion to the rest of him. This will right itself after a few days.

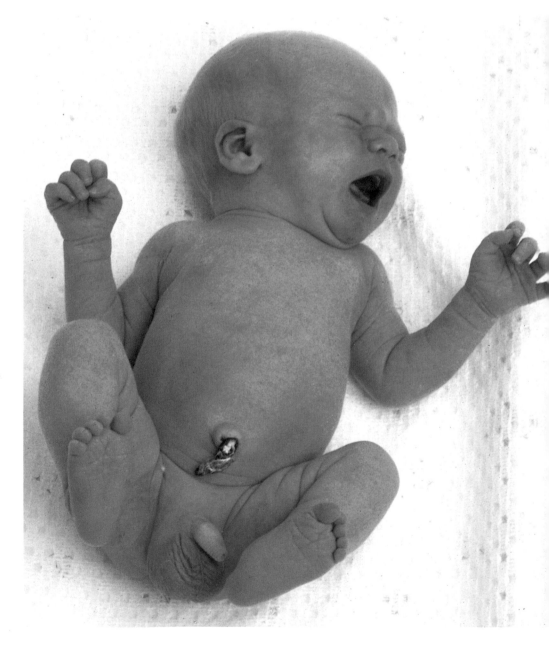

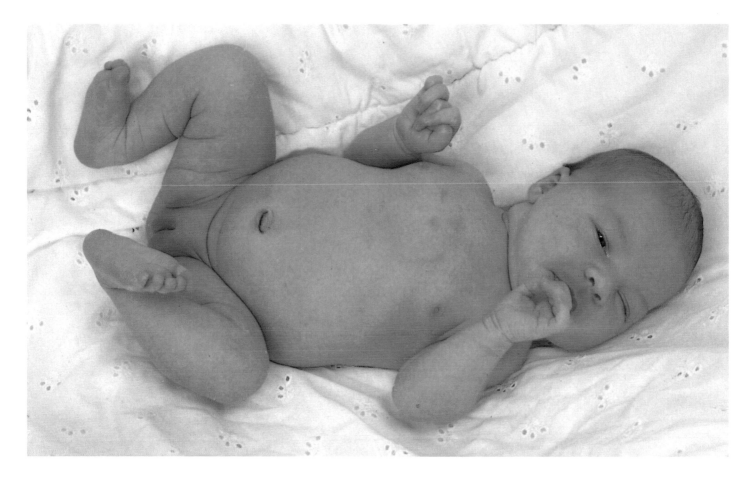

A newborn baby loses the stump of her umbilical cord usually within the first few days after the birth.

the cord will shrivel up and after about a week it will drop off completely. During this time the area around the cord should be kept dry and clean to avoid the risk of infection. Try to let the air get to the healing navel as much as possible so that moisture from wet nappies doesn't affect it.

Your baby has soft spots known as fontanelles on the top of the head. These are the spaces between the skull bones, where they have not yet joined. There is usually a large one on top of the skull and a smaller one further back. They will gradually fuse over the next two years or so. The fontanelles are covered with a tough membrane to protect the brain and you should never press them hard. If you notice a bulge or the skin seems

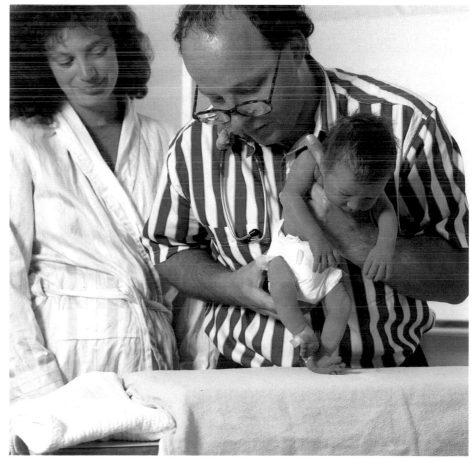

Sometime during the first couple of days your newborn baby will be given a complete physical examination to check that all the organs and limbs are functioning correctly.

very tight over the fontanelles you
should get in touch with your doctor immediately.

Some babies are born with a lot
of hair, others arrive almost bald.
Any first hair that a baby has will rub
off within a couple of months, but
this will be replaced with new hair
growth. The new hair may be a different colour.

Most white babies are born with
eyes that appear to be blue-grey in
colour. This is because melanin, the
body's natural pigment, is not present in the eyes until some weeks
after birth. Babies with brown or
black skins may have brown eyes at
birth. If your baby's eyes are going to
change colour this will gradually
happen over a period of weeks or
even months. Although a new baby
may cry quite a bit during these
early weeks there probably won't be
any tears. Some babies don't produce

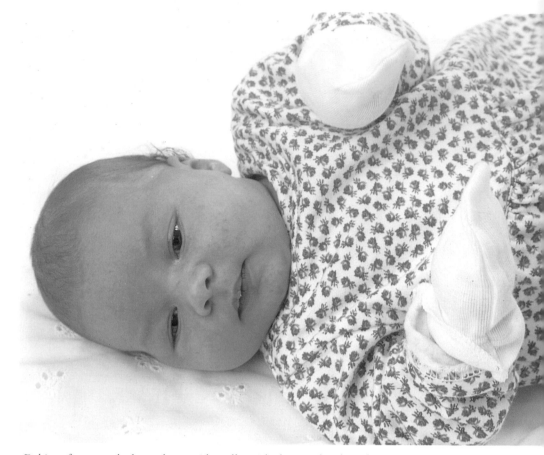

Babies often scratch themselves accidentally with their nails when they are very young. Scratch mitts will stop your newborn from catching her face with her fingernails.

How to hold your new baby

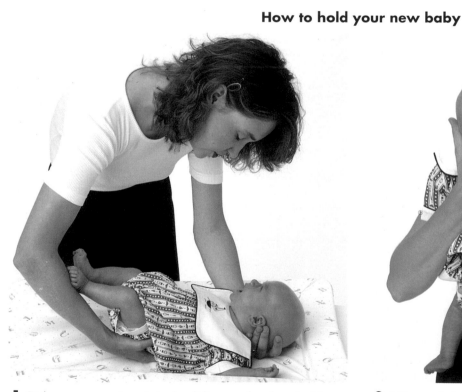

1 *Pick up your newborn baby by sliding one hand under his neck and head and then placing the other hand under his back and bottom to support his body.*

2 *Lift your baby so that he is cradled against your chest with one arm supporting the head and the other holding the lower back. Holding him close to your body will make him feel secure.*

Right: Touch is very important to a newborn and a gentle massage with a special baby oil can be soothing.

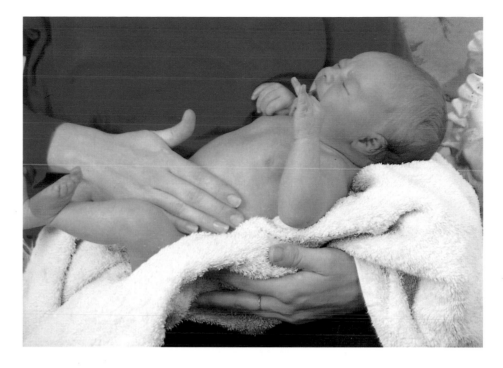

tears until they are six months old – this is not a cause for concern.

Slightly swollen or bloodshot eyes are common in newborn babies. This is caused by pressure from the birth and will disappear within a week or two. The muscles controlling a new baby's eye movements are still very weak so he may look slightly cross-eyed at first. After a month or so the muscles will have developed sufficiently for the eyes to work together. However, even when looking cross-eyed, a baby can focus on things up to 20-25 cm/8-10 in away, so hold your face close when you are feeding or talking.

Enlarged genitals and breasts are common in both boys and girls when they are first born. In some cases the breasts may even ooze a little milk and baby girls can have a slight vaginal discharge. This is caused by your hormones, which are still in your baby's bloodstream. In a few days these effects will disappear.

GENERAL HYGIENE
Young babies often object noisily to being undressed and immersed in a bath full of water, so don't feel you have to bathe your baby every day if the infant is unhappy about it. A top and tail wash every other day is quite sufficient until you both feel more comfortable. Always start by washing the baby's face with cooled boiled water using several pieces of cotton wool. Never use any kind of soap on the baby's face or near his eyes. If you wipe the eyes, use separate pieces of cotton wool for each one and start from the inner corner wiping outwards. A baby's ears and nose

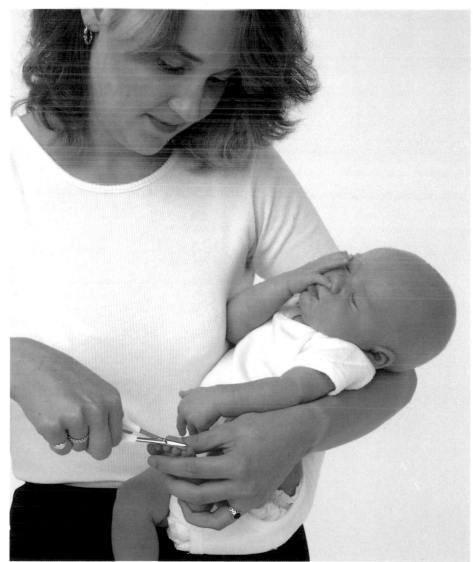

Above: Your baby's fingernails will grow quickly and you will need to keep them short to stop him scratching himself. You may find it easier to cut the nails while your baby is asleep.

are self-cleaning so never try cleaning inside them with cotton wool or buds. Just gently remove any visible mucus or wax. Once you have washed his face you will need to lift up his head and clean the folds of his neck, making sure that you dry the area carefully afterwards. Using

another piece of cotton wool, wash between your baby's fingers and then dry his hands carefully.

When you have finished the top half you need to remove his nappy, wiping away any solid matter before gently cleaning his bottom. You can use lotion to do this, or some warm

water. Once the area is dry, you can apply a barrier cream to help prevent nappy rash.

Cradle cap is very common in the early months and can sometimes continue for a while. Dry white or yellow scales form a crusty cap on the scalp. Rub olive oil, baby oil, or

Topping and tailing

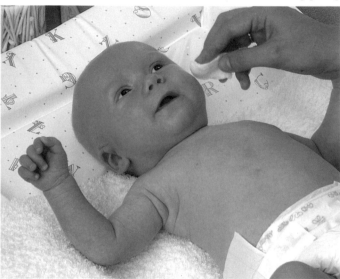

1 *Undress your baby down to his nappy. Using cooled boiled water, and several pieces of cotton wool, gently wash his face. Never use any kind of soap on your baby's face or near his eyes.*

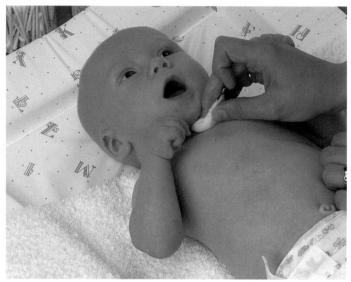

2 *Take a piece of cotton wool and gently lift his chin so that you can wash in the folds of his neck. When you have finished, use another piece of cotton wool and carefully dry between the folds.*

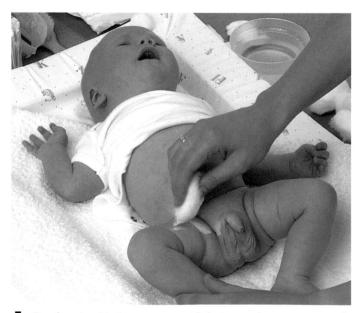

5 *Gently wipe his bottom area with lotion or damp cotton wool making sure that you clean in all the folds and creases of his legs.*

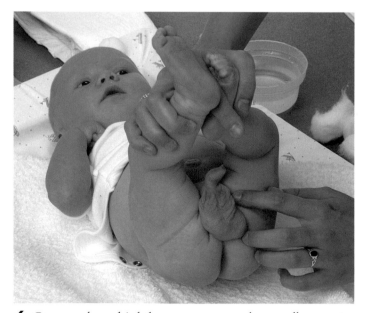

6 *Once you have dried the nappy area, apply a small amount of barrier cream to help prevent nappy rash.*

a specially formulated treatment into the scalp and then comb out the loosened flakes. Wash the baby's head afterwards with baby shampoo and dry thoroughly. You may need to repeat this treatment several times to remove all the flakes. As soon as the condition is under control you will only need to do this once a week. Cradle cap usually disappears by the time a baby reaches about eight or nine months.

A young baby's nails will grow very quickly and if not cut can cause scratches, especially on his face. You should keep his fingernails and toe-nails short by cutting them straight across with a pair of blunt-ended scissors. If your baby objects to this, or you find it difficult to cut his nails while he is wriggling about, try doing it while he is asleep or get someone else to hold him steady while you quickly cut his nails.

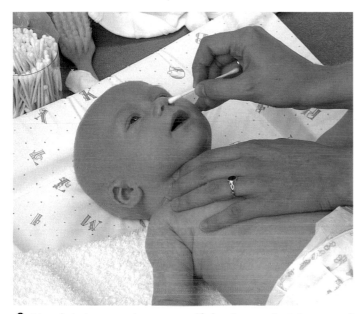

3 *Your baby's ears and nose are self-cleaning, so don't be tempted to clean inside them with cotton buds. Take a dampened cotton bud and carefully remove any visible mucus from his nose.*

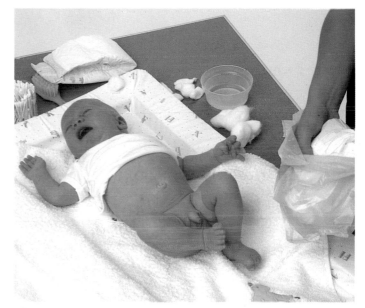

4 *Put your baby in a clean vest and then remove his nappy, wiping away any solid matter with a clean corner before placing the dirty nappy in a bag.*

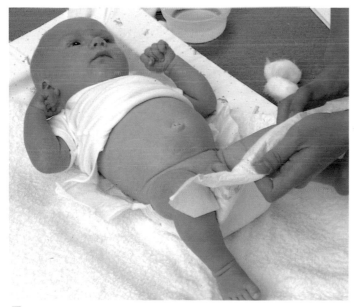

7 *Now that your baby is clean and dry he is ready to have his nappy put on. Place the nappy under his bottom and draw it up carefully between his legs.*

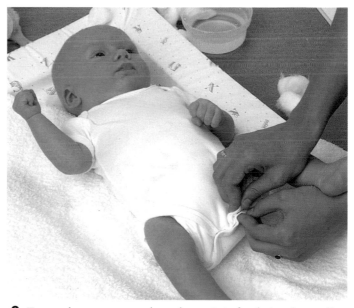

8 *Fasten the nappy securely and once it is firmly in place pull down your baby's vest over the top of it. He is now clean and ready to be dressed again.*

BREAST-FEEDING

Breast-feeding is the ideal way to feed a baby because breast milk is a baby's natural food containing all the required nutrients in the right proportions for the first months of life. But like any new skill, breast-feeding has to be learned and you may find it more difficult than you expected. Don't give up though, because breast-feeding really is best for your baby and for you and, once it is established, it can be a real pleasure. If you are having problems, talk to your midwife or health visitor.

Ideally, you should put your baby to your breast as soon after birth as possible. The sucking will start a reaction that leads to the release of the hormones that cause both the milk to be manufactured in the breast and the let-down reflex, which allows the milk to pass through the breast to the nipple.

Immediately after the birth and for the first few days, the breasts

Getting your baby latched on

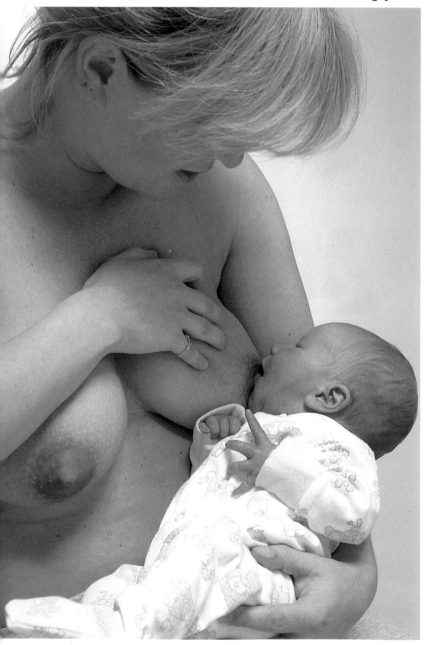

Hold your baby in a comfortable position. Offer her the breast making sure that her mouth is open wide enough.

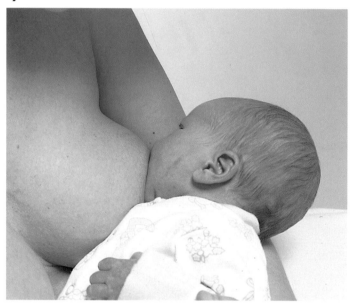

Make sure that your baby's body is in a straight line with your breast so that she doesn't have to turn her head to feed.

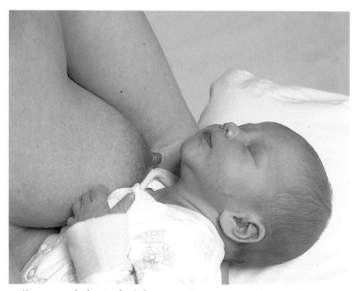

Allow your baby to feed from one breast for as long as she wants. She will let you know when she has had enough.

produce colostrum, a high-protein liquid full of antibodies. This is followed by the actual milk coming in, which often makes the breasts feel heavy and uncomfortable. This discomfort will soon wear off once breast-feeding has become established.

At the first stage of a feed your baby gets foremilk from the breast; this has a high water content to satisfy thirst. Foremilk is followed by calorie-rich hindmilk which satisfies your baby's hunger and helps her to grow. To make sure that your baby always gets the hindmilk, you should allow her to feed for as long as she wants from one breast before you offer her the other one. If your baby has had enough when she has finished feeding from one breast, remember to start with the other breast at the next feed.

Your breasts produce milk in response to your baby's feeding, so the more your baby feeds the more milk you will produce. By letting your infant feed for as long as she wants you should be able to produce the amount of milk that is needed.

FINDING THE BEST POSITION
Finding the position which best suits both you and your baby is one of the most important factors for successful breast-feeding, so don't be afraid to experiment. Immediately after the birth, when you are still sore, you may find that sitting on a low chair with plenty of soft cushions is more comfortable than sitting in bed. You can raise your knees slightly by resting your feet on a low stool, or put a pillow on your lap to raise your baby and cushion your abdominal muscles.

Hold your baby so that her body is in a straight line with your breast so that she does not have to turn her head to feed. Sit up straight and lean

Breast-feeding techniques

Aim the nipple towards your baby's nose and allow her to take it into her mouth herself. When supporting your breast try not to apply pressure which can block the milk ducts.

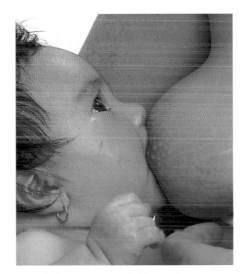

Your baby may try to hold your breast or simply clench and unclench her fists while feeding. Her ears will move as she swallows.

When you want to remove your baby from the breast, insert a finger into her mouth to release the suction.

Advantages of breast-feeding

• Breast milk is designed especially for babies and it contains all the nutrients your baby needs. It is always available, at the right temperature, and it is free.
• Breast milk is easy for your baby to digest, so she is less likely to suffer stomach upsets and constipation.

• Breast milk contains antibodies which will help protect your baby against some infections.
• Breast-fed babies are less likely to develop allergies.
• Breast-feeding will help you get your figure back more quickly.

will let you know when she is hungry and your milk supply will be regulated by supply and demand.

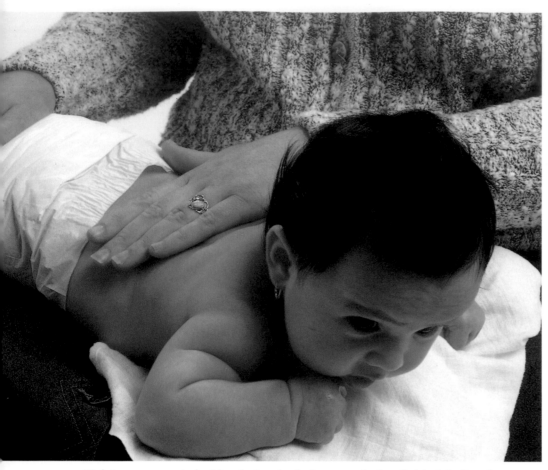

To bring up any wind, either during the feed or once she has finished feeding, lay your baby across your knees and stroke her back gently.

EXPRESSING MILK

Expressing milk allows someone else to feed your baby with your breast milk. You can express milk with your hands or you may find it easier to use a breast pump. The best time to express is when you have the most milk, which is either in the morning or, once your baby has dropped her night feed, it may be in the evening. Milk can be expressed from your breast and kept in a sterile container in the refrigerator for up to 48 hours, or it can be frozen and kept for up to six months. Any feeding equipment or containers you use must be sterilized.

BREAST-FEEDING PROBLEMS

If you are concerned that you are not producing enough milk, breast-feeding more often will automatically increase your supply, so don't be afraid to let your baby suck for as long as it is comfortable.

You may have a sleepy baby who needs to be woken for a feed. If your baby needs encouragement, gently brush her mouth with your nipple but don't force it into her mouth. Your baby may fall asleep at the breast after a feed but this only means that she is contented, well fed and doing all right.

Breast-feeding may hurt during the first few weeks because your milk supply has to become established and your nipples are not yet used to your baby's sucking. If the discomfort persists, however, then the positioning of your baby on the breast may not be right and you should experiment. Also check that your baby is latched on properly. If

You may prefer to wind your baby by sitting her upright on your knee, supporting her head, and gently patting her back.

slightly forward so that the nipple drops into your baby's mouth. Make sure that she is then properly latched onto the breast. This means that your baby takes as much as possible of the areola (the dark area surrounding the nipple) into her mouth, along with the nipple. The milk ducts lie just under the areola and your baby's sucking action on these effectively draws the milk from the breast. You may well be told to check that your baby's nose is not pushed against your breast so making it hard for her to breathe. However, if your baby is positioned properly, she will be able to breathe easily.

There is no set pattern for feeding. Some babies want to be fed every couple of hours, others can happily go for four to six hours before requiring a feed. Your baby not, your baby may just be sucking the nipple which means she won't be getting enough milk and the more she sucks the more painful it will actually become.

You may experience engorged breasts. This is when your breasts become over-full and painful. Feeding your baby frequently will help and you can ease the swelling by bathing your breasts with warm water or having a hot bath. Smooth out some milk with your fingers, stroking the breast downwards towards the nipple.

If you experience a shooting pain when your baby sucks, you may have a cracked nipple. If your baby is in the correct position even if your nipples are sore, they shouldn't hurt when you are feeding, so check your positioning. Keep sore nipples clean and dry and let the air get to them as much as possible. A nipple shield which fits over your nipple may help, but don't wear it for more than a day or two. Occasionally sore nipples can be caused by thrush in a baby's mouth. If you think this may be the case, discuss the problem with your doctor.

Finally, some nursing mothers can develop a condition called mastitis. This is an infection of the milk ducts and your breast will be inflamed, hot, and flushed in places. Bathing your breast in warm water, or holding a cold flannel against it, will help to ease any discomfort. You may also need a course of antibiotics to clear up the infection, so consult your doctor.

Sore, cracked nipples and mastitis are usually caused by your baby sucking just the nipple. Make sure your baby takes the nipple and surrounding area well into her mouth when she is feeding.

Breast-feeding equipment

Although no equipment is essential, there are some items which will make life easier, such as feeding bras. There are other things that you may require if you decide to express milk so that you can bottle-feed occasionally. You will need:

• At least two well-fitting cotton nursing bras which allow access to a large area of the breast when your baby is feeding.

• Breast pads for use inside the bra to absorb any leaks of milk.

• Nipple shields to protect your sore nipples.

• Breast shells to fit over the nipple and collect excess milk.

• Breast pump, bottles, and teats.

• Sterilizing equipment if you intend to express breast milk.

Breast milk can be expressed by hand, or using a manual breast pump like this. Electric pumps are also available.

Various accessories may help with breast-feeding. Breast pads will absorb any leakage, freezer bottles can be used to freeze breast milk, and nipple shields will protect sore nipples.

BOTTLE-FEEDING

If you decide to bottle-feed you should be content with your decision. Do not feel guilty, or think that you are giving your baby second best. Such feelings will only take away the pleasure you should get from feeding your baby. Make the most of each feed by settling comfortably and giving your baby all your attention.

FORMULA MILKS

Formula milk has been specially produced to provide all the vitamins and minerals your baby needs. Most formula milk is made from cows' milk, which has been specially treated to make it easily digestible, and its nutritional quality is as near to that of breast milk as possible. There are several brands to choose from and the midwife will be able to advise you. If your baby is known to have a lactose intolerance, or there is a very strong family history of allergies that are connected to cows' milk, you may be advised to use an alternative to regular formula milk. Often this is a soya-based milk, but others are available. It is important that these alternatives are only introduced if recommended by your doctor.

Formula milks are available in powder forms, which are made up with cooled boiled water. It is important to follow the instructions on the tin or pack because the amounts have been carefully calculated to make sure that a baby gets the correct balance of nutrients. Never be tempted to add more powder than is recommended because feeds that are too strong can be harmful to your baby. Ready-prepared formula milks are also available in cartons and bottles. Ready-prepared formula is more expensive than powdered milk but it's useful when you are out with your baby.

HOW TO BOTTLE-FEED

Prepare the formula milk according to the instructions, making up enough for 24 hours. Store the bottles in the refrigerator until needed

Feeding equipment

All feeding equipment needs to be kept scrupulously clean. Bottles and teats should be washed out immediately after use and then sterilized thoroughly before you make up the next batch of feeds. You will need to have:
• Enough bottles, teats, and caps to enable you to make up feeds for a 24-hour period.
• Sterilizer – there are four main ways of sterilizing feeding equipment: the chemical method, using a container filled with sterilizing solution; an electric steam sterilizer; a microwave steam sterilizer, or boiling on the stove.
• Bottle brush for cleaning inside all the bottles.
• Sterilizing solution or tablets for chemical method.
• Bottle warmer – this is optional, but can be very useful, especially when doing night feeds.

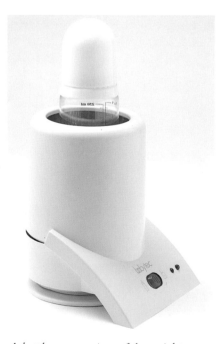

A bottle warmer is useful at night.

Sterilizing equipment for bottles.

A microwave steam sterilizer.

Bringing up wind is something a father can do whether you breast- or bottle-feed.

An older baby may prefer to hold the bottle himself, but he will still need to be cuddled and you should check that the teat is always full of milk.

Feeding should always be a special time for a baby as it helps him bond with the people closest to him. Here a father takes his turn at bottle-feeding.

and make sure that any unused formula is thrown away after this time. Never reuse leftover milk because it is a potential breeding ground for bacteria. Some babies are quite happy to take their bottles at room temperature but if yours prefers warm milk, heat the bottle either in a normal bottle warmer, or by standing it in a jug of hot water. Always test the temperature on the inside of your wrist to make sure that it isn't too hot before giving the bottle to your baby to drink.

Check that the milk is coming through the teat at the right speed. If your baby is having to work hard to get the milk, the flow is too slow and you need a teat with a bigger hole. If, on the other hand, your baby seems to be gulping a lot and the milk is leaking out of the corner of his mouth, the flow is too fast and the teat should have a smaller hole. If the teat flattens while you are feeding, pull it gently out of the baby's mouth to release the vacuum, then insert it again.

All your baby's feeding equipment must be thoroughly washed before sterilization.

Chemical sterilizing

1 *After washing the equipment fill the sterilizing unit with cold water.*

2 *Add sterilizing tablets to the water and place the bottles, teats and caps in the unit.*

3 *Check bottles are filled with water, then place tray in unit. Leave for time specified.*

Electric steam sterilizer

1 *Wash and rinse the feeding equipment and then place it in the sterilizing unit.*

2 *Add water, taking care to follow the manufacturer's recommendations.*

3 *Place lid on unit and switch on. The steam destroys any bacteria present.*

Making up a formula feed

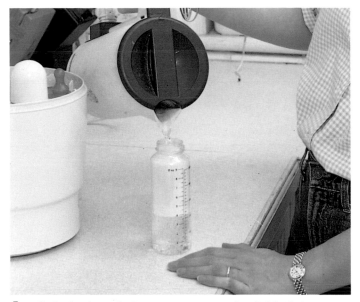

1 *Fill the bottle with the correct amount of cooled boiled water. Never use water that has been boiled more than once.*

2 *Using the scoop provided, measure the required amount of milk, levelling off each scoopful with the back of a knife.*

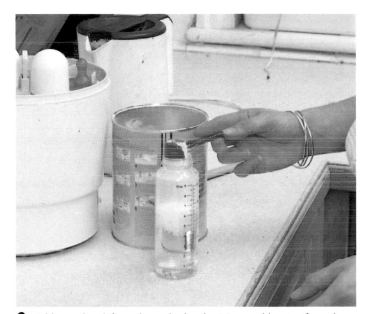

3 *Add powdered formula to the bottle. Never add extra formula as this can make the mixture too concentrated and could be harmful.*

4 *Secure teat and place lid on bottle. Shake until the powder has dissolved. Check the milk temperature before giving it to your baby.*

You may want to encourage feeding by stroking the teat across your baby's mouth. Once his mouth has opened, place the teat between his lips and your baby should start sucking. Keep the bottle tilted so that formula fills the teat completely and your baby doesn't suck in air, which can cause wind. Never leave your baby to feed from a bottle on his own because he could vomit and choke. Don't add solids such as rusk, cereal, or baby rice to bottle feeds – this could cause choking.

The amount of milk your baby needs at feeds will change as he gains weight. At first he may take only a couple of ounces but this will increase. Your health visitor will give you a growth chart to check on progress.

Wind can sometimes be a problem, so try stopping halfway through a feed and wind your baby by holding him against your shoulder, or propping him up on your lap while you rub his back. You may want to do this after the feed has finished as well. The baby may bring back a small amount of milk during or after a feed; this is called possetting and is quite normal. If the vomiting becomes frequent or violent, you need to consult your doctor.

INTRODUCING SOLIDS

Once milk alone no longer satisfies your baby you will need to start introducing solids into her diet. This can be any time between four and six months of age – in general, babies younger than this shouldn't be put on solids. Your baby will let you know she is still hungry by wanting more after the feed is finished, or she may start chewing her fists. A baby may also begin to demand feeds more often and if she normally sleeps through the night, you may find that she starts waking up early wanting to be fed.

Breast and formula milk give babies all they require for the first six months so you don't have to worry if your baby seems satisfied with milk alone until this age. By six months of age, your baby needs the additional nourishment provided by solids, and she also needs to learn how to eat.

HOW TO START

First solids are really just tasters to get a baby used to different textures and flavours; the main nourishment will still come from breast or formula milk. The first food should be bland and smooth, like baby rice mixed with either cooled boiled water, or formula or breast milk. To begin with offer a small amount on the tip of a clean spoon, midway through a feed, once a day. Once your baby has accepted this, you can introduce a small amount of fruit or vegetable purée, for example, banana, potato, or carrot (with no added salt or sugar), mixed with formula or breast milk.

As soon as your baby has got used to taking solids off a spoon, you can begin to introduce new foods and other solids at a second meal. If your baby obviously doesn't like the taste of something don't force matters. Try another food and reintroduce

the rejected food at a later stage. At first the baby will simply try to suck anything off the spoon. But it won't take long to master getting the food off the spoon and into the back of her mouth. Once your baby can do this she will be able to cope with lumpier textures, so you can begin to mash rather than purée food. Your baby will also be able to enjoy a wider variety of tastes and textures.

ADVANCED FEEDING

By six to nine months, you can introduce food combinations such as baby cereal and fruit, or egg yolk and tomato – remember to remove the seeds from the tomato and to cook the egg thoroughly. Food can be lumpier and more solid so that it encourages your baby to start chewing. Try mincing or mashing the food with a fork.

At nine months and over, your baby is likely to be on three meals a day as well as milk, unsweetened diluted fruit juice, or water. Giving your child food at grown-up meal-

Making your own purée

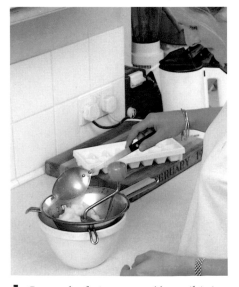

1 *Steam the fruit or vegetable until it is thoroughly cooked and soft, then place it in the food mill or blender.*

2 *Without adding any sugar or seasoning, blend to a smooth consistency then remove a portion for your baby.*

3 *Pour the remaining purée into an ice-cube tray to freeze in baby-size portions. Label and use within one month.*

times will encourage her to learn social skills by watching others. As her appetite grows you can gradually increase the amount given at each meal. Offer finger foods such as slices of peeled apple, and banana; this will encourage her to feed herself. Always stay with your child while she is eating in case of choking.

As with younger babies, don't force unwanted foods; your child may simply not be ready for that particular taste. Don't ever fight over it. Take the food away, but don't offer alternatives or provide snacks between meals or let the child fill up on drinks, especially non-nourishing drinks, such as squash.

THE VEGETARIAN BABY

The principles of weaning are the same as for a non-vegetarian baby with the first solids being cereal, puréed fruit, and vegetables. However, vegetarian diets tend to be high in fibre and too much fibre is not suitable for young babies. And it can also interfere with the absorption of minerals such as calcium and iron. So your child will require a combination of cereals, milk, and vegetables which contain the right balance of energy and other nutrients for healthy growth. The diet will also need to include iron-rich foods such as dried fruit, fortified breakfast cereals, bread, lentils, eggs and green leafy vegetables. Vitamin C helps the absorption of iron from vegetables so you should give fresh orange juice, fresh fruit, or raw vegetables with every meal.

A vegan diet excludes milk and all dairy products, as well as meat and fish, and it may be unsuitable for babies. If you are considering a vegan diet it is essential that you talk to your health visitor or community

Equipment

First foods need to be puréed, preferably using a blender or liquidizer, although a sieve and spoon will achieve the same results. As your baby gets older and is able to cope with lumpier foods you can use a fork to mash the food. Your baby should have his or her own feeding utensils, which you will need to keep very clean.

To prepare and feed your own puréed foods you will need:
- Blender or liquidizer.
- Unbreakable bowl, spoon, and feeding cup.
- Bib (preferably two or three) and several face cloths.
- Ice-cube tray or similar for freezing small portions of purée.

Use an unbreakable bowl, plastic teaspoon and feeding cup when weaning your baby.

A blender or sieve will purée first foods. Freeze baby-size portions in an ice-cube tray.

Left: By eight months a baby will be enjoying finger foods. At first he will examine the food, squashing it between his fingers as he explores its texture. Right: Once he's examined the food he will probably concentrate on trying to get it into his mouth.

Below right: Using both his hands to help him, he eventually manages to get the food into his mouth. These are the very early stages of how a child learns to feed himself.

dietician before beginning to wean your baby onto solid food.

BABY FOODS

You can make your own first foods by puréeing ripe fruit or vegetables. Remove the skin and any seeds or stones, then boil, steam, or microwave until thoroughly cooked. Allow the cooked fruit or vegetable to cool, then purée. Fruits with seeds such as strawberries will need to be sieved. Make a batch of purée, and freeze in small portions for convenience. Reheat thoroughly before use and allow it to cool before giving it to your baby. When your baby is older and has progressed to lumpier, mixed foods she can eat the same foods as you, but remove a small portion for your baby before you add any seasoning or sugar.

Warming food for babies in a microwave is not recommended because it can result in uneven heating which could scald the child's mouth. If you have to use a microwave, stir the food well after cooking to ensure the even distribution of heat and allow it to stand for at least one minute. Check the temperature again before offering the food.

The alternative to home-made baby food is to choose from the prepared baby foods that are widely available. One of the

Choking

If your baby chokes while eating try to hook out the obstruction with your finger (being careful not to push it further in) while gently slapping on the back. If this doesn't work, lay your baby face downwards with her chest and abdomen lying along your forearm and your hand supporting her head. Then slap the infant gently on the back to dislodge the obstruction.

main advantages of prepared baby foods is that they are quick and convenient. They have been formulated to make sure that, in conjunction with breast or formula milks, a baby receives a nutritionally balanced diet. Available in jars, packs, and tins, there are commercially prepared baby foods available for each stage of weaning. Check the labelling for the age range for which it is suitable and, if you wish, whether it is acceptable for a vegetarian diet.

Introduce new combinations of prepared baby food with the same care as you would home-made food. Different food combinations contain several ingredients, some of which may be new to your baby. Always place the amount you require in a dish rather than feeding straight from the tin or jar. The digestive substances in your baby's saliva can find their way from the feeding spoon into the container, which can make any remaining food unsuitable for another meal. Once tins and jars are opened, they should be stored covered in the fridge and kept for up to 48 hours.

FOODS TO WATCH
You must think carefully about the foods you introduce to your baby's

Always feed your baby her food using a plastic spoon. Keep the dish away from her until she learns not to put her hands in it.

diet. Some must be avoided altogether; others simply need special care in their preparation.

High-fibre foods Babies and young children shouldn't be given high-fibre foods such as bran because their digestive systems are too immature to cope with them.

Salt Never add salt to any food that your baby is going to eat. An infant's system can't cope with more salt than is found naturally in food. Remember too that some products, such as crisps, are usually quite salty, so you need to be aware of any salt intake from these foods.

Sugar Sugars occur naturally in fruit and vegetables so you should never add sugar to your baby's food or drinks as this can lead to tooth decay later and the possibility of obesity. Some manufacturers' pre-

pared foods may contain sugars, so read food labels: sugars may be listed as glucose, sucrose, dextrose, fructose, maltose, syrup, honey, or raw/brown sugar.

Additional fats Babies shouldn't have much additional fat added to their food – although the occasional knob of butter added to mashed potato will do no harm.

Nuts Whole nuts should never be given to a child under five years of age because of the risk of choking. Nuts that are finely ground may be given to children over six months.

Spices Strong spices such as chillies, ginger, and cloves are not suitable to be given to babies.

Eggs Eggs should always be cooked until solid. Since eggs can also cause allergic reactions, start by offering a small amount of well-cooked yolk.

Egg white is not recommended for babies under 12 months.

FOOD ALLERGY
If either you or the baby's father have a family history of food allergies, eczema, asthma, or hayfever, your baby may have an intolerant reaction to the following foods: wheat, oats, and barley cereal; citrus fruits, eggs, nuts, and fish; dairy products, including cows', goats' and sheeps' milk. Intolerance to cows' milk is usually the result of an allergy to one of the proteins in milk or an intolerance of lactose (milk sugar). When you buy commercially manufactured food, always check the ingredients for any foods that may cause an allergic reaction.

Symptoms of food intolerance or allergy include diarrhoea, vomiting

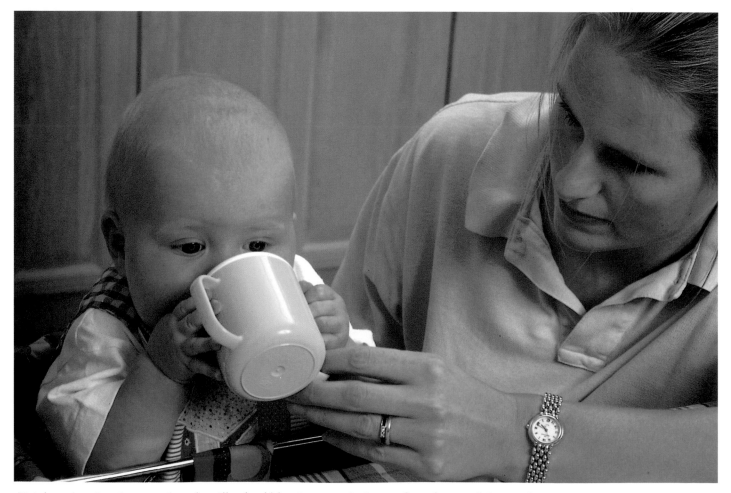

Drinks, other than breast or formula milk, should be given in a feeder cup from the age of six months.

At around one year a baby will be able to manage finger food and a feeder cup without help. Never leave your baby alone when he is eating in case he chokes. Give drinks at the end of a meal or they will fill your baby up before eating.

Vitamin drops

If you are breast-feeding, it is recommended that vitamin supplements are given to children from six months. Bottle-fed babies do not usually require supplements until they switch to cows' milk at a year old. These vitamin supplements should be given to children up to the age of five. They are available from your health visitor at the baby clinic or you can get them from the pharmacist.

after eating, or occasionally blood in stools. In extreme cases the reaction can be a generalized blotchy skin rash which occurs within an hour or so of eating the food. Your child's lips may also become swollen, the eyes puffy, and breathing a little wheezy. If breathing becomes restricted you will need to get medical help immediately. The blotchiness and swelling will disappear quickly but it should always be reported to your health visitor or doctor. These extreme responses to an allergy are rare, but may occur from time to time; if they do you should avoid that particular food.

If your child shows an intolerance to any food it is important that you seek advice from your health visitor or doctor. It may be that you need to change your child's diet, but this should always be done with the advice of a health professional.

MILK AND OTHER DRINKS
As the amount of food increases, your baby's intake of milk will decrease. However, the recommendation is at least 600 ml/1 pt of breast, formula, or follow-on milk (after six months) a day, until the baby is one year old.

Follow-on milks have been produced to help meet the nutritional needs of growing babies from six months to two years. They contain more iron than other milks, plus a healthy balance of other nutrients.

In the past cows' milk was introduced into the diet at around six months, but it is now thought that it is unsuitable until the baby is at least one year old. This is because cows' milk is low in vitamins like C and D, and is particularly low in iron, all of which your baby needs for healthy growth. After a year full-fat milk should be give to the under-fives as

it provides energy, protein, and calcium, even though it has more saturated fat than breast or baby milks.

Reduced-fat milks are not suitable as they are low in calories and vitamins. Skimmed milk should not be given to a child until she is at least five years of age. However, if your child has a good appetite and varied diet, you may offer semi-skimmed milk at two. Always check with your health visitor first.

If your baby seems thirsty and you are still breast-feeding, your milk will provide all the liquid needed. Otherwise, offer cooled, boiled water between feeds after the age of four weeks. Try giving your baby these additional drinks from a teaspoon; this will make the idea of a spoon familiar before you start weaning onto solids. From the age of six months, any drinks other than breast or formula milk should be offered from a feeder cup.

Any water you give your baby needs to be boiled and cooled until the child is at the age when you no longer sterilize feeding equipment. Only use boiled water or bottled water sold specifically for babies – never make up a feed with, or offer your baby, bottled mineral water.

NAPPIES

Nappies are produced in a variety of types, styles, and sizes, but the basic choice is still between disposable and towelling nappies. Ideally, you should decide which type of nappy you are going to use before your baby arrives. You will need to take into account a number of factors: your lifestyle, the amount of time and money you have available, and the type of washing and drying facilities you will be using.

CHANGING

Whichever nappy you choose, the techniques required for changing and cleaning a baby's bottom are the same. You should change your baby whenever he is wet or dirty. The number of changes may vary from day to day, but generally you will have to change your baby first thing in the morning, after each feed, after a bath, and before bed at night. Get everything you need together before you start so that there is no reason to leave your baby unattended while you are changing the nappy. Make sure that the room where you are changing your new baby is warm and free from draughts. Lie your baby on a folded towel or changing mat, placed on the floor, a table, or on the bed, making sure that a

---

Folding towelling nappies/Triple absorbent fold

This is particularly good for newborn babies because it makes a small, neat shape while giving extra absorbency between the legs.

1 *Fold the nappy into four sections with the two folded edges nearest you and to your left.*

2 *Pick up the top layer by the right-hand corner and pull it out to make a triangle.*

5 *Fold these layers over again to make a thick central panel.*

6 *Place a nappy liner over the top of the central panel.*

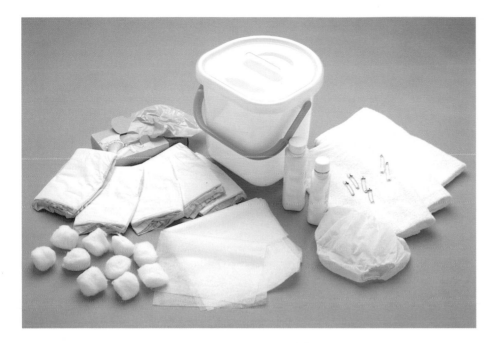

Changing equipment:
• Changing mat or towel.
• Clean towelling nappy, nappy liner, pins, plastic pants. Or a disposable nappy.
• Baby lotion or wipes, cotton wool.
• Bowl of warm water.
• Barrier cream.
• Bucket for dirty nappy or a plastic bag for a disposable nappy.

3 *Turn the nappy over.*

4 *Fold the vertical edge into the middle by a third.*

7 *Bring the middle fold between the legs, then fold one corner across your baby's stomach and hold while you bring the second corner across. Pull taut and then pin all three layers together.*

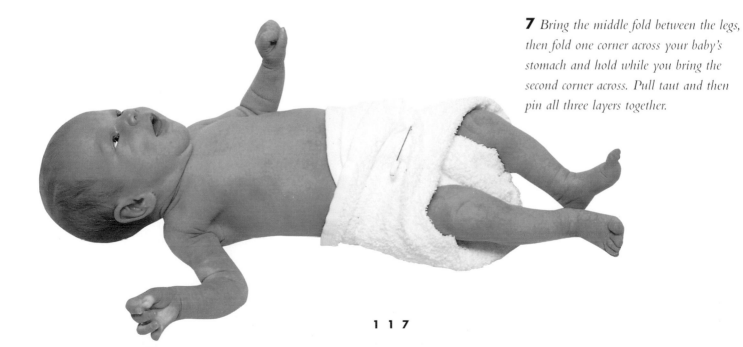

Kite fold

This is suitable from about three months onwards. You can adapt the size of the nappy by varying the depth when you fold the point up, before positioning the liner.

1 *Lay the nappy out flat in front of you so that it is in a diamond shape with one of the corners nearest you.*

2 *Fold the sides into the centre so that you form a kite shape with the nappy.*

5 *Bring the nappy up between the baby's legs and carefully fold one side and then the other into the middle. Secure the nappy with one pin in the centre for a small baby and two pins, one on either side, for a bigger baby.*

wriggling infant cannot roll off if you are changing the nappy on a raised surface.

Remove the soiled nappy. Then clean your baby's bottom thoroughly, wiping away any solid matter with a clean corner of the used nappy, or with a damp tissue or cotton wool soaked in warm water. A baby wipe, or some baby lotion, can be used to finish cleaning the area. Once you have dried your baby's bottom, apply a small amount of a specially formulated barrier cream to protect the skin. Then put on a clean nappy.

WHAT'S IN A NAPPY

You may find the nappy of your new baby is stained dark pink or even

3 *Fold the point at the top down towards the centre so that there is a straight edge along the top.*

4 *Fold the bottom edge up towards the centre, adjusting the fold so that the nappy is the correct size for your baby.*

red. This is because the urine of newborns contains substances called urates. Your newborn's immature bladder cannot hold urine for very long so he may urinate as frequently as 20 times in every 24 hours. This will gradually lessen.

Your baby's first stools will be a blackish-green colour because the meconium from your amniotic fluid is working its way out of his system. Once feeding begins, the stools will change to greenish-brown and then to a yellowish-brown colour. The number of stools passed varies from baby to baby, but generally breast-fed babies pass fewer stools than bottle-fed babies.

DISPOSABLE NAPPIES

There is no doubt that disposables are more convenient than towelling nappies. They are quick and easy to put on and remove and they don't require washing, which is a strong consideration when you think about

the extra washing your baby is likely to produce without even including nappies. Their main disadvantages are that they are more expensive than their towelling counterparts and, despite their name, are cumbersome to dispose of. Most end up being wrapped and put in the dustbin; there are special plastic bags that will neutralize strong odours, and these are widely available.

Alternatively, there are a number of portable units available which will wrap and seal the dirty nappy in strong film, so that they can be stored for a number of days and then be disposed of in bulk.

Disposables work by allowing moisture to soak through a top sheet into an absorbent filling, which is protected on the outside by a waterproof backing. They come in a wide range of shapes and sizes and most are also available in boy/girl styles. Most disposables have elasticated legs to ensure a snug fit, and reusable

tapes so that you can check whether the nappy needs changing and adjust the leg size. Disposables need to be checked frequently because many of them are so good at keeping your baby dry that you may forget to change them.

TOWELLING NAPPIES

These are a once-only buy which makes them more economical than disposables. Towelling nappies come in a variety of absorbencies and qualities. As a general guide the more absorbent the nappy the more expensive it is, so buy the best you can afford. The nappy can be folded in a number of different ways to fit your baby. It is held together with special pins and covered with reusable plastic pants to prevent leakage. One-way liners can be placed inside the nappy to help keep your baby dry; this method also has the added advantage of allowing you to flush any motions down the lavatory

Putting on a towelling nappy

Towelling nappies can be folded in a variety of ways to suit the age and sex of your child.

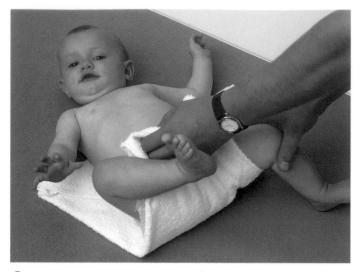

1 *Fold nappy and place a liner in the centre. Lay your baby on the nappy with top edge at waist. Now bring nappy up between her legs.*

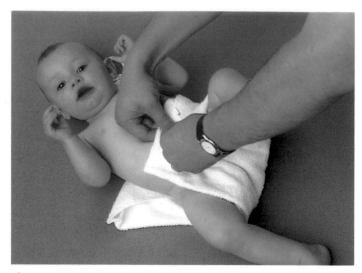

2 *Holding the nappy in place, fold one side over the central panel and secure with a nappy pin.*

3 *Fold the other side into the middle and secure. Always keep your finger between the nappy and your baby's skin when inserting the pin so that there is no risk of pricking your baby.*

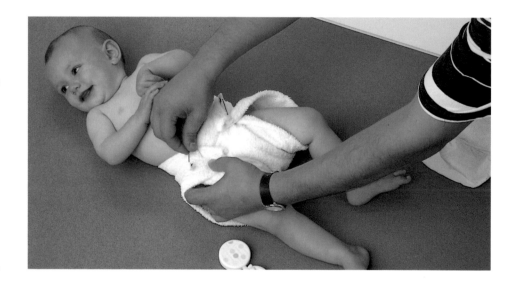

4 *Once the nappy is securely in place you may want to put on a pair of protective plastic pants. Try not to get cross if your baby wets her clean nappy immediately and you have to start all over again.*

with the minimum of bother.

When working out the price of towelling nappies you need to take into consideration the extra cost of washing powder, the electricity used for washing and drying them, sterilizing solution, plastic pants, nappy liners, and pins. Towelling nappies are harder work than disposables because they need washing, so a washing machine and tumble dryer will make life easier for you. The nappies will need to be sterilized, rinsed, and then well washed and dried. Then they should be aired before being reused.

SHAPED WASHABLE NAPPIES
These wash like towelling nappies but are shaped like disposables with re-sealable fastenings and elasticated legs. They come in various sizes, and have a waterproof backing.

CONVENIENCE AND HELPING THE ENVIRONMENT
The choice of nappy is influenced by environmental considerations. Disposable nappies are a great convenience for busy parents, but there are hidden costs to the environment. Some manufacturers of disposables try to minimize the bulk of their products without cutting down their efficiency. This uses fewer natural resources for materials, but some portion of the nappy still will not break down after being discarded. Towelling nappies would seem environmentally friendlier, but you must assess the cost of energy resources and the impact on the environment of the sterilizers and detergents needed to wash the used nappy.

Whichever type of nappy you choose, you can arrange for services to handle them. You can have disposables delivered regularly for a nominal charge, at a price reduced for bulk ordering. Or, with towelling nappies, you can pay to have the used ones picked up and replaced with clean, sterile ones.

NAPPY RASH
Whichever nappy you choose, it is unlikely that your baby will get through the nappy years without experiencing a nappy rash at some time. The key to avoiding the problem is cleanliness and frequent nappy changes, so that urine and faeces

Putting on a disposable nappy

Disposable nappies are available in a variety of shapes, sizes and absorbencies. Always select the size which is recommended for your baby's weight.

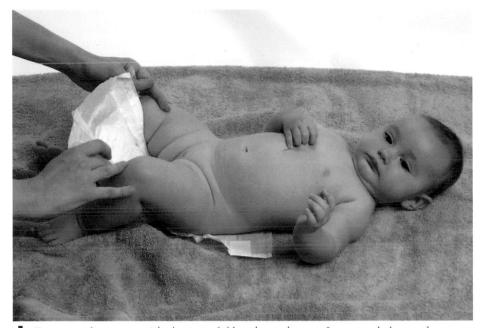

1 *Open out the nappy with the re-sealable tabs at the top. Lay your baby on the nappy so that the top aligns with her waist. Bring the front of the nappy up between her legs.*

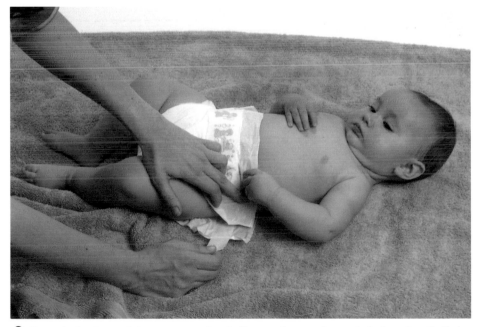

2 *Smooth the front of the nappy so that it fits snugly round your baby's waist. Pull the adhesive tabs firmly towards the front of the nappy and fasten them to secure.*

don't remain in contact with the skin too long. Allow your baby to spend some time naked each day; this will help keep the skin clear.

Nappy rash is sometimes caused by the fungus thrush, and if so an anti-fungal cream will be needed, so consult your doctor if the rash persists.

DRESSING YOUR BABY

There are clothes to fit every size of newborn, from the tiny premature baby to the bouncing 10-pounder. Most baby clothes are sized by the approximate age and height of the child. Your baby probably won't require a great number of first-size clothes and may well grow into the next size within a matter of weeks – some babies are even big enough when born to go straight into second-size clothes.

Dressing and undressing your newborn can be difficult enough without having to worry about doing up complicated fastenings, so keep first clothes simple and save buttons and bows until later. Choose well-designed baby clothes which allow you to dress and undress your baby with the minimum of fuss. Look for garments which have wide, envelope necks that will stretch, so that you can slip them over baby's head easily. Stretchsuits which have fastenings up the inside leg will allow you to change a nappy without having to remove all your baby's clothes. All-in-one bodysuits, which fasten between the legs, will prevent your baby from getting cold around the middle and are ideal if you dress your baby in separates.

If you have a girl you may well be tempted to put her in dresses from the beginning, but dresses are not practical everyday wear for a young baby. They ride up and can be uncomfortable to lie on, they will allow draughts in around her middle, and they get in the way when she is starting to crawl. It is better to save them for special occasions or for when she's older. Lacy jackets and

shawls are best avoided too, as little fingers can get caught in the holes.

As your baby grows, colourful rompers and dungarees can take the place of stretchsuits. They are versatile and are suitable for both boys and girls. Rompers, which are really stretchsuits without feet, are easy to wear as they allow your baby freedom of movement. When you buy dungarees make sure that they have generous turn-ups and adjustable shoulder straps so that you get the maximum wear out of them.

When the weather is warm, babies need to be dressed in clothes that will keep them comfortably cool, and you should always cover their heads with a sun hat if you are out and about. Outerwear for cold days should be roomy enough to fit easily over everyday clothes.

EASY-CARE FABRICS

Your baby is quite likely to get through as many as three or four changes a day so it makes sense to buy clothes made in easy-care fabrics that will wash and wear well. Check the labels before buying and avoid any garments that are going to need special treatment. Choose natural fabrics as these are best for warmth and absorbency. Pure cotton is ideal for your baby's underwear and also her stretchsuits.

Whether you are machine- or hand-washing garments, always follow the instructions on the labels so that your baby's clothes retain their shape, colour, and texture. Avoid using "biological" washing powders as these may irritate your baby's skin. It is important that all clothes are

well aired and completely dry before being put away.

FOOTWEAR

It is very important that a baby's toes are never restricted by tight footwear. Check regularly that all-in-one-suits, leggings, and tights have enough room in them for the baby to wiggle her toes. Socks, bootees, and tights that have shrunk or been outgrown should be discarded. (The same care should be taken with tight collars, cuffs, mittens and also gloves.)

Your baby will not need proper shoes until she is walking and her feet need protection from the hard ground. If you do put your child in soft shoes before this, these should be made from a lightweight breathable material such as cloth or very soft leather and they must be flexible enough for you to feel her toes through them.

When you come to buy your baby's first shoes always have them fitted at a shop which offers a special fitting service for children. Both your baby's feet should be measured for length and width. If you can afford them, shoes with leather uppers are best. It is essential to check regularly that the shoes still fit and have not become too tight.

For a first layette you will need:
- 3 baby gowns.
- pair of scratch mittens.
- shawl.
- 7 stretchsuits.
- 2 pairs of bootees or socks.
- 4 vests or bodysuits.
- warm outer wear for chilly days.
- sun hat.

How to dress your newborn

Dressing and undressing a newborn can seem difficult at first. Always dress a newborn baby on a flat surface so that you have both hands free.

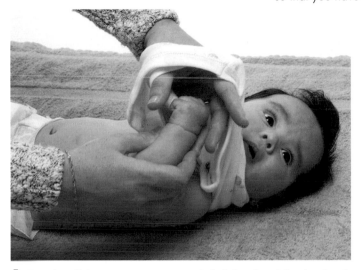

1 *Put the all-in-one vest over your baby's head, raising her head slightly. Then widen one of the arm holes with your hand.*

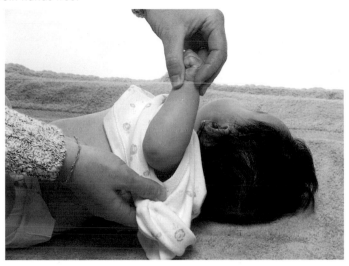

2 *Using your other hand, gently guide the arm through the sleeve. Repeat with the other arm.*

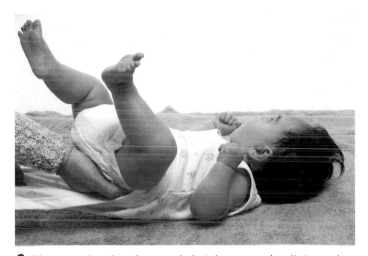

3 *Place your hand under your baby's bottom and pull down the back of the vest.*

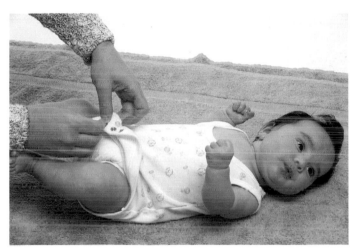

4 *Do up the poppers between the legs and make sure that the vest isn't too tight anywhere when fastened.*

5 *Concertina up the leg of the sock and then hold it wide as you ease it over your baby's foot.*

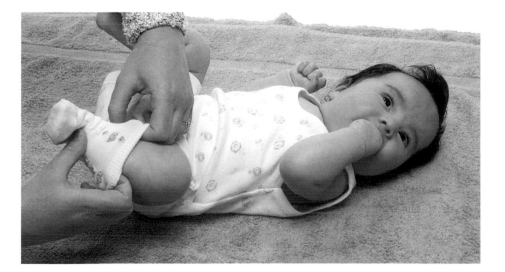

6 *Gently place one foot in the trouser leg and then the other and pull the trousers up.*

7 *Place your hand under your baby's bottom and lift so that you can pull the trousers up over the nappy.*

8 *Adjust the trousers and make sure that the vest is smooth and that there are no puckers that could be uncomfortable to lie on.*

9 *Hold the neck of the T-shirt wide as you slip it over your baby's face and then pull it down over the back of her head.*

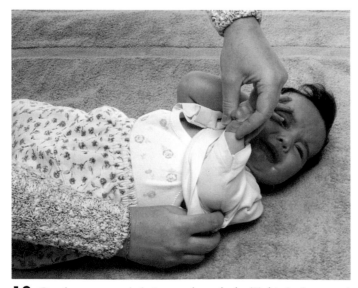

10 *Gently ease your baby's arm through the T-shirt's sleeve and then pull the sleeve down.*

11 *Put her other arm into the sleeve, then pull down top and tuck into her trousers. Your baby is now ready to face the day!*

An all-in-one suit with leg fasteners is ideal for a new baby. The leg opening allows you to change the nappy easily without having to remove any of her clothes.

Rompers and a top are ideal for an older baby and are practical for both boys and girls. The romper straps hold the rompers in place even when your baby is being very active and will help prevent gaps occurring around the middle.

A more mobile baby will be happiest in trousers that will protect her legs as she learns to walk. Make sure the trouser legs clear the floor so that she doesn't trip.

Choose clothes carefully

You will be surprised at how quickly your baby grows during the first 12 months. Select clothes that will mix and match and allow some room for growth. Once she begins to crawl, your baby will need sensible easy-care clothes that will withstand endless washing. Make sure that neck openings are large enough and that garments are easy to unfasten for quick nappy changes. Not all clothes have to be practical; it is nice to buy a couple of special outfits that can be used for parties and days out too.

Dresses look pretty, but are not really practical everyday wear for very young babies or once your baby becomes mobile. Keep dresses for those special occasions.

Rompersuits with short sleeves made in natural fibres are ideal for the summer. Synthetic fibres don't allow the skin to breathe properly and may make your baby feel hot and uncomfortable.

Babies don't need proper shoes until they have started to walk. Soft shoes like these are perfect for little feet in the meantime.

BATHING

When you bath your baby you need to get all you require together before you start. It helps if you can keep all the nappies, pins, pants, and toiletries either in a changing bag or box. A nappy bucket is essential because you'll need somewhere to put the dirty nappy and used cotton wool. A second bucket is also useful for dropping the dirty clothes into as you undress the baby. Any clean clothes and towels should be well aired before you begin and the room where you undress your baby should be warm (a minimum of 21°C/70°F) and draught-free.

When babies are tiny it is easier to bath them in a baby bath on a stand, or one which fits into the big bath.

This way they will be at a comfortable height for you to hold them. Before undressing your baby, fill the bath with warm water, putting the cold in first then the hot, and mix well. Add any bath preparation at this stage. Test that the water is at the right temperature. A special bath thermometer will give you an accurate reading or you can use your elbow.

For bathing you will need:
- Bowl of cooled boiled water, cotton wool and cotton buds (optional) to clean your baby's face before bathing (see topping and tailing).
- Changing mat.
- Bath towel.
- Baby bath preparation.
- Baby shampoo.
- Baby powder.
- Nappy changing equipment and a clean nappy.
- Clean clothes.

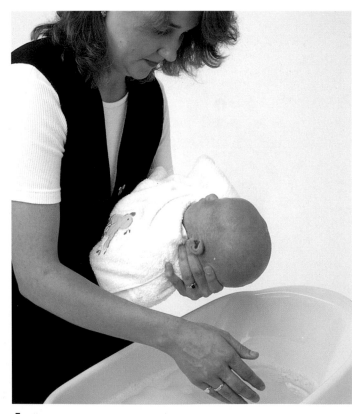

1 *Wrap your baby firmly in a towel. Test the temperature of the bath water again then, having tucked his legs firmly under your arm, hold your baby's head over the bath, supporting his neck and back with your hand.*

2 *Wet his head and apply a mild baby shampoo. Wash the hair with gentle circular movements, keeping the water and shampoo well away from his eyes. Once washed, rinse off the shampoo and lift your baby back onto your knee and towel his hair dry.*

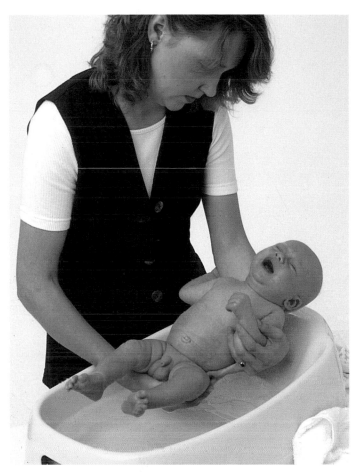

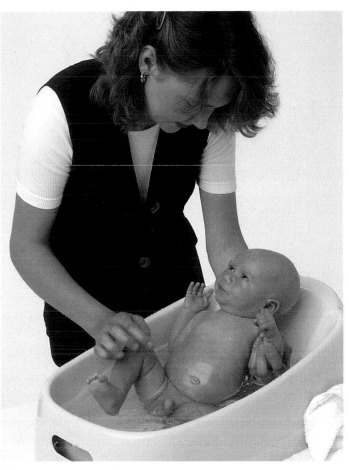

3 *Lift your baby gently into the bath, supporting his head and back on your arm, while holding the arm that is the furthest away from you.*

4 *This leaves your other hand free to wash under his arms and in all the folds and creases. When you have finished, lift your baby out of the bath and into a warm towel.*

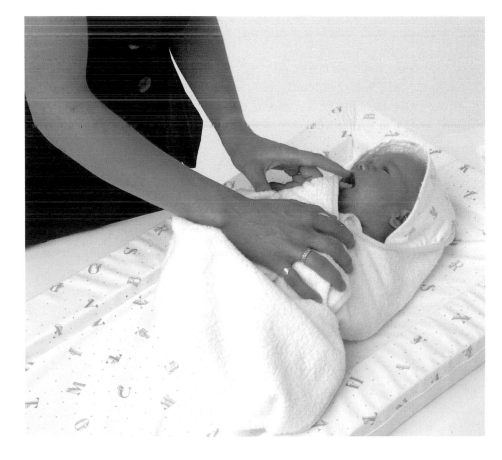

5 *Once you have dried your baby, you may want to apply some baby powder. Put a little powder on your hands and then rub it onto the baby's body, making sure you close the lid tightly after use. Don't sprinkle it on straight from the container in case it gets into your baby's mouth or eyes. It can be dangerous for young infants to inhale powder into their lungs.*

You may find it easier to bath a very young baby in a baby bath. Some of these have their own stand; others, like the one above, fit over a big bath.

A sponge inlay which fits snugly into the bottom of the bath will prevent your baby from slipping, and will make it easier for you to hold him.

An older baby will be happy to spend time in the bath if he has bath toys to play with. Containers that can be filled and emptied and toys that float and bob about will give hours of fun and entertainment.

Once your baby is old enough to be bathed in the big bath you should cover the taps with a folded towel before putting him in the bath. This will prevent him from accidentally burning himself on the hot tap.

Never leave your baby or toddler alone in the bath. It only takes a few seconds for a child to drown in as little as 5 cm/2 in of water.

• When drying or dressing your baby never leave him unattended on a raised surface. He could easily roll off and hurt himself.

• Always check the temperature of the bath water before putting your baby in the bath.

• If you bath your child in a conventional large bath, place a cover over the taps so that he can't burn himself. A folded towel will do.

• Use a non-slip bath mat in the bath.

• Always put the cold water in first when running the bath.

• If you are using a bath and stand, make sure that it is sturdy and secure before lifting your baby into it.

Above: Your child may enjoy sharing his bath with others, or he may prefer to have a bath alone. If you are intending to bath two or three children together it is often easier to put the smallest into the bath first and then let the others join him one at a time.

Right: Not all children enjoy spending time in the bath. If one child is unhappy about bathtime don't force him to stay in longer than he wants. Always stay in the bathroom with your children so that you can be sure that they are safe.

SLEEPING

Your new baby has no understanding of day and night so during the first weeks of her life she will sleep and wake at random. You may find that she sleeps for 20 hours out of every 24 or for only 12 hours out of 24. Whatever pattern your baby adopts, she will be getting as much sleep as she needs.

Average sleep pattern

Birth	17 hours in every 24	
	Day	**Night**
3 months	5 hours	10 hours
6 months	4 hours	10 hours
9 months	3 hours·	11 hours
12 months	2 hours	11 hours

Your baby's biological clock will dictate when she is ready for sleep in the evenings and this is a good start-ing point for establishing a regular bedtime. From the very beginning

Try not to let your baby fall asleep before putting him in his cot as he may wake feeling distressed if you are not there.

you should make the hour before bed quiet and relaxing. You may choose this time to give your baby a bath, and you will certainly want to feed and change your baby before putting her down in the cot. You may need to rock or sing to the child until sleep comes, especially if she is very young. During the first three months your baby may sleep better if swaddled in a blanket or sheet – this will prevent tiny limbs from jerking and twitching. These sudden involuntary movements often wake a very young baby. As your child gets older she will begin to settle on her own and you can help by pro-viding things for amusement, such as a mobile and cot toys. Follow the same routine every night so that the

Your baby will enjoy being outside from an early age. Keep her out of direct sun in the shade and have the hood up to protect her from draughts.

baby gradually begins to associate the cot with night-time and sleep.

A baby's room needs to be warm – around 18°C/65°F – so that the child doesn't wake up cold in the

Cot death

All parents are worried about the possibility of cot death, technically known as Sudden Infant Death Syndrome (SIDS). Although the chance of this happening to your baby is remote, it is sensible to take a few simple precautions that are known to reduce the risk.
• Make sure that your baby sleeps either on her back or side, with the lower arm forward to stop the child rolling onto her stomach.
• Keep your baby warm, but not too warm. Check her temperature regularly by feeling the back of her neck or tummy, and use several lightweight blankets so that you can add or take them away to adjust the temperature.
• Don't use a duvet or baby nest because these could be too warm for your baby.

• Do not smoke near your baby and keep her out of a smoky atmosphere.
• If your baby seems unwell, take her to the doctor immediately.
• Try, if you can, to breast feed. It is believed to help reduce the risk of cot death.
• Make sure your baby's room is well ventilated. Leave the door ajar or a window open (but ensure that the baby is not in a draught). Don't leave room heaters on at night. The temperature should be around 18°C/65°F.
• Research is being carried out into the possible link between chemicals found in mattresses and cot death, but as yet no proven link has been found. However, you can safeguard your baby by making sure that her mattress is kept clean, dry and well aired.

Bedtime tips

• Encourage your baby to sleep while there are background noises going on. This way she won't expect silence at bedtime.

• Put a selection of toys in the cot to provide amusement if she wakes early.

• Make night feeds as quick and quiet as possible, keeping the lights low and changing the baby first. Don't do anything stimulating.

• Put the baby down to sleep in the cot at night so that she comes to associate it with sleep.

• Wrap up a newborn baby firmly so that she feels secure.

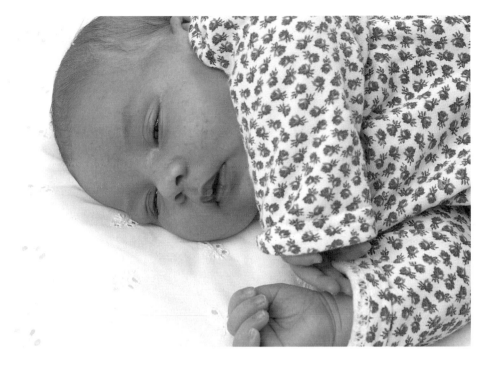

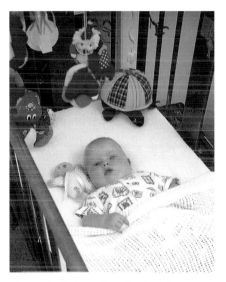

An older baby will enjoy looking at a mobile when he is awake in his cot.

the day. Stimulate your baby by talking and playing with her in the daytime when she is awake. Keep feeding and changing down to a minimum amount of time during the night so that your baby learns that this is not a time for being sociable.

Above: If your baby prefers to sleep on her side, make sure her lower arm is in a forward position to stop her rolling onto her stomach.

Below: Check your baby's body warmth regularly at night, and remove some blankets if she feels too warm.

night. Put your baby down to sleep in a vest, nappy, and stretchsuit and cover her with a sheet and several layers of blankets. You can check for body warmth during the night by feeling the tummy or the back of the neck, then you can add or take away blankets accordingly. If your baby seems worried by the dark, leave a nightlight on near the cot.

You can help your infant develop a better sleeping pattern by encouraging her to be more awake during

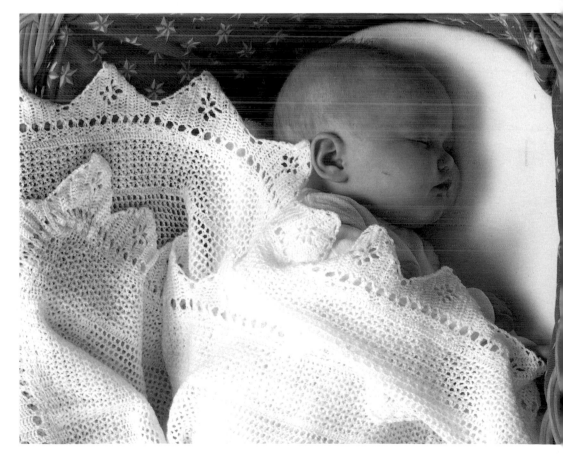

CRYING

Your response to your child's crying and the way you comfort him can influence the bond that grows between you. There is no risk of spoiling your child by responding to his cries. It is impossible to give a young baby too much love. By going to your baby you will be showing him that you care and this in turn will help to form a deep, loving relationship between you.

WHY BABIES CRY

Babies cry for a lot of different reasons and you need to understand what makes your baby cry so that you can provide comfort. Your newborn may cry a lot because this is the main means of communicating with you. The infant needs to be able to let you know that the world he is now in is a strange and sometimes frightening place. Once he has adapted to the new environment and you have developed a routine that takes account of his likes and dislikes,

the amount of crying will gradually start to decrease.

Hunger is the most common cause of crying and you will soon learn to recognize when your baby is hungry. The first action is to feed on demand – a very young baby may need feeding about every two or three hours.

Being too hot or too cold can also make a baby cry. A young baby can't regulate his own temperature and he can easily become too hot or too cold, so it is important to keep a check on an infant's temperature. You should make sure that your baby's room is kept at a constant 18°C/65°F. Wet or dirty nappies do not cause crying except when the wet nappy gets cold.

Your new baby will probably hate being undressed, even in a warm room. This is because the feel of clothing on the skin creates a secure feeling, so when it is removed the infant cries. Keep undressing to a

minimum in the first few weeks. Top and tail rather than bath your baby so that you only need to remove a bit of clothing at a time. When you do undress him completely, wrap him in a towel to give him a feeling of security.

Pain is a definite cause of crying, but it may be hard for you to locate the cause of the actual pain. If you

Crying cures

• Movement soothes a baby so try rocking him or walking around holding him on your shoulder.
• Put your baby in a bouncing seat that will move very gently.
• Push him backwards and forwards in the pram.
• Put the baby in his car seat and go for a drive.
• Talk, sing, or croon soothingly.
• Put on the radio or TV or turn on the vacuum cleaner.
• Distract the baby with a noisy toy.
• Play a tape of calm music.
• Carry a young baby next to your body in a sling.

Not being allowed to do what he wants, when he wants, can lead to a child's tears of frustration.

Waiting for a bottle to cool down can be tiresome and can lead to angry tears from a hungry baby.

can, remove the source of the pain –
for example an open nappy pin. If
you can't find a reason for the pain,
don't just leave your baby to cry;
pick him up and comfort him. Stay
with your baby until he is completely calm. If your baby seems feverish
or just generally unwell, always seek
medical advice.

Any baby will normally start crying when he is tired. If you think
that this is the cause, put your child
down to sleep in a dimly lit, warm
room. If necessary, rock or sing a
soothing song to him until he has
completely calmed down and starts
to become sleepy.

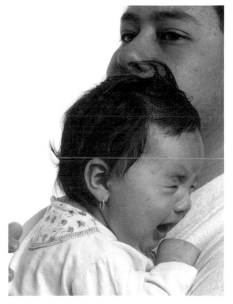

*Tiredness is a common reason for tears
before bedtime.*

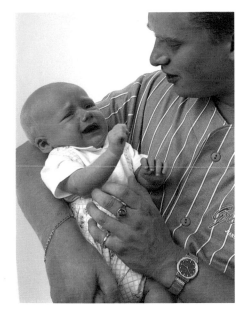

*The discomfort of wind after a feed can
cause a baby's tears.*

Sometimes it all gets too much for a young child and the only way to show his feelings is to scream.

COLIC

Young babies sometimes have prolonged periods of crying during the day which are frequently attributed to colic. These crying spells often take place around the time of the evening feed, although they can happen at any time of day. Colic, if it is going to occur, usually starts within the first three weeks after birth and normally lasts until around three months, although it can go on for longer. It generally stops as abruptly as it starts, having caused your baby no harm.

Although no one knows exactly what colic is, or what causes it, many doctors believe that it is a type of stomach ache that occurs in spasms, and makes the baby draw up her legs in pain. The pattern of crying would indicate cramp-like pains; the baby is miserable and distressed, then calms down for a few minutes before starting to scream again. This may continue for several hours at a time, which can become very wearing and upsetting for both of you.

POSSIBLE CAUSES

Colic has been blamed on many things and it is certainly worth investigating all the possibilities if your baby suffers from it. Since colic affects both bottle- and breast-fed babies the method of feeding is not thought to be the cause. However, if you are breast-feeding it could be something that you are eating which is causing the problem. Try cutting out of your diet anything you have eaten during the previous 24 hours which you think might have affected your baby. It has been suggested that the amount of feeds offered – both too little and too much – could be to blame, or that the milk, if bottle-feeding, could be too hot or too cold, or the feeds too weak or too rich. Remember, when you make up bottle feeds it is essential to follow the manufacturer's instructions.

Other possible causes are constipation, diarrhoea, indigestion or intestinal cramps. Vigorously crying babies are almost always healthy, but if your baby looks pale or ill, seek medical advice.

There may also be a link between tension and colic, which can lead to a chain reaction. The end of the day is usually a busy time in a household and you may be tired and tense as you try to prepare the baby for bed, tidy up, and get a meal ready. Your baby is sensitive to your moods and may respond to tension by crying which, of course, increases your anxiety, with the result that the crying becomes prolonged and ends when you are both exhausted.

WHAT TO DO

There is no reliable treatment for colic and, although there are some over-the-counter medicines available you should always consult your doctor before giving them to your baby. On a practical level you can rearrange your day by preparing the evening meal earlier, so that you have time to spend comforting your baby during this crying period. Although there is little you can do to ease your baby's discomfort completely, holding him against you, so that there is gentle pressure and warmth on her stomach, and rubbing her back soothingly may be of some help. Try to share the comforting with your partner to spread the strain, and remember that colic doesn't last for more than a few months so, although it is awful at the time, it will not last for ever.

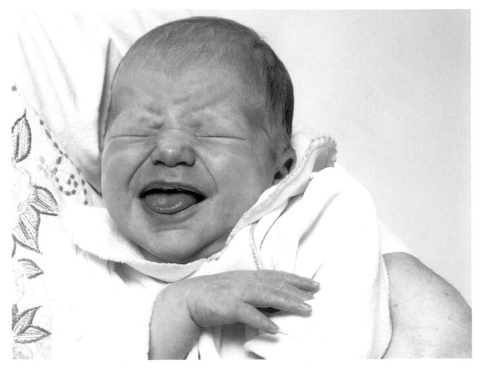

Colic can start as early as three weeks and may last until your baby is three months old. Be patient; it will pass and it won't do your baby any harm.

TEETH

At around six months your baby's milk teeth will start to emerge and by the age of two-and-a-half all 20 first teeth will usually have appeared. Every tooth has two parts: the crown, which can be seen in the mouth; and the root, which anchors

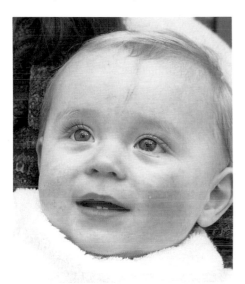

Your baby's first teeth will start to emerge at around six months old, and you should start to clean them as soon as they appear in the gums.

the tooth to the jaw. The outside of the tooth is made of enamel which protects the crown and provides a strong surface for chewing. Because the enamel is not fully formed when the teeth first come through, calcium and other minerals are required over the next six to 12 months to strengthen it. These minerals are found in the saliva and plaque in your child's mouth and, under normal conditions, will steadily accumulate in the teeth. But calcium and phosphates in the enamel frequently come under attack from acids that are formed by the bacteria living in plaque. These bacteria use carbohydrates, such as sugar, to generate the acid.

Your baby needs carbohydrates, but food and drink containing a lot of simple sugars such as sucrose, fructose, and glucose will speed up the production of the acids which can damage

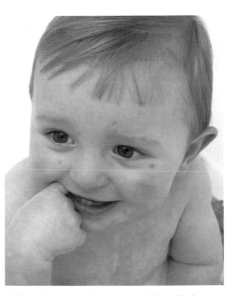

When he is teething your child will chew anything, even his fingers. Try offering her finger foods, such as a stick of raw carrot, as something different to chew on.

teeth. It is not just the amount of sugar she eats that affects your child's teeth, it is also the frequency of her consumption of sugary food and drink. Drinks taken slowly, or sugary foods eaten over a long period of time, keep the sugar content of the

Chewing and biting on things is often one of the first signs of teething in a baby, and this may occur some weeks before any teeth appear.

Before you start trying to brush your baby's teeth, it is a good idea to let him play with his toothbrush so that he becomes familiar with it and does not cause a fuss when you put it in his mouth.

Your child will find it good fun attempting to brush his own teeth from a very early age.

You will need to clean your child's teeth until he is old enough to do it himself. A fluoride toothpaste will help protect his teeth and gums.

mouth high, which means that calcium and phosphates are being removed for longer and less time is available to replace them. Generally, the lower the sugar content of food and drink the better they are for the teeth because it is the total sugar levels, not just added sugar, that counts. This is why you should never add sugar to your baby's food or drinks and you should always dilute concentrated drinks and give them in a trainer cup rather than a feeding bottle.

CLEANING TEETH

As soon as your baby's first teeth appear, you should clean them every morning and night. Cleaning the teeth at night, before bed, is especially important because the flow of protective saliva decreases when your baby is asleep, which means that any sugar in the mouth allows the plaque to stay acidic for a prolonged period.

In the morning, brushing your baby's teeth will help to remove any build-up of plaque that has occurred during the night.

The main point of cleaning teeth is to remove as much plaque as possible, and toothpaste does this with the aid of abrasives; there are toothpastes specially formulated to be suitable for young children. A pea-sized amount of toothpaste on the brush is all that is required to clean a mouth full of teeth. You'll probably find it easiest at first to use your finger wrapped in a soft cloth and then, when your baby has got used to the idea of having his teeth cleaned, you can start to clean his teeth with a soft baby toothbrush.

Since the introduction of fluoride toothpastes, children's teeth have been healthier. Fluoride, which is present in most toothpastes, works by making the enamel stronger

As your child starts to get teeth she will experiment with the chewing action on her favourite toys.

against attack from plaque. The amount of fluoride children should use varies according to their age and the fluoride levels already present in the water.

THE DENTIST

Take your baby with you when you go for your own dental check-ups so that he will become familiar with the dentist and the surgery. By getting your child used to having his teeth inspected before he needs treatment, he will then experience no alarm at the thought of going to the dentist. A child usually won't need to have an actual dental check-up until he is about three years of age, when your dentist will check to see that the teeth are developing properly. The dentist will also be able to advise you about any special protective treatments available for your child.

Cleaning your young baby's new teeth at bedtime is essential to prevent the build-up of plaque as he sleeps.

IMMUNIZATION

Diseases such as measles, mumps, whooping cough, rubella (German measles), diphtheria, tetanus, polio, and Haemophilus influenzae type b (a cause of meningitis) can be very serious and, in very young children, can be fatal. Immunization offers long-lasting protection against these diseases. If you are concerned about your child having the immunizations, or are worried about allergic reactions, or because there is a family history of convulsions, don't just decide not to have your child immunized, discuss it with your doctor.

The triple vaccine or DPT, which immunizes against diphtheria, whooping cough (the P in DPT stands for Pertussis – the medical name for whooping cough) and tetanus, is usually given as one injection at two months, three months, and four months of age. Hib vaccine, which immunizes against Haemophilus influenzae type b, the most common bacterial meningitis in the under-fives, is given by injection at the same time as DPT. Polio vaccine is given by mouth in three doses also at the same time as the DPT injections. With all of these it is important to complete the course of three doses to ensure the maximum immunity. MMR immunizes against measles, mumps, and rubella and is given in one injection – normally between 12 and 15 months.

Your newborn baby may also be offered immunization against tuberculosis (TB) with a BCG vaccine if you are in or from a high-risk area, or if you come from a family that has a history of TB.

SIDE-EFFECTS

Many parents worry about possible side-effects of these vaccines, especially from the whooping cough vaccine and MMR. However, research shows that the risk of harmful complications from any of the vaccines on the schedule is extremely small. In fact, a child is much more at risk from the diseases themselves than from immunization.

After any immunization your child may feel a bit off-colour for a while and may even run a slight temperature. It is quite normal for the skin around the site of the injection to become red and sore or slightly swollen. But if you are at all worried about your child you should contact your doctor.

Any side-effects from the triple vaccine are usually mild. Your baby may be slightly feverish and appear unhappy for up to 24 hours after the injection. Very occasionally a convulsion occurs as a result of the fever, but this is over very quickly and has no lasting effect. The whooping cough part of this vaccination is the one that most parents worry about, but the latest research suggests that there is no proven link between the vaccine and brain damage. The Hib vaccination has similar side-effects to the triple vaccine: some redness and swelling at the injection site and slight fever and irritability.

The MMR immunization has no immediate side-effect, although some children develop a mild fever and rash seven to ten days after the injection, others sometimes get a very mild form of mumps. If either of these reactions occur they are not infectious. In rare cases, a child may have an extreme reaction to the vaccine, such as a convulsion with fever or encephalitis (inflammation of the brain). But the vaccine that was associated with this reaction has now been replaced.

If your baby is feverish or acutely unwell or has had a severe reaction to an earlier immunization, you should not have her immunized again without talking first to your doctor. Always remember to tell the doctor who is doing the immunization if your baby is taking medication or if she has a severe allergic reaction to eggs. If the baby is vomiting or has diarrhoea it is better to put off giving the polio vaccine until she is better.

THE DISEASES

Immunizations have developed over the years and many diseases which were formerly feared are no longer threats. This is the result of a sound immunization programme applied to virtually all children. Often parents

At 2 months:	
Diphtheria	}
Whooping cough	}DPT one injection
Tetanus	}
Hib	}one injection
Polio	}by mouth

At 3 months:	
Diphtheria	}
Whooping cough	}DPT one injection
Tetanus	}
Hib	}one injection
Polio	}by mouth

are vague about the actual disease themselves, so it is worth familiarizing yourself with the conditions and their symptoms:

Diphtheria starts with a sore throat and then quickly develops into a serious illness which blocks the nose and throat, making it difficult and sometimes nearly impossible for a child to breathe. It can last for weeks and can often be fatal.

Tetanus is caused by germs from dirt or soil getting into an open wound or burn. It attacks the nervous system causing painful muscle spasms. Immunization has made it rare, but there is still a real chance of getting it and it can be fatal.

Whooping cough is a highly infectious disease which causes long bouts of coughing and choking, leaving the sufferer exhausted. These bouts can occur up to 50 times in one day and the cough can last two to three months. Whooping cough can cause convulsions, ear infections, pneumonia, bronchitis, and even brain damage. It can prove fatal, especially in children who are under one year of age.

Haemophilus influenzae type b is the commonest form of bacterial meningitis in the under-fives. It causes epiglottitis (a severe form of croup), pneumonia, blood poisoning, and infections of the bones and joints. It affects babies under a year most severely and can be fatal.

Polio attacks the nervous system and causes muscle paralysis. If it affects the breathing the sufferer will need help to breathe and could even die. Thankfully, polio is extremely rare in most western countries because of immunization, but there is still a risk of contact with the disease through foreign travel, which is why immunization is still important. Adults should check to see if they need a polio booster when they take their baby for immunization.

Measles can be much more serious than people think because it is the disease most likely to cause encephalitis (inflammation of the brain). It begins like a bad cold with a fever and then a rash appears which is often accompanied by a bad cough and high temperature. Measles can cause convulsions, ear infections, bronchitis, and pneumonia; it can sometimes be fatal.

Mumps is usually a mild illness, but it can have serious complications which affect both boys and girls, and it can cause permanent deafness.

Rubella (German measles) is a mild disease, but one which can harm an unborn baby if a woman catches it when she is pregnant. The risk is particularly high during the first four months of pregnancy. Babies whose mothers get rubella during pregnancy can be born deaf, blind, and with heart and brain damage.

Tuberculosis (TB) usually affects

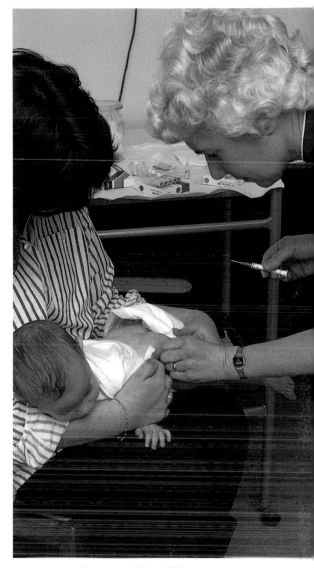

At two months your child will be given his first immunizations. Although they will probably cause some momentary discomfort it will all soon be forgotten with a cuddle.

the lungs; symptoms include a cough, fever, or night sweats. Children are vulnerable and develop TB meningitis more often than adults.

Immunization timetable

At 4 months:		At 12-15 months:		At 3-5 years (pre-school booster):	
Diphtheria	}	Measles	}	Diphtheria	}one booster
Whooping cough	}DPT one injection	Mumps	}MMR one injection	Tetanus	}injection
Tetanus	}	Rubella	}	Polio	}by mouth
Hib	}one injection				
Polio	}by mouth				

CHILDHOOD ILLNESSES

Knowing what to do when your child is ill and when you should call the doctor is something that comes with experience. Common symptoms that indicate that your child is unwell include sickness, diarrhoea, or a high temperature. These may be accompanied by unusual behaviour such as listlessness, refusing to eat, and crying for no apparent reason. However, it is not always easy to tell when a very young baby is unwell so you should trust your instincts – you know your baby better than anyone. Signs indicating that a baby is ill and that you should call the doctor include refusing feeds, a fit or convulsion, extreme drowsiness, difficulty in breathing, severe diarrhoea, vomiting, high fever and the appearance of unusual rashes.

DEALING WITH ILLNESS

Fever occurs when the body temperature rises above normal and is usually caused by an infection. If your child is feverish he will need a lot of cold fluids to drink and a dose of paracetamol syrup to bring his temperature down (aspirin should not be given to children under the age of 12, unless specifically prescribed by your doctor).

If your child is very feverish, keep him in bed and cool him down. This can be done by sponging him all over with tepid water, then covering him with a light sheet and making sure that he drinks plenty of liquids. Alternatively, put a cool fan next to the bed – but safely out of reach.

The easiest way of detecting feverish illness is by taking your child's temperature. This can be done by using a clinical thermometer which is placed under your baby's arm, or in the groin – older children can hold it under their tongue. Alternatively, you can hold a fever strip on your child's forehead. Whichever method you use, make sure that you start with a low reading. A clinical thermometer should have the mercury shaken down close to the bulb. A normal temperature is 37°C/98.6°F, but a child's can vary between 36°C/96.8°F and 37.5°C/99.5°F. You must phone your doctor if the temperature goes over 39°C/102°F, or if it remains above normal for more than two days.

Medicines for young children usually come in liquid form and can be given to them by dropper, or by using a specially designed spoon; older children can manage with an ordinary spoon. It is important that you know what the medicine is, what it does, and the correct dosage before you give it to your child. If you are in any doubt, check the details with your pharmacist.

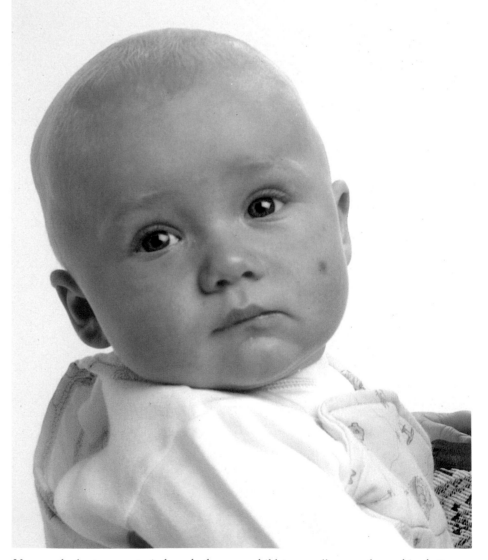

You are the best person to judge whether your child is unwell as you know him better than anyone else. As you become more experienced as a parent you will know whether you need to call the doctor. If you are unsure, it is always better to seek medical advice.

It may be easier to take a young baby's temperature using a fever strip. Place the strip on your child's forehead and hold it there for 15–20 seconds to get the necessary reading.

A more accurate way of taking a temperature is with a clinical thermometer. Place it under your child's arm, in the armpit, and hold it in position for two or three minutes.

SPECIFIC CONDITIONS:
COUGHS AND COLDS

Colds are caused by air-borne viruses, not bacteria, so antibiotics can't be used to help relieve the symptoms. If your child is suffering from a blocked or runny nose, you may need to buy a nasal decongestant or your doctor may prescribe some nose drops, particularly if the cold is hindering your baby's feeding. Always seek advice from your doctor or health visitor if a cold is affecting your child's breathing. It is better to be safe than sorry.

Irritating coughs often occur with a cold so if your child has a dry cough ask your pharmacist to recommend a soothing linctus that is suitable for children.

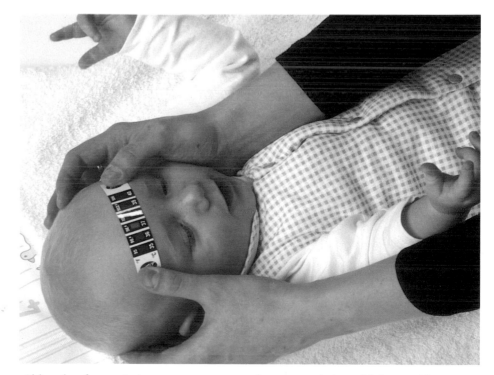

Although a fever strip is not as accurate as a thermometer it is useful for a quick assessment. It will show a raised temperature so that you can take the appropriate action.

necessary. Including more water, fruit, vegetables, and fibre will help solve the problem. If the problem still continues to persist, a mild laxative may be required. Consult your health visitor for advice.

Diarrhoea is the frequent passing of loose, watery stools. If a baby is being bottle-fed or being weaned, you should omit one or two milk feeds and solids and offer plenty of clear fluids instead, including an oral rehydration mixture if the loose stools continue. Breast-fed babies can continue their milk feeds as normal.

You should contact your doctor if the diarrhoea persists after a period of 12 hours, or if it is accompanied by vomiting because the baby could become dehydrated.

TEETHING

The first signs of teething in a young child are often a red area on his cheek, excessive dribbling, and he starts chewing on his fingers. A teething gel, containing a local anaesthetic, will help to give some relief, but you will need to watch out for any sign of allergic reactions to the gel. These can include a noticeable reddening or swelling of the gums.

VOMITING

If your baby starts to vomit frequently or violently, and if there is any other sign of illness, you should always contact your doctor immediately as young babies can very quickly become dehydrated if they are sick.

Older children can be sick once or twice without suffering any lasting effect. Give your child plenty of clear fluids to drink and don't bother about trying to offer him any tempting food until he is feeling better.

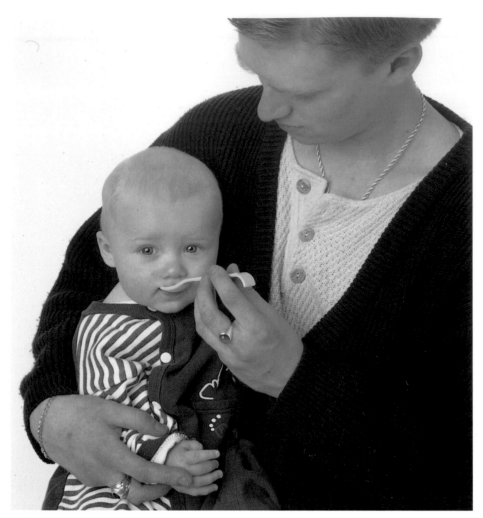

Medicines for young children usually come in liquid form and can be given on a teaspoon. Sit your baby on your knee and hold his hands out of the way as you spoon the medicine into his mouth.

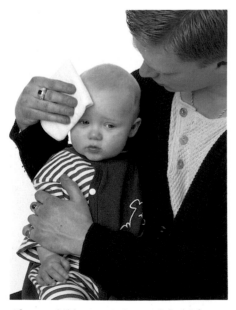

If your child appears hot and feverish you can help to cool him down by wiping his forehead with a face cloth that has been wrung out in cold water.

EAR INFECTIONS

Problems with a child's ears often accompany a cold. One of the first signs is if your baby starts pulling at one of his ears, which might appear red, but he may also just cry a lot and seem generally unwell. Paracetamol syrup will help relieve the pain, but an antibiotic may also be required to clear up any infection, so you will need to consult your doctor for advice. Do not take your child swimming with an ear infection.

CONSTIPATION AND DIARRHOEA

If a child is having difficulty passing stools because they are hard, the problem is most likely to be constipation. A change in diet will be

CHILDHOOD DISEASES

There are a number of diseases that affect most children. If treated promptly, they pose no serious threat and will probably give immunity to the sufferer. The key thing for the parent is to recognize the condition as close to its onset as possible and take the appropriate action.

GERMAN MEASLES (RUBELLA)
This is usually a mild illness which causes few problems. It is rare for a child to get German measles in the first six months if the mother has had the infection or has been immunized. The incubation period is 10-21 days and the virus is spread through the coughing and sneezing of an infected person. It is infectious from the day before the rash appears and for two days after its appearance. It is very important to keep your child away from any woman who might be pregnant if you suspect German measles because it can seriously damage an unborn baby.

Symptoms: The first sign is usually a rash that starts on the face and then spreads to the trunk. The spots are pink, pinpoint in size, separate (not blotchy), and are not raised above the level of the skin. The rash is not

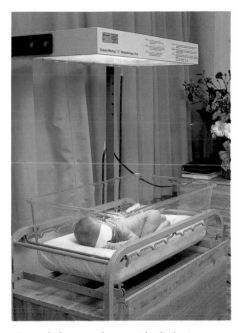

Some babies are born with slight jaundice, a yellowing of the skin, which may need treatment with ultra-violet light. It is usually carried out in the post-natal ward.

The polio vaccine will probably be given to your baby on a spoon at the same time as he has his other injections.

itchy and lasts for only two or three days. It may be accompanied by a slightly runny nose and a little redness around the eyes and swollen glands in the neck, the back of the head, and behind the ears. These may remain swollen for a few days.

Treatment: Check your child's temperature at least twice a day and give plenty of fluids if the temperature is at all raised.

Call the doctor: If you think your child has German measles, contact your doctor to confirm it. Do not take your child to the surgery because of possible contact with a pregnant woman.

MEASLES

It is rare for a child under six months to get measles if the mother had measles as a child, because the mother's immunity is passed on to the baby. The incubation period is 10-15 days and your child is infectious about six days before the rash appears and for five days afterwards. The virus is spread through droplets from the nose and throat of an infected person.

Symptoms: The first symptoms are a slightly raised temperature, runny

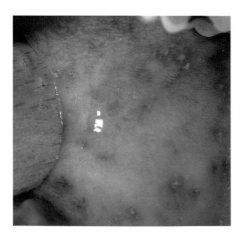

One of the first signs of measles are Koplik's spots which appear inside a child's cheeks. The spots are small and red and have a white centre.

nose, cough, redness of the eyes, lethargy, and loss of appetite. Two or three days later white spots about the size of a pinhead, with a surrounding red area, can be seen on the inside of the cheeks. These last for a few days then a blotchy, slightly raised, red rash appears behind the ears and on the face and then spreads to the chest during the next 24 hours. By the third and fourth day it will have spread over the arms and legs and will have reached the feet. The rash is not itchy but it will be accompanied by a high temperature. As the rash fades so the temperature falls.

Treatment: Bring the fever down. If your child's eyes become crusted, wipe them gently with cotton wool dipped in cooled boiled water. Your child can get out of bed as soon as she is feeling better.

Call the doctor: If your child is no better three days after the rash develops; if the child's temperature rises very rapidly; if earache or breathing difficulties develop.

MUMPS

This affects the glands in the neck and in front of the ears and causes swelling. Sometimes mumps causes inflammation of the testicles, but this is rare in boys before puberty. Mumps is unlikely to affect a baby under the age of six months. The incubation period is 12-21 days. Mumps is spread by droplet infection and it is infectious from two days before the swelling appears and until it disappears.

Symptoms: Pain and swelling in one or both of the parotid glands which are situated just in front of the ears. The swelling makes the face appear puffy and reaches its maximum in about two days. It subsides within about five days.

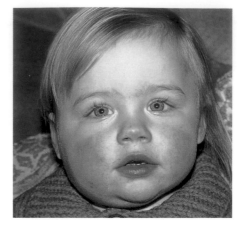

With mumps, your child's face will become swollen and he may find it hard to swallow. Make sure he drinks plenty of liquids and give him jelly and ice cream to eat.

Treatment: Give a suitable painkiller to reduce discomfort. Give your child easy-to-swallow foods such as ice cream and jelly and plenty of liquids, but avoid acidic drinks. If opening the mouth is painful, try getting her to drink through a straw. Warmth will help to soothe the swelling, so heat a soft cloth and hold it gently to her cheeks.

Call the doctor: If your child develops bad pains in her stomach or, if a boy, has a red testicle. Your doctor should be told if you suspect that your child has mumps.

WHOOPING COUGH

This can occur at any age and is one of the most serious common infectious diseases. The incubation period is 7-10 days and the germ is spread through droplet infection. A child is infectious from about two days before the onset of the cough until about three weeks later.

Symptoms: Whooping cough starts with a slight cough and sneezing and is often mistaken for an ordinary cold. It develops into severe bouts of 10-20 short, dry coughs which occur during the day and night – these are often worse during the night. In children over 18 months of age a long attack of coughing is followed by a sharp intake of breath which may produce the crowing or whooping sound. Not all children develop the whoop. During bad bouts of coughing your child may vomit, become red in the face and sweat. The cough can last for two to three months.

Treatment: Stay with the child during her coughing fits because they are distressing and she will need you to comfort her. Try lying her face-down across your lap while she coughs. Sleep with her at night when the cough is at its worst. Keep a bowl near her in case of vomiting and clean it afterwards with disinfectant so that the infection isn't spread. Try to keep your child entertained to distract her from coughing.

Call the doctor: Immediately if you suspect that your child has whooping cough. The doctor may prescribe a cough suppressant and an antibiotic. A very young baby may need to be admitted to hospital if the coughing is affecting breathing.

CHICKENPOX

This is a highly infectious but usually mild disease in childhood (it can be serious if it occurs during adulthood). It is caused by one of the herpes group of viruses and is transmitted through direct contact with an infected person. The incubation period is 14–21 days and it is most infectious before the rash appears, which makes it difficult to isolate an infected child from others.

Symptoms: Chickenpox often starts with a fever, which may be accompanied by a headache and is then followed by a rash. Sometimes the only sign is the rash, which appears mainly on the trunk and

then spreads to the rest of the body and may even occur in the mouth. The rash consists of small red spots that quickly turn into itchy blisters. These gradually dry to form crusts which can remain for a few weeks. New spots appear in batches so an area may be covered in both crusty spots and new blisters. Scars only occur if the spots are scratched or if they become infected. Your child is infectious to other children until new blisters have stopped appearing,

which normally takes about one week.

Treatment: Treat any fever as previously described. Keep your child's nails very short to prevent her from scratching and infecting the spots. Apply calamine lotion to help reduce the itchiness. A handful of bicarbonate of soda added to a cool bath will also ease itchiness.

Call the doctor: If the itchiness is really causing a serious problem or if any of the spots have become infected or are very painful.

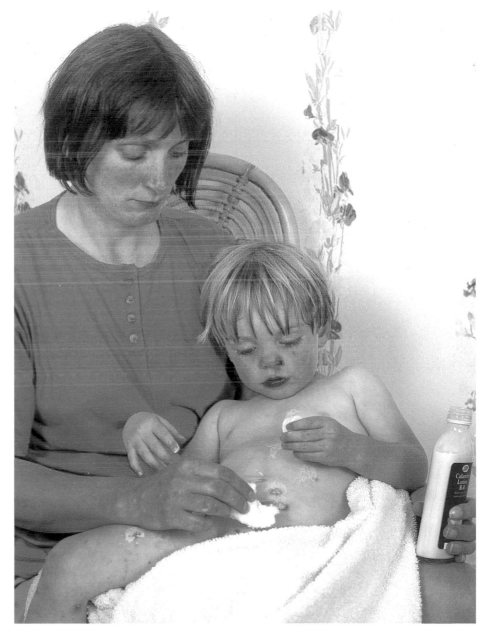

Your child will probably feel miserable if he has chickenpox. Try to prevent him from scratching the spots as this will lead to scarring. Applying some calamine lotion to the spots will help reduce the itchiness and irritation.

LEARNING WITH TOYS

Playing with toys is important in children's development because through play they learn about themselves and the world in which they live. During the first few months your child isn't capable of manipulating objects so he learns through sight, sound, and touch. A young baby likes to see things from close up and will enjoy objects that are colourful and that move or make a noise. A baby doesn't need a lot of toys because in these early months you will be his best plaything and your baby will be endlessly fascinated by your face and will study it during feeding. Sing and talk to your baby because, even though he can't understand, he will love the sound of your voice. As your baby gets older he will start imitating you and making different sounds. Encourage him by playing games such as Pat-a-cake or singing "Old MacDonald had a farm" and getting him to help with the animal noises. Your child may be able to remember simple concepts too, such as putting things in and taking them out of a container. Bath toys will give a lot of pleasure as your baby learns the fun of playing in water.

Toys will help your child learn to develop new skills, and they offer stimulation at each stage of development. For example, a very young baby will gain a lot from a simple pram toy; he can see it, touch it, suck, and smell it and by doing so will be discovering a number of new sensations. It won't take long to learn that a toy pushed out of the pram will just disappear. By performing this trick over and over again your baby will start to realize that he can make things happen which influence his world.

In the first year, toys can be used to help a child to learn hand and eye co-ordination, recognition, and then crawling and walking. As a child gets older, toys become useful props in imaginative games that teach him how to communicate with others, and help him to discover different aspects of life.

A baby will enjoy a play mat that offers her different textures to play with. She will also be fascinated by the bright colours and bold designs featured on the mat.

An activity gym will keep a baby amused from a young age. At first he will just look at the hanging objects, but he will soon start to reach for the toys.

Left: An activity centre is always fascinating to a young baby and this one can be used as a walker too. Toys which will help your child to balance as she begins to pull herself up and then take her first steps will give her confidence.

Below: Although there are many attractive, well-designed toys available, don't be surprised if your baby decides that a wooden spoon and a metal pan are her favourite play things.

There are so many toys to choose from that it's often difficult to decide which ones are right for a child at any particular stage. You should always buy the correct toys for the age of your child. Toys designed for an older child may well have loose parts on which a baby could choke. You should check all the toys a child plays with regularly to make sure that there are no loose or broken parts that could hurt him.

Your young baby will enjoy looking at a toy hung from the pram or above the cot.

Toys for 0-6 months
- Mobile.
- Rattle.
- Soft toys.
- Baby mirror.
- Squeaker.
- Baby gym.
- Play mat.

Toys for 7-12 months
- Cloth or card books.
- Big ball.
- Soft blocks.
- Beakers.
- Bath toys.
- Pop-up toys.
- Musical toys.
- Push-along toys.

This rollaball can be rolled along and will help your baby's hand/eye co-ordination.

As your baby learns to co-ordinate his hands, he will like to hold and feel toys that are easy to handle. This frog also has a baby-safe mirror. Your baby will be fascinated by his own reflection.

A play telephone with push buttons that make different noises will intrigue your baby and keep him amused for hours.

Simple toys which are colourful, tactile and chewable will interest a young baby.

This colourful activity octopus has eight different-textured tentacles for your young baby to grasp and pull at. The caterpillar can be bent into different positions.

Your older baby will enjoy playing with different-sized, coloured stacking beakers.

This stacker has different coloured rings to help an older baby recognize colours and learn how to stack the rings.

This shape sorter offers your child the opportunity to explore different shapes as well as colours.

Once your baby can sit unaided he will enjoy toys such as this train that he can push along the floor.

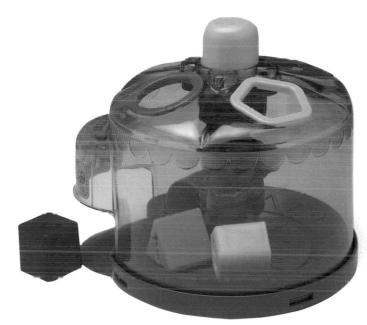

A simple shape sorter will give your older baby hours of entertainment as he discovers how to put the squares into the holes and then watch them drop inside.

All babies enjoy an activity centre and one that can be fixed to the side of the cot will keep your baby amused when you put him down for a rest.

Pull-along toys will develop and encourage your baby's mobility. They will also help him gain confidence as he learns how to push and pull the toy back and forth along the length of the floor.

BABY MASSAGE

Touch is an important part of your baby's physical and emotional growth, and massage is an ideal way of extending your natural inclination to caress and cuddle your baby. Massage has been used on babies in India and Africa for hundreds of years, not only to help form a bond between mother and baby, but also as a means of relieving colic, helping the digestive system, and making the developing muscles supple. It is thought that gentle stroking encourages the abdominal walls to relax, which helps to alleviate wind and ease colicky pain; massaging the young limbs will also help to strengthen them.

There are a number of specific massage techniques that can be learned, but initially your instinctive touch will be enough, just as long as you are gentle and don't try to manipulate your baby's limbs. You need to be sensitive to your baby's moods and should only massage her

when she is content, perhaps between feeds or after a bath. Before you undress your baby for massage, make sure that the room is very warm and draught-free – this is important because babies lose their body heat 10 times more quickly than adults.

Remove any rings or bracelets before you begin and make sure that your fingernails are short and that there are no jagged edges that could scratch or irritate your baby. Relax your hands by stretching and shaking them, then warm them up by rubbing them together. Place a small amount of baby oil on your hands and, with your fingertips, gently massage the baby's skin using light, rhythmic movements. Start at the head and gradually work down to the feet.

Remember, a newborn needs only a feather-light, extremely gentle touch, and you must be careful when stroking the head and around

the still-healing navel. The tiny infant will naturally revert to the fetal position, so you shouldn't try to straighten out her arms and legs too much. As your baby gets older you can start to apply a slightly firmer touch, using the whole of your hand in the massage. When you have finished and your baby is dressed, allow her to have a sleep if that is what she seems to want.

Massaging tips

• Don't attempt to massage your baby if she is tired, hungry, or fretful.
• Allow yourself plenty of time so that the massage is not hurried or stressed.
• Get everything you need ready before you begin.
• Don't massage for more than 10 minutes or your baby will start to become bored.
• Talk or sing to your baby during the massage so that it is a pleasurable experience.
• If your baby isn't enjoying the massage, stop immediately and try again another time.

How to massage your baby

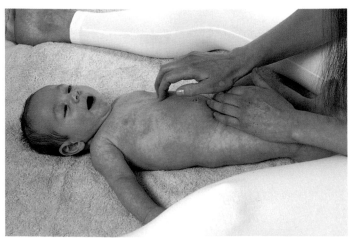

1 *Your baby will love the feel of massage. Place him on a towel in a warm room. Take some warmed baby oil into your hand and lightly massage his chest with circular movements.*

2 *Move on to the arms. Hold your baby's hand in one hand and with the other squeeze down his arm from the shoulder to the wrist. Repeat three times and then work on the other arm.*

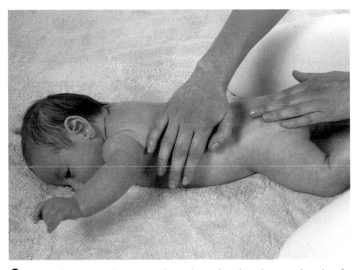

3 *Turn him onto his stomach and, with a hand on each side of his body, massage him from his bottom up to his shoulders, crossing your hands from side to side. Work down again and repeat.*

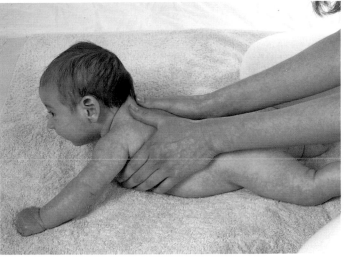

4 *Placing your hands on either side of his shoulders, bring your thumbs together and gently massage around your baby's neck and shoulders with a circular movement.*

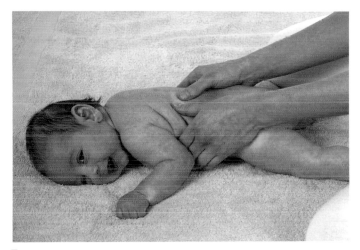

5 *Move both your hands down to your baby's left-hand side and softly knead his skin for a short time between your fingers. Repeat on his right-hand side.*

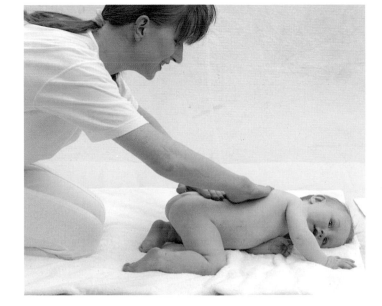

6 *Move your hands into the centre of your baby's back and do some light kneading movements with your fingers up and down the length of his spine.*

To finish your baby's massage, make some soft circling strokes with both hands up and down the back.

TRAVELLING WITH A BABY

The secret of successful travelling with children, no matter how long or short your journey, is careful planning. Young children are surprisingly adaptable, so providing that you take the essentials – food, nappies, and a favourite toy or two – your child should be quite happy to go with you.

The car is probably the easiest form of transport with a baby as you can use it as a kind of nursery on wheels, packing into it everything that you and your child are likely to require. Prepare a survival kit for the journey before you set off and keep it where it is easily accessible. The kit should include spare nappies, a change of clothes, baby wipes, changing equipment, and a mat or towel. If you are bottle-feeding or giving solids, you will also need to include some feeds plus some feeding equipment.

From birth your child should travel in the car in an approved safety restraint suitable for his age and weight. These restraints must be fixed and used properly to obtain maximum protection for your child in the event of an accident.

An older baby will need to be kept amused on the journey and the easiest way to do this is with a selection of toys. Choose toys that have been specially designed for use in the car, or ones which have suction pads that will stick on the window or the back of the front seat. These are better than loose toys, which you may find you have to retrieve each time they are dropped.

Try to make the journey as relaxed as possible by checking the route before you set out and allowing extra time to get there. This way you won't arrive late and anxious because you've had to make a number of unscheduled stops. If you are going on a long journey consider travelling at night. If you are fortunate, your child will be soothed by the motion of the car and will sleep for at least half the journey.

If the journey you are taking involves public transport, you will need to be selective about what you take with you as you'll have to transport your luggage as well as your baby. Take a similar survival kit to the one already mentioned, but make sure it is packed into an easy-to-carry holdall. If possible, take a lightweight pushchair, which you can fold with one hand, leaving the other free, or put your baby in a baby carrier, either strapped on your front if he is still very young, or on your back if he is old enough to sit up on his own.

If you are booking a seat on a train, coach, or plane, always mention the fact that you are travelling with a young child when you arrange your ticket and ask for the most convenient seating accommodation available. If the rail or coach station has a lot of steps to be negotiated ask one of the staff to help you, or find out if there is a lift you can use.

Some airlines have sky cots and others will allow you to take a buggy onto the plane as hand luggage.

They may even allow you to use your car seat (if it is of a suitable type) as a restraint for your child. Ask the airline or your travel agent what facilities are available for babies and older children before you set off.

Whichever method of transport you use, always shield your child from the sun, and make sure that any exposed skin is protected by a high-factor sunscreen. Keep your baby as comfortable as possible by putting him in clothes that are loose and easy to change. A number of layers of fairly thin clothing are best as this will allow you to add or take away a layer depending on how warm it is. Cars can get very hot in the summer, with the temperature creeping up considerably without you realizing it, so keep a constant check on your child while travelling.

Once your baby can support his head, you can put him in a carrier on your back. But always make sure that it is a comfortable fit.

A baby sling is an ideal way for either parent to carry a young baby, both inside the house, or when they are out and about.

KEEPING YOUR CHILD SAFE

Although there is no such thing as a completely safe home, many accidents can be prevented by taking a few safety precautions. High-risk areas can be made safer by installing devices that have been specially designed to prevent your child getting into danger.

HALL, STAIRS AND LANDING
The most common accident in these constantly used corridor areas is a child falling down the stairs, so keep staircases blocked off at both the top and bottom.
What you can do:
• Ensure that there is no loose floor covering or any trailing wire at the top of the stairs on which either you or a child could trip.
• If you have carpet on the stairs make sure that it is securely fitted and in a good state of repair.
• Make sure that the gaps between the stair spindles are no more than 10cm/4 in so that a child's head cannot get stuck between them.
• Fix gates at the top and bottom of the stairs to prevent young children from having access to them.
• Check that the lighting is good, so that there is no risk of tripping on some unseen object on the stairs.
• Fit safety film or safety glass to any glass doors in these areas.
• Make sure that the front-door latch and letterbox are out of reach.

LIVING ROOMS
These rooms are more difficult to keep safe because the environment is constantly changing as people come in and out and items are moved. Frequent safety checks are needed because the danger areas change as your child becomes more mobile. Try looking at the room from your child's level. One of the biggest dangers in the living area is fire.
What you can do:
• Install a circuit-breaker.
• Install smoke alarms throughout your home.
• Fit all fires with guards.
• Use electrical plug socket covers to prevent a child poking something into the socket.
• Unplug electric fires when they are not in use.
• Make sure that all fabrics and upholstery are made from fire-resistant materials.
• Keep matches, lighters and cigarettes out of reach and regularly empty ashtrays.

Stairs can be hazardous for your child and should ideally be blocked off top and bottom. Teach him to hold on to the spindles or wall to keep his balance.

A safety gate is an essential piece of baby equipment. Fitted to the top or bottom of the stairs it will prevent your baby from climbing the stairs and falling. Placed across a doorway it will keep your child out of a room, such as the kitchen, where he could be in danger.

As your baby becomes more mobile he will use anything he can hold on to when pulling himself up. Once he is standing, things that were safely out of the way while he was still only sitting or crawling can now be reached.

Ideally, don't smoke at all!
• Fit safety protectors to the corners of tables and cupboards.
• Use mats instead of tablecloths so that your child can't pull things off the table on top of her.
• Place all ornaments and breakables out of reach.
• Check the floor regularly for small objects that could be swallowed.

KITCHEN
This is potentially the most dangerous room in the house for a young child. The most common accidents to occur in the kitchen are scalds from hot water, burns from cookers, and poisoning from cleaning products. What you can do:
• Keep the doorway blocked with a safety gate so that your child can't get in unnoticed.
• Put all sharp objects, such as knives, well out of reach of children.
• Fit safety catches to all low-level

cupboards, drawers, the fridge, and also the freezer.
• Use a shortened coiled kettle flex.
• Cook on the back rings of the hob with the pan handles facing inwards.
• Use a pan guard on the cooker.
• Never leave containers of hot liquid, such as cups or pots of tea, where your child can reach them.
• Make sure that all household chemicals and cleaning materials are kept out of reach and that their lids are always tightly screwed on.

Kitchen cupboards have a fascination for most young children. Safeguard your child by fitting cupboards with safety catches so that he can't open them.

BATHROOM
Among the most common accidents to happen in the bathroom are scalds from hot water, falls in the bath or shower, poisoning from medicines, and cuts from razors, scissors and broken glass.
What you can do:
• Make sure that all medicines and other dangerous objects, such as razors, are locked away in a cabinet which is placed out of easy reach of a child.
• Use a non-slip mat in the bottom

of the bath to prevent your child from slipping.
• Fit a lock to the toilet seat.
• Make sure that your child cannot reach the bathroom window by climbing on the toilet or the bath.
• Always run cold water into the bath before adding hot water and then check the temperature before putting your child into the tub.
• Make sure the hot water thermostat is not too high. The water should not be above 32°C/90°F.
• Hang a towel over the taps to prevent a child burning herself.
• Check that a child can't reach the door lock and lock herself in.

NURSERY
This is the one room where a child will spend time alone, so regular

Equipment
• Make sure any equipment you buy conforms to the safety regulations established by the European Union (EU) and the British Standards Institute (BSI).
• Only use equipment for the age of the child it has been designed for.
• Second-hand equipment needs to be checked thoroughly for safety.
• Always use safety straps when you put your baby in a pram, pushchair, highchair, or bouncing cradle.
• Never put a bouncing cradle on a raised surface because your baby's active movements could easily make it fall off.
• When travelling in a car, always put your baby in a car seat approved for the child's weight and age.
• Use child locks on the doors.
• Don't leave your child alone in the car, even if she is firmly strapped into her seat.

safety checks need to be carried out as your child grows and becomes more adventurous.

What you can do:

• Make sure that your baby's cot and mattress conform to safety standards and that the mattress fits snugly into the cot base.

• If your child sleeps in a bed, always use a bed barrier and make sure there is a safety gate fitted at the top of the stairs.

• Use a cot light, nursery light, dimmer, or plug light to give your child reassurance at night and to allow you to look in on her without causing any disturbance.

• Install a nursery listening device so that you can monitor your child.

• Place a thermometer in the nursery to help you keep a check on the temperature. The room needs to be around 18°C/65°F.

• If you, or your partner, must smoke, protect children from coming into contact with cigarette smoke, which could put them at risk from coughs, chest infections, and even cot death. There is also some evidence linking passive smoking with the development of childhood asthma.

• Fit any windows with locks.

• Make sure you place the cot or bed away from the window.

OUTSIDE

Many accidents happen outside the home. Even if you have your own garden you should never leave a young child outside unattended.

What you can do:

• Keep all garden tools and chemicals locked away.

• Fit locks to garden sheds and garage doors.

• Make sure that the gate to the road outside is secure.

• Always use a harness and reins, or a wrist link, when you are out on the pavement with your child.

• Make sure that the surface under any play equipment is safe for children to fall on.

• Cover up a pond or a water butt.

A bouncing cradle can be used from around three weeks, and your baby will enjoy reclining in the soft fabric seat. He will quickly learn that by kicking his legs hard he can make the cradle bounce.

Many infant carriers double as car safety seats for at least the first six months. They are usually light and portable so that a newborn will fit into them snugly.

The rear-facing infant carrier can be fitted on both the front passenger seat and the rear seat. The seat is held in place in the car with any approved three-point adult seat belt.

FIRST AID

Many accidents can be dealt with when and where they occur. Adults with a sound knowledge of first aid can not only calm a distressed child, but they can also help to limit the effects of an accident, aid recovery, and could save a child's life. First of all you need to assess the situation and establish whether basic first aid is sufficient to treat the injury, or whether you think professional help might be required.

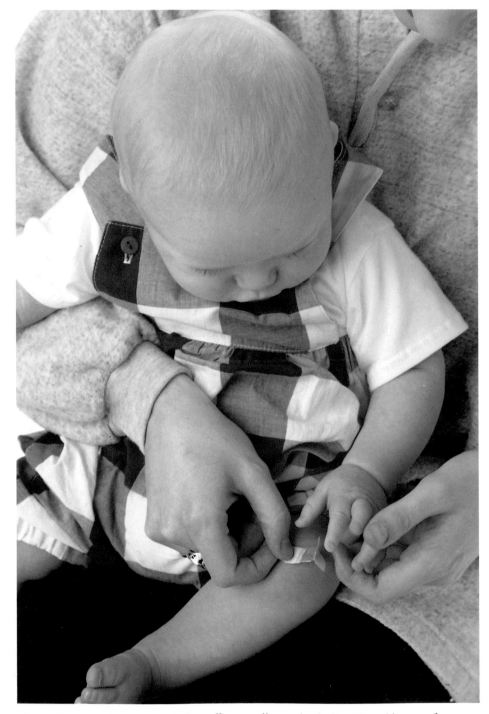

Any minor cuts that a young baby suffers usually can be dealt with on the spot from your first aid box.

GETTING MEDICAL HELP

If your child is unconscious or you think that he may have suffered spinal injury, after a fall, for example, always call an ambulance. If there is even a small possibility of spinal injury, do not attempt to move your child as this could cause severe damage. The best thing you can do is to keep your child warm, still, and calm until the ambulance arrives.

Time is of the essence in dealing with an emergency case that requires immediate medical attention. Should you need to get your child to the hospital urgently, and he can be moved safely, it may be quicker to take him there yourself. If possible, find someone else to drive, so that you can sit with your child in the back seat and give first aid if required. Although it is difficult, it is most important that you try to remain calm and to reassure your child. If you are unsure where the nearest hospital emergency department is, however, or have no suitable transport, then you should call an ambulance; the driver will quickly take you to the nearest suitable hospital.

If you fear that your child has injured his neck or back, call an ambulance and do not move him unless he is in immediate danger. If your child must be moved, you need extra pairs of hands to help turn him onto his back in one movement while holding his neck, shoulders and hips steady.

BREATHING

If your child has stopped breathing, start resuscitation at once and continue until breathing resumes. Get someone else to call an ambulance.
Mouth-to-mouth resuscitation:
1 Position – lay your baby or child on his back on a firm surface.

First aid kit checklist

It is important to have a fully stocked first aid kit in your home and you should also carry a basic kit in the car. You can buy ready-made kits, or you can make up your own by buying the items separately and storing them in an airtight container, out of the reach of children. You should check the contents regularly and replace items as they are used, so that you will always be ready for an emergency. Your home first aid kit should contain:

- assorted plasters.
- cotton wool.
- sterile gauze dressings.
- sterile eye pad.
- roll of 5 cm/2 in gauze bandage.
- crepe bandages.
- triangular bandage.
- safety pins.
- surgical tape.
- scissors.
- blunt-ended tweezers.
- paracetamol syrup.
- antiseptic solution or wipes.
- calamine lotion.
- clinical thermometer or fever strip.
- doctor's telephone number.
- details of your nearest hospital casualty department.

4 Check breathing – once his airway is open he may breathe spontaneously. Place your ear near the mouth and look along the body for movement. If there is no breathing after five seconds, give artificial ventilation.

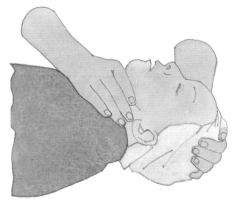

5 With a baby, cover his nose and mouth with your lips and breathe gently into his lungs until the chest rises. With a child, tilt his head back and bring the chin forward. Pinch his nostrils, take a deep breath and seal your lips around the child's mouth. Blow steadily until his chest rises.

6 Monitor recovery – your child's chest should rise as you blow air into the lungs, and fall when you take your mouth away. Look for this each time you raise your head to take a new breath of air. The first two breaths should be given quickly, then

2 Clear his airway – tilt his head on its side and remove any obstruction from the mouth with your fingers.

3 Open his airway – if your child is unconscious the airway may be blocked or narrowed, making breathing difficult or impossible. With a baby, tilt his chin using one finger. With a child, place one hand on the forehead, pushing his head backwards while you tilt his chin gently with the other hand.

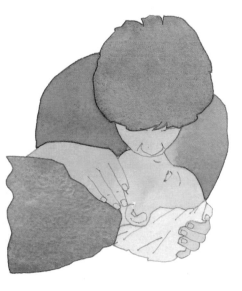

continue at a rate of one breath every three seconds. Keep this up until a medically qualified person can take over.

If your child's chest fails to rise the airway may not be fully open, so readjust the position of his head and jaw and try again. Check a baby's pulse on his upper arm. With a child, check the pulses in his neck or groin. If the heart is not beating, external chest compression is needed.

EXTERNAL CHEST COMPRESSION

If your baby is under one year old and you can't feel a pulse or hear a heartbeat, start chest compressions:

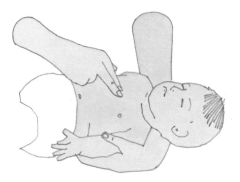

1 Place two fingers on the middle of your baby's breastbone, just below the nipples. (Use the heel of your hand on an older child.)
2 Press your fingers 1.3 cm/½ in into his chest five times in three seconds, making the compressions smooth and rhythmic.
3 Give a breath into his lungs and then five more chest compressions.
4 Continue with five compressions followed by one breath until the heart starts beating, or emergency help arrives.
5 Check every few minutes to see if the heart has started beating. When it does start you must stop the chest compressions immediately.
6 Continue with artificial respiration until your baby begins to breathe on his own.

UNCONSCIOUSNESS AND THE RECOVERY POSITION

If a baby is unconscious but breathing, cradle him in your arms, tilting his head so that his airway is kept open, and phone for medical help. An older child should be put in the recovery position. This prevents your child's tongue from slipping back into his throat and obstructing his airway, and avoids choking if he vomits. Put your child into this position if unconscious, but still breathing:
1 Lie your child on his back, face turned towards you, keeping the chin pulled down.
2 Place the arm near you at right angles to his body, elbow bent, with the palm upwards.
3 Fold the other arm over your child's chest with the back of his hand against his opposite cheek.
4 Lift the furthest knee, keeping this foot flat on the ground.
5 Keeping your child's hand pressed against his cheek, pull on the thigh furthest away from you, to roll him towards you.
6 Tilt your child's head back with his hand supporting it. Adjust his upper leg so that it supports his body.

7 Cover the child with a blanket and stay with him until help arrives, checking constantly for breathing and heartbeat.

CUTS AND GRAZES

You should seek medical help if there is a serious risk of infection, even with small wounds. But treat minor wounds yourself:
1 Clean the wound and surrounding area under running water.
2 Use an antiseptic cream or saline solution to reduce the risk of infection.
3 Apply a plaster or dressing once the surrounding area is dry.
Never:
• use a tourniquet.

Larger, more serious wounds must be treated immediately to control the bleeding and to minimize the risk of infection. Once the blood flow has been stemmed you should take your child to hospital:
1 Control any severe bleeding by applying direct pressure to the wound. If possible use an absorbent sterile dressing.
2 If the wound is on an arm or leg, raise and support it.
3 Cover the wound with a sterile dressing and attach it firmly with a bandage or adhesive tape to help control the bleeding.

BURNS AND SCALDS

Burns are caused by dry heat like flames and hot electrical equipment. Scalds are the result of wet heat, such as steam or boiling water. There is always a risk of infection with both burns and scalds because of the damage they do to the skin.
1 Cool the damaged area of skin under running cold water for at least 10 minutes.
2 Try to remove anything that might constrict the area if it swells,

for example, rings or tight clothing.

3 Cover with a sterile dressing.

4 Always seek medical advice for all minor burns and scalds.

Never:

• apply butter, oil or grease to the damaged area.

• burst any blisters.

• use adhesive dressings or tape.

• remove anything that is sticking to the burn.

BRUISES AND SWELLING

If your child falls and hits himself, or receives a blow, bleeding may occur under the skin that causes swelling and discoloration. This should fade over about a week. You should hold a cloth that has been wrung out in cold water, or wrapped around an ice pack, to the bruised area for about half an hour to help reduce the swelling.

STRAINS AND SPRAINS

A strain is a tear or rupture of a muscle which causes swelling and discomfort. However, a sprain is more serious because it involves damage to the joint itself or the ligaments that surround it. Symptoms of a sprain include swelling, acute pain, and restricted movement. Both strains and sprains require the same treatment:

1 Avoid any activity that may overstrain the injured area until the swelling has gone down. Do not massage the injury because this may cause further damage.

2 Cool the injury with a cold pack, a bag of ice wrapped in a towel, or a cold, wet towel. This will reduce the pain and control inflammation.

3 Use a bandage to apply gentle compression to the injured area. This will give support and help to lessen inflammation.

4 Raise and support the injured area as this will help reduce swelling.

APPLYING A BANDAGE

Select the width of bandage appropriate to the area to be covered.

1 Support the injured limb while you are bandaging.

2 Start below the injury site, and wrap the bandage around the limb, using a spiral action, overlapping by two-thirds each time.

3 Secure with a safety pin or some adhesive tape.

4 Check to make sure that the bandage isn't restricting the circulation.

5 Bandage injured joints by wrapping the bandage around the joint in a figure-of-eight pattern, overlapping by two-thirds each time.

Never:

• bandage too tightly because this can affect the circulation. If the fingers or toes of the bandaged limb are cooler or darker than the other limbs the bandage is too tight. It should be removed and then reapplied, fixing it in position more loosely.

• ignore a limb injury. Always seek medical help if the leg is too painful to take your child's weight, if he is not using his arm, or if any swelling hasn't gone down after 48 hours.

BROKEN BONES

Technically, a broken or cracked bone is a fracture. All fractures should be treated with great care because any undue movement could cause further damage:

1 Keep your child still and cover with a coat or blanket.

2 Remove anything which might constrict any swelling around the injured area.

2 Get medical assistance.

BITES AND STINGS

Bites from mosquitoes and midges or stings from wasps and bees can be extremely painful, causing hard, red,

swollen lumps which itch intensely. A small number of people are allergic to wasp and bee stings. If your child appears to be having difficulty breathing as the result of a sting you must seek medical help immediately. In ordinary circumstances:

1 If the sting has been left in the skin, remove it with tweezers, taking care not to squeeze the poison sack because this would force the remaining poison into the skin.

2 Apply a cold compress to the site for quick relief from pain.

3 Massage sting-relief cream into the area for longer-term relief.

EYE INJURIES

Eyes are delicate organs which can be damaged very easily, so immediate first aid treatment is required if an injury occurs:

• Remove any foreign object from your child's eye using a damp piece of cotton wool. If you can't do this or the pain remains after the removal, cover the eye with a clean pad and then take your child to hospital.

• If your child's eye has been injured by a blow, apply a sterile dressing, and take him to hospital for immediate treatment.

• Chemicals that are splashed into the eye should be washed out completely by flooding the eye with some clean, cold water for at least 15 minutes. Then cover the damaged eye with a clean pad and get your child to hospital.

CHOKING

This happens when a foreign object gets lodged in the throat and obstructs the airway.

For a baby:

1 Lay your baby face downwards, with the chest and abdomen lying

Choking

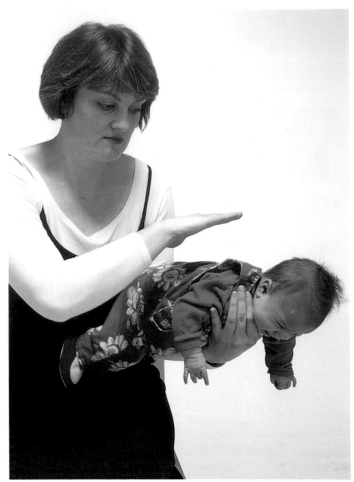

If your baby is choking, you will need to take immediate action. Lay a young baby face down with her chest and abdomen lying along your forearm with your hand supporting her head. Slap her gently on the back several times.

With an older baby or toddler the action would be slightly different. You will need to lay her horizontally, with her head facing downward. To remove the obstruction, slap her firmly between the shoulder blades.

along your forearm and your hand supporting his head.

2 Slap him gently on the back.

Note: if your baby or child doesn't start breathing normally once the blockage is completely removed, call an ambulance and begin artificial ventilation immediately.

For a child:

1 Lay your child across your knee, with his head down, and slap him sharply and firmly between the shoulder blades.

2 If the above fails to remove the blockage, use your finger to try to hook out the object, taking care not to push it further down your child's throat.

CROUP

Croup is a noisy barking cough which may be accompanied by fever and, in severe cases, your child may breathe with a grunting noise called "stridor". Croup can be quite frightening for both you and your child, so it is very important to stay calm and to reassure him. To help remedy the situation:

• Treat simple croup with warm drinks and paracetamol syrup to bring down any fever.

• Ease severe croup by getting your baby or child to inhale steam from a kettle, or sit near a running hot tap in the bathroom or near wet towels over a radiator. Make sure that he

cannot scald himself on the source of the steam.

• If your child is very distressed or has trouble breathing or swallowing, call your doctor immediately, or take him to hospital.

DROWNING

If possible get your child out of the water straightaway, otherwise you will need to give emergency first aid in the water.

1 Empty your child's mouth and, if his breathing has stopped, start to give him mouth-to-mouth ventilation. Do not attempt to remove any water out of your child's stomach or from his lungs.

2 If you carry your child, keep his head lower than the rest of his body to reduce the risk of him inhaling any water.

3 Lay him down on a coat or blanket. Open the airway and check his breathing and pulse.

4 Once your child is breathing normally again, remove all his wet clothes and cover him with some warm, dry ones. Give him a reviving hot drink.

5 Always take him to hospital for a thorough check-up, even if he appears to be fine and to have completely recovered.

ELECTRIC SHOCK

Most electrical accidents occur in the home, so it is vitally important to ensure that household appliances are wired correctly and kept out of the reach of young children. Severe injuries and even death can result from electric shock. But if a shock does still occur:

1 Switch off the current and pull out the plug before touching the child. If this is not possible, use something wooden, such as a broom handle or chair that will not conduct the electricity, to move him right away from the power source.

2 Check his breathing and heartbeat. If your child is unconscious, immediately place him in the recovery position.

3 Treat any burns.

4 Cover your child to keep him warm and reassure him by talking to him calmly.

5 Phone to get some medical assistance immediately.

Never:

• touch your child until the power source has been turned off.

• apply water to a burn that occurs from an electric shock while your

child is still attached to the source of the electricity.

NOSEBLEEDS

Bleeding often follows a blow to the nose, or may occur as a result of blowing the nose too hard. Sometimes there is no apparent reason for the nosebleed. The flow of blood can be quite heavy, which can be frightening, although it is not usually a serious problem:

1 Sit your child upright with his head positioned slightly forward. Putting the head back can sometimes cause choking and cause some discomfort.

2 Get your child to breathe through his mouth while you pinch the soft part of his nose firmly for 10 minutes until the flow of blood slows down and stops.

3 If your child's nose is still bleeding, hold a very cold cloth or an ice pack wrapped in a cloth to his nose for a couple of minutes, then pinch his nose again.

4 Try to ensure that your child avoids blowing his nose for several hours after a nosebleed has finally been staunched.

POISONING

This occurs when harmful substances are inhaled or swallowed. It is important to keep all such substances out of reach of young children. Always be on the alert and see that your child does not eat any poisonous berries or plants in the garden, or when you are out in the countryside. If you suspect poisoning, ring for an ambulance and then take immediate action:

1 Check breathing and be ready to resuscitate if necessary.

2 If your child is breathing, but is unconscious, place him in the recov-

ery position and phone for help.

3 If his lips or mouth show signs of burning, cool them by giving water or milk to sip slowly.

4 Keep the bottle or container the poison was in, or a similar berry or fruit to take to the hospital. This will enable the medical staff to administer the correct antidote to your child as fast as possible.

Never:

• try to give fluids to your child if he is unconscious.

• try to make your child sick. This can be extremely dangerous as the poison could find its way into his lungs and cause severe damage to these organs as well as endangering his breathing.

SHOCK

Severe bleeding, burns, and even fear can bring about a state of shock. You can recognize shock by an extreme loss of colour along with cold and clammy skin. The child may also be shivering and sweating at the same time. This may be accompanied by rapid breathing and dizziness, and possibly by vomiting. Shock often occurs after a major accident, so all casualties must be treated for shock, even if they are not showing any of these symptoms. In extreme cases shock can be fatal, so it requires some immediate action and should always be taken seriously:

1 Lay your child down on his side and make sure that his breathing isn't restricted.

2 Loosen any restricting clothing at his neck, chest, and waist. Then cover your child with a blanket or a coat, but take care not to allow him to overheat.

3 Try to get your child to remain still and to be calm while you seek medical help.

PART THREE

THE FIRST YEAR

YOUR NEWBORN arrives in the world a helpless, totally dependent baby, yet, with your help, within a year she will have learned all the basic skills that she needs to build on for her future growth and development. This section takes you, month by month, through the first year of a child's development. It is, however, important to realize that your child is unique, so there is little point in comparing her with others in anything other than a general way at this stage.

You will want to help and encourage your child as she masters each new skill. Understanding how she learns to talk, crawl, walk and play will enable to you to assist her at each stage. The five senses - hearing, vision, taste, smell and touch - are all extremely important from the time your child is born. As each sense develops, your child will be discovering something new about the world in which she's living.

Being able to participate in this fascinating time in your child's life is a very special privilege. You will be part of the most exciting process in the world: the development of your child from a helpless baby to a confident, independent toddler.

NEWBORN

Your newborn baby will probably look wrinkled and slightly blotchy at first. When he is born his skin may have a bluish tinge and the legs may even be a different colour to the rest of his body. This will only last for a short time, until oxygen from the lungs has had time to reach the bloodstream. You may also find patches of dry skin. Eyes may be reddish and slightly swollen and your baby may still be covered with vernix, the greasy white substance which has been protecting the skin from becoming waterlogged by the amniotic fluid. There may also be a covering of lanugo, fine hair which covers the shoulders, upper arms, and legs.

Your baby's head may look too big for his body. It is usually about one-quarter of the total body length and it may be a slightly odd shape because of the pressure that was put on it during the birth. His features may also appear slightly flattened from being squeezed through the pelvis. Your baby's head may be covered with very thin hair or have a thick thatch that stands up on end.

Milestones

Your child is immediately able to:
• Hear and respond to noises.
• Focus on objects that are within 20-30 cm/8-12 in.
• Grip your finger tightly.
• Suck vigorously.
• Make walking movements when held on a hard surface.
• Turn towards you when you stroke his cheek.

An increase in female hormones from the placenta just before birth affects both boys and girls and your baby's genitals may be enlarged and breasts may appear slightly swollen.

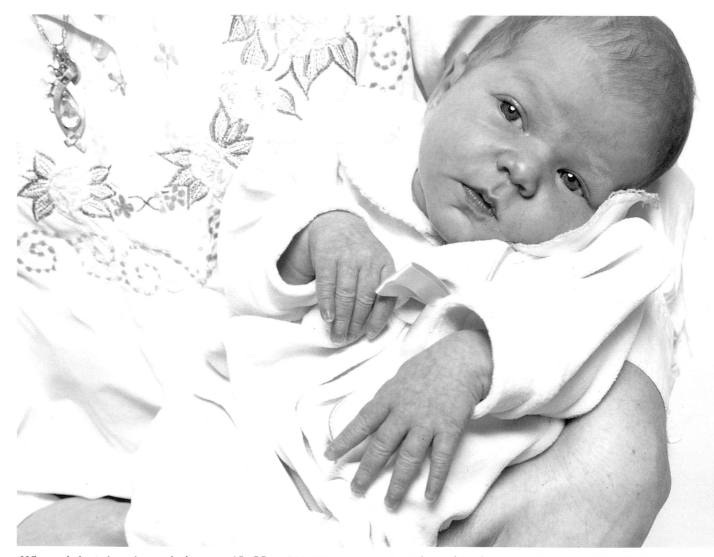

When a baby is born he can be between 45–55 cm / 18–22 in long and weigh anything between 2.5–4.5 kg / 5½–10 lb.

It is quite usual for the breasts of both boys and girls to have a milky discharge; girls may have a slight vaginal discharge as well. All these features will disappear over the next few weeks.

SIZE

Although the average weight of a baby at birth is 3.4 kg/7½ lb, wide variations occur so, assuming that your baby was born around the estimated date of delivery (EDD), it could weigh anything between 2.5-4.5 kg/5½-10 lb. Your baby's weight is determined by a lot of factors, including your size and the size of your partner, how much weight you put on in pregnancy, and your general health.

Your baby is quite likely to lose weight during the first week. This is because it takes a little while for regular feeding to become properly established. Once an infant is feeding well his weight should remain stable for a couple of days and then, within seven to 10 days, he will regain his birth weight. A baby's weight gain is one of the easiest ways of telling whether he is thriving.

The average length of a newborn is between 48-51 cm/19-20 in, but as with weight, this can vary, although most babies are somewhere between 45-55 cm/18-22 in.

REFLEXES

A baby is born with a number of reflexes. The rooting reflex means that your child's mouth automatically searches for your nipple; grasping is seen when your baby demonstrates a surprisingly strong grip. When on his back, your baby may adopt the tonic neck reflex – the head is turned to one side and the arm and leg on that side are extended while the opposite ones are flexed. A loud noise or the sensation of falling causes the startle or Moro reflex: the newborn extends legs, arms, and fingers, arches the back and throws the head back and then draws back the arms, fists clenched, into the chest. All these initial reflexes will gradually diminish over the next weeks and months as voluntary movements take their place.

In addition to these reflexes, every baby is born with the ability to suck, swallow, and gag so that they can feed as soon as they are born. The gagging reflex prevents a baby from choking on too much liquid and allows the child to get rid of any mucus that may be blocking up his airways.

Your newborn will probably hiccup and snuffle a lot at first. Hiccups occur because the baby's breathing rhythm is still rather jerky. They

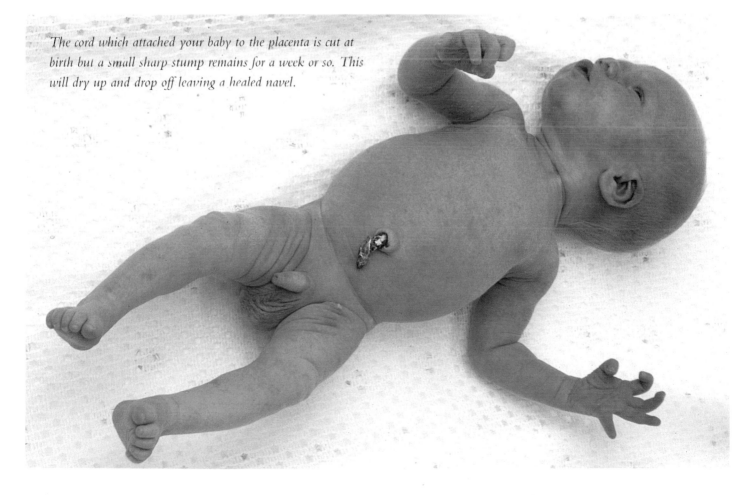

The cord which attached your baby to the placenta is cut at birth but a small sharp stump remains for a week or so. This will dry up and drop off leaving a healed navel.

don't hurt, or even particularly bother them in fact, so you need not worry about them at all. Your baby will also make some snuffling noises. This is from learning to breathe through his nose and because the nasal passages are still very small. As the nose gets bigger the snuffling will stop.

All babies are sensitive to bright lights and this may make them sneeze when they first open their eyes. This is because the light stimulates the nerves in their nose as well as their eyes. Sneezing is also a way of clearing the nasal passages and it will prevent any dust from getting into the baby's lungs.

CRYING

Your baby may make his first cry as soon as his chest has been delivered, others wait until they have been born or until they start to breathe normally. These first cries are often not much more than a whimper and the full-bodied cry follows later. A baby may look red and angry while crying, but this is quite normal. Crying is a baby's way of communicating as well as a means of exercising his lungs.

Hunger is the main reason for a newborn to cry, but being lonely, wet, or tired will also make a baby cry. Some babies cry because they don't like being undressed, others

when they are immersed in water. Some babies are more fretful than others so they cry more. You will quickly learn to recognize why your baby is crying and the best way to soothe him.

NEWBORN TESTS

The first test your baby will be given is the Apgar test. The scores are recorded at one minute after birth and then again at five minutes and they reflect your newborn's general condition. Babies who score between 7 and 10 are in good to excellent condition, those who score between 4 and 6 are in fair condition, but may need some resuscitative

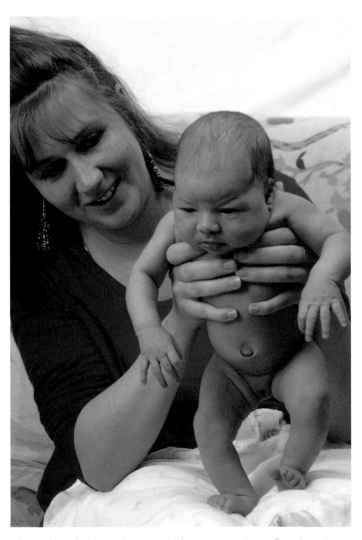

A newborn baby might initially have a stepping reflex, but this will soon be replaced by voluntary movements.

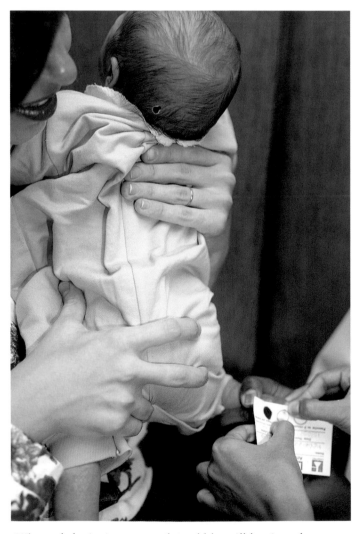

When a baby is six or seven days old he will be given the Guthrie test to test for a range of rare diseases.

Apgar table

Score	0	1	2
Appearance (colour)	pale or white	body pink, extremities blue	pink
Heart rate	not detectable	below 100	over 100
Grimace (reflex irritability)	no response to stimulation	grimace	cough, sneeze
Muscle tone	flaccid (no or weak activity)	some movement of extremities	moving
Respiration (breathing)	none	weak, gasping, irregular	crying, regular

measures. Babies who score under 4 will need some immediate emergency treatment.

Sometime during the first 24-48 hours your baby will be thoroughly checked. A doctor will check your baby's head circumference, the fontanelles, and the roof of the mouth to see if there are any abnormalities. The doctor will listen to the heart and lungs and feel your baby's abdomen to check that the internal organs such as kidney, liver, and spleen, are the right shape and size. The genitals are also checked for abnormalities and, if your baby is a boy, the doctor will look to see that both testicles have descended. Hips will be checked for possible dislocation and all the limbs will be inspected to see that they are the right length and are moving correctly. The doctor will run his thumb down the baby's spine to make sure that the vertebrae are in place. The baby's reflexes will also be checked.

The Guthrie test is usually done six or seven days after birth. A blood sample will be taken from the baby's heel. The blood is then tested for phenylketonuria (PKU), a rare disease which causes severe mental handicap, and other rare diseases.

SPECIAL CARE

If your baby is born several weeks early, the birth weight is low, or your child needs extra care for any other reason, he may be put in the Special Care Baby Unit (SCBU). Here the infant will be monitored so that he gets all the special treatment required. It can be distressing to see your baby in a special care unit, especially if he is surrounded by an array of strange equipment. Ask the staff to explain what the equipment is for and why your baby needs it. Try to spend as much time as you can with your baby in special care because, even if you can't pick him up and hold him, your baby will be able to hear your voice and it will soothe him. You will probably be able to touch your baby through the side of the incubator.

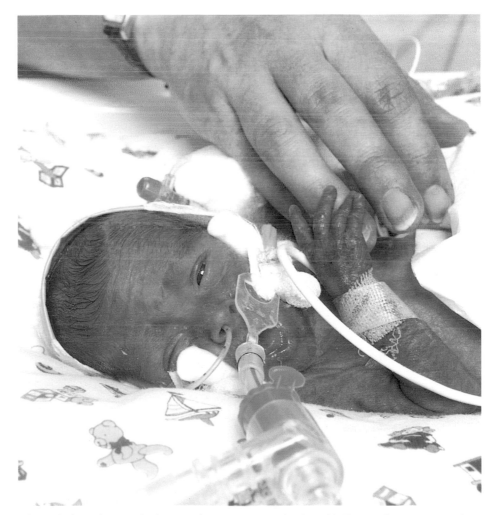

If your baby is born early, he may have to go into the Special Care Baby Unit. Don't be afraid to ask about all the equipment he is attached to, and let him know you are there by touching and talking to him.

ONE MONTH

Your baby's movements are still dominated by the primary reflexes so when placed on her back your infant will adopt the tonic neck reflex posture, with her head to one side and the limbs on that side extended while the ones on the other side are flexed. If you place your baby on her front her head will turn to one side, then your baby will pull her knees under the abdomen and hold her arms close to her body, with her hands curled into fists. The fingers and toes will fan out when she straightens her arms or legs. If you hold your baby to stand on a hard surface she will press down and make a forward walking movement.

Although your baby was born with vision and can see colours and shapes at close range, her sight is still immature. Images which offer a high contrast and simple patterns, for example black lines on a white background, are easier for a baby to understand than paler, more complicated designs. Hold your baby upright or in a half reclining position

Milestones

Your child may be able to:
• Lift her head briefly while lying on her stomach.
• Focus on your face while feeding.
• Respond to a small bell being rung by moving her eyes and head towards the source of the sound.
• Follow with her eyes an object which is moved in an arc 15–25.5 cm/6–10 in away from her face.
• Turn her head towards you when you speak to her.

Even at this early age your baby will be interested in things around him.

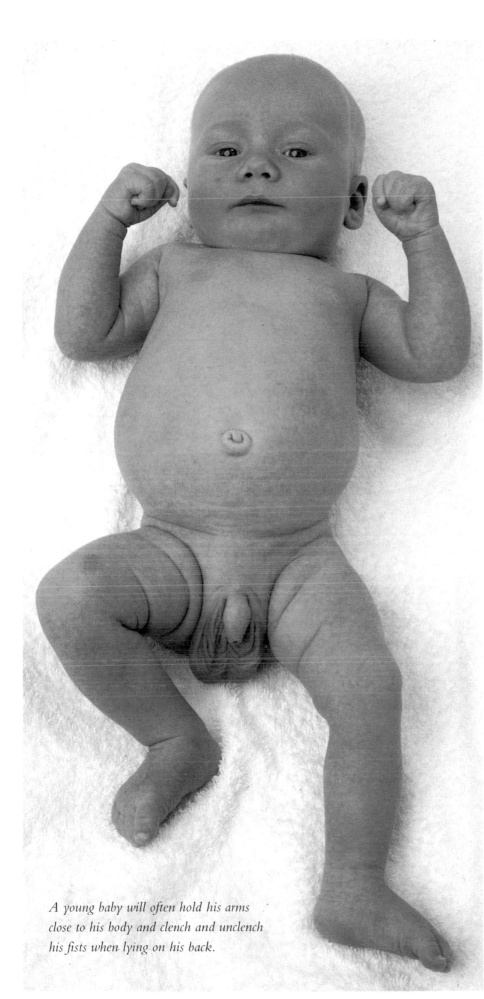

A young baby will often hold his arms close to his body and clench and unclench his fists when lying on his back.

if you are showing her something; this will help to keep the child's interest and will stop her dropping off to sleep. Cot books, with bold patterns and shapes which attract very young eyes, placed where a baby can see them will help develop visual powers.

Babies can recognize their mother's smell from the earliest days and your baby will be able to distinguish between the smell of your breast milk and that of any other mother. She can also tell the difference between the smell of formula or cows' milk and your milk.

MINOR BLEMISHES

Occasionally babies may be born with some minor skin blemishes. These are usually harmless and require no treatment; they disappear on their own as the skin matures. *Milia* are tiny white spots on the face, caused by blocked oil glands. They should fade after a few days. *Stork marks or bites* are red marks which occur around the back of the neck, on the eyelids, or across the bridge of the nose. They usually disappear during the first few months. *Strawberry marks* are raised red marks that sometimes appear in the days after the birth and they may grow rapidly during the first few weeks. These usually disappear after about six months, although they can sometimes last until the child is much older. Treatment may be required if the mark has not disappeared by the time your child is in her teens. *Port wine stains* are red or purple marks which are usually found on the face and neck. These are permanent and will require treatment once your child is older. *Urticaria, or nettle rash* has a raised white centre surrounded by an

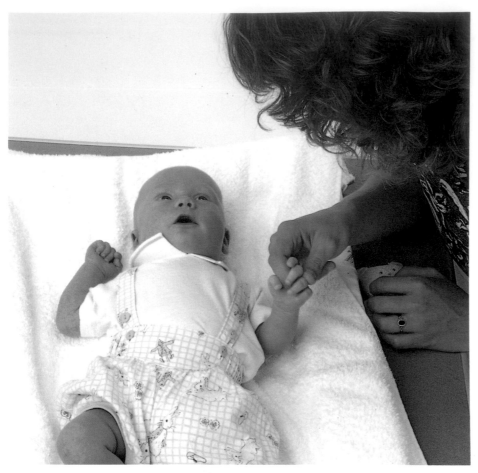

When you are changing your baby, always make time to play and talk to him. This will make him feel secure and at ease.

FRESH AIR

A baby needs fresh air so if you have a garden or secure outside area and the weather is warm enough you can let your infant sleep outside in the pram from the first week or so providing that the child is well covered up and away from draughts. When it is hot, use a canopy rather than the pram hood so that the air can circulate, and make sure that the pram is in the shade. When outside, protect your baby from cats and insects with

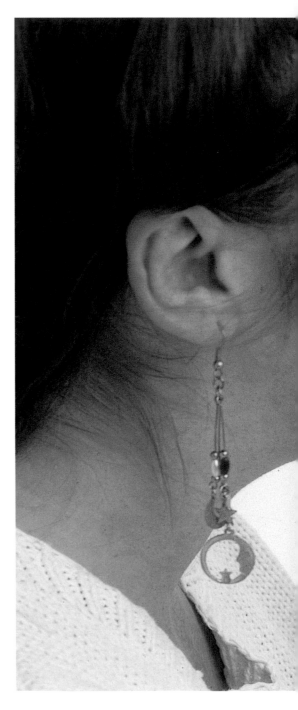

inflamed red area and quite commonly occurs during the first weeks. This rash doesn't require any treatment and will usually clear up after the first month.

INFECTION

Thrush is a fungal infection that produces white patches on the baby's tongue, the roof of her mouth, and in her cheeks. It can be caught from unsterilized feeding teats and dummies or from the mother if she was suffering from vaginal thrush at the time of the birth. Thrush can also appear on the baby's bottom as a red rash which spreads from the anus over the buttocks. Oral thrush is treated with anti-fungal drops and thrush on a baby's bottom needs to be treated with antibiotic cream. Both can be obtained from your doctor.

Above: White patches on the tongue are one indication that your baby has thrush. This is easily treated.

a fine mesh pram net. If you have no place to leave the baby outside, put her in the cot or crib and open the window to let fresh air into the room. Don't leave a baby in her cot or pram for too long when she is awake because she will get bored. Babies need other activities to stimulate them as well as exercise.

Taking your baby on outings in a baby sling or carrier is another way of giving your baby fresh air and a convenient way for you to carry her

if you don't want to push a pram. Your baby will enjoy being close to you and will be able to see the world from a different viewpoint.

NOISE

There is no need to tiptoe around or to get people to whisper while your baby is asleep. If you do, it could mean that your baby won't be able to go to sleep if there is any noise and will wake at the least little sound, which can cause sleep prob-

lems when your child is older. A very young baby will quickly learn to sleep through the everyday noises that go on in a home, such as the television and vacuum cleaner. Sudden loud noises may wake your baby, but reassurance and a cuddle should soon settle her down again.

When newly born your baby's vision is not well developed, so hold her up to talk to her and let her focus on your face.

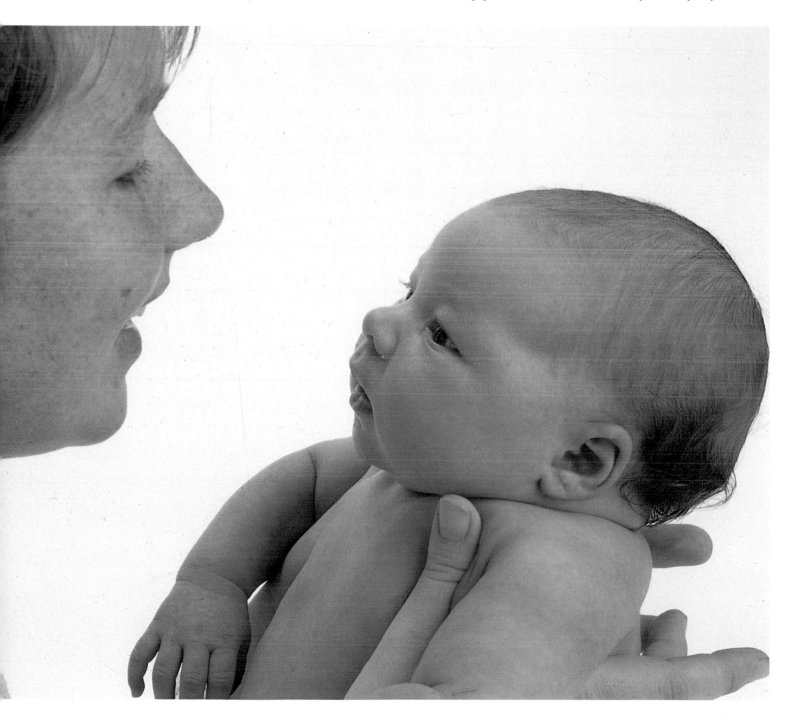

TWO MONTHS

Your baby is developing quickly and, although you may not realize it, he is already trying to talk to you by making a number of vowel sounds and throaty gurgles. At first it may not seem as though these noises are actually directed at you because your baby will enjoy practising these vocal exercises as much for his own benefit as for yours. Each new noise is helping your baby discover which combinations of throat, tongue, and mouth actions make which sounds. As your baby masters each new sound you will begin to notice that he uses them to communicate vocally with you.

CRYING

Your baby now stays awake for longer periods between feeds and is usually more awake in the evenings. It is quite likely that your baby will use some of this extra waking time to cry. Of course not all babies are the same and yours may cry very little, but on average babies usually cry for two to three hours a day and

Milestones

Your child may be able to:

• Smile.

• Begin to make cooing noises.

• Lift his head 45° when lying on his stomach.

• Grasp a rattle for a few seconds if one is put in his hand.

• Follow an object which is moved in a 180° arc above his face.

much of this takes place in the evening. Very often this is blamed on colic, thought to be a type of stomach or abdominal ache occurring in spasms, which makes a baby draw up

At two months, your baby will start to smile at you and will turn her head to follow objects moved above her head.

his legs in pain as he screams. No one knows exactly what colic is, but if it is going to occur it usually starts within the first three weeks of birth and lasts until around three months, although it can go on longer. There is no reliable treatment for colic and, although there are some over-the-counter medicines available, you should consult your doctor before giving them to your baby.

Colic isn't always the cause of excessive crying; some babies cry for no obvious reason for some time each day. If your baby does this you may be able to offer comfort by rocking, letting him suck, or by distracting him with a toy. Don't leave

When you support your baby in a sitting position, she can hold her head up for a minute.

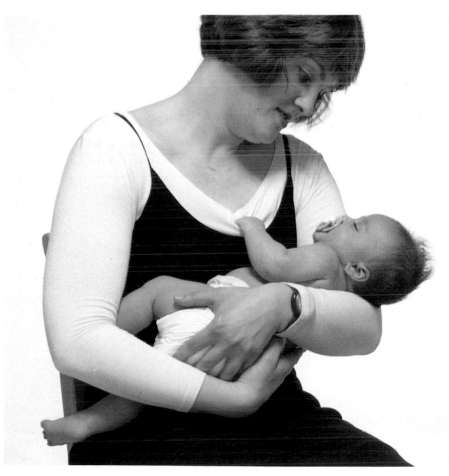

Holding and cuddling your young baby is an important part of her getting to know you.

him to cry for more than a few minutes; at this age crying is the only way to let you know that he is miserable and needs comforting.

LEARNING CONTROL

Your baby is gradually gaining control of his body. When you place the child on his stomach he will be able to lift his head, keeping the nose and mouth free to breathe. If held in a sitting position, your baby will be able to hold his head up for about a minute, and if you touch his hand with a rattle your baby will jerk his hand towards it. This is the first stage of learning when he reaches out to hold something.

SIX TO EIGHT WEEK DEVELOPMENT CHECK

The ages at which developmental screening takes place vary within each health authority and with the individual needs of the child. But in general, you can expect your child to have an initial developmental check sometime between six and eight weeks. This will be carried out

Immunization

Your baby should be given the first round of immunizations for diphtheria, tetanus, and whooping cough (DPT), polio and Hib. After the immunization your child may feel a bit off-colour for up to 24 hours and may even run a temperature. Rarely, a convulsion may occur as a result of the fever, but this is over quickly and has no lasting effect. It is also quite normal for the skin around the site of the injection to become red and sore or slightly swollen. If you are at all worried about your child's reaction, contact your doctor immediately.

Learning head movements

1 *At this stage of development, your baby is gaining control of her body. When lying on her stomach, with her arms supporting her, she can start to lift her head.*

2 *As she manoeuvres herself into position, she pushes hard with her legs and starts to put her weight on her arms.*

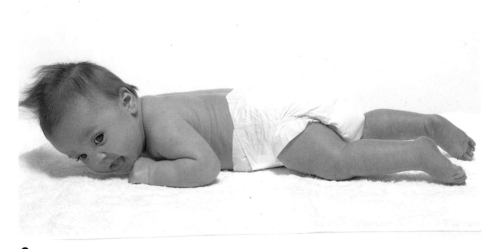

3 *As she raises her head, pushing up with her arms, she will find she can hold it up, keeping her nose and mouth free to breathe.*

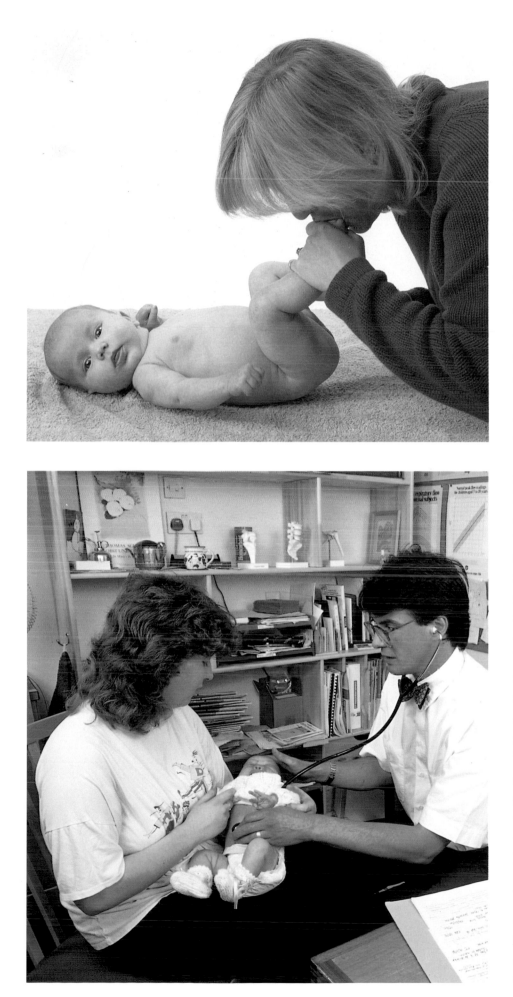

Make sure you allow enough time to play and have fun with your baby, so that you can really get to know her.

at the child health clinic by a doctor or health visitor, or at your doctor's surgery. These checks are part of the child health surveillance programme and their aim is to detect any problems early, to prevent illnesses, and to promote good health. If the checks detect any early signs of delayed development, or health or behaviour problems, treatment can be begun at once. A number of routine checks take place between now and when your child reaches school age. They are all important because the checks are designed to reveal hidden disabilities as well as more obvious ones.

This early check will include measuring your baby's weight, length and head circumference and noting the changes since birth. You will probably be asked questions about how your baby is feeding and sleeping. General progress will be assessed and the doctor may also carry out a series of tests to evaluate your baby's head control, use of hands, vision, hearing, and social interaction. You may be given guidance about what you should expect during the next month in relation to feeding, sleeping, and development. You may also be asked questions about how you, the baby, and the rest of the family are managing with your new baby at home. This is the time to voice any concerns or problems that have been worrying you.

At six to eight weeks your baby will be given a developmental check-up at the health clinic or your doctor's surgery. This will detect any early problems.

THREE MONTHS

Below: As you pull your baby up at this age, he will now be in more control of his head movements.

Your baby will probably have begun to control her head movements, so that when held in a sitting position she can keep her head up for several seconds before it drops forward. As her neck strengthens your baby will be able to look around and turn her head to watch something moving within 15-20 cm/6-8 in.

EARLY LEARNING

As babies begin to understand their own body, they will spend hours studying and moving their fingers. Their hands have opened out now and they can clasp and unclasp them, pressing the palms together. Babies enjoy playing with them and may even be able to hold a small toy for a few seconds. When your baby is lying down you will probably notice that her arms and legs make a lot of

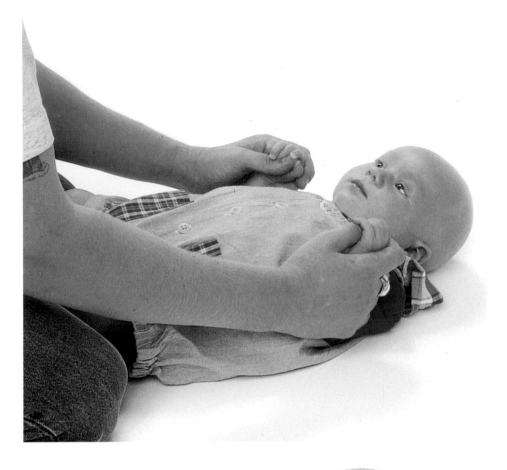

Below: When your baby lies on the floor, he will often raise his head for several seconds before it drops forward.

Below: As your baby sits up, he can hold his head steady more easily because his neck has strengthened.

Bottom: Your baby will be fascinated by any toys in bright, primary colours that are hung over her cot.

Milestones

Your child may be able to:

- Smile and coo when she sees you.
- Control her head.
- Show anticipation when food is on the way by licking her lips.
- Enjoy looking at brightly coloured objects such as a mobile hanging over the cot.
- Play with her hands.
- Hold a small toy for a few seconds.

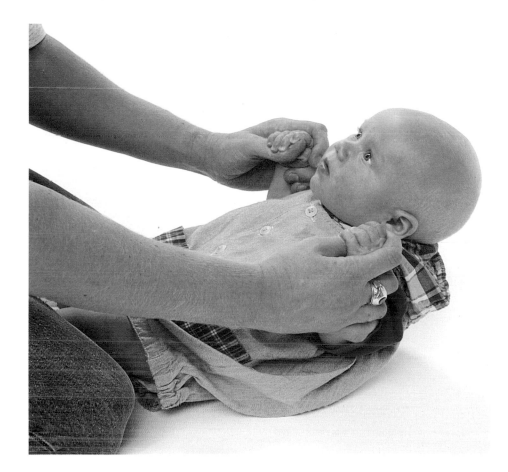

movement. A child will kick vigorously, usually with alternate legs, but occasionally with both legs together.

The first smiles are reflexive, but they very quickly become social and the baby will smile at you in response to your smile or voice. The smiles will come in clusters, four or five at a time, followed by a pause of maybe half a minute before the next cluster. The baby will also respond vocally when you speak to her. Talk

to your baby and she will answer you back in her own way, using her lips and tongue as she coos and tries to imitate you. She uses her whole body to express the way she feels, making excited movements when pleased, expressing happiness and delight with gurgles and squeals. When she is angry, uncomfortable, or lonely she will tell you by crying loudly and even angrily. To encourage your baby, you should respond to her behaviour with exaggerated gestures and praise, using a slow singsong voice and lots of repetition.

A baby will react to familiar situations and will show excitement when she recognizes preparation for things that she enjoys. She responds with obvious pleasure to friendly handling, especially when it is accompanied by play and a friendly voice. Bathtime and other caring routines, where she has your undivided attention for quite a while, are likely to become her favourite times of the day.

Left: Plastic stacking toys in bright colours will soon attract the attention of your inquisitive baby who will try to grasp hold of them.

Below: Lying on his back, your young baby will enjoy kicking vigorously with alternate legs and sometimes with both legs together.

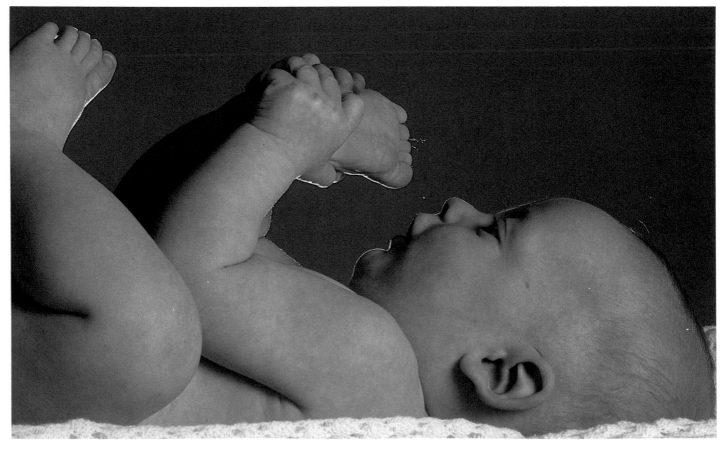

If you haven't already done so, introduce a regular bedtime routine now so that your child starts to realize that a bath, a story, and a cuddle are a prelude to being put into the cot to sleep. By about three months many babies begin to sleep for long periods at night. If your baby has started to sleep through the night you will probably find that she needs less sleep during the day and that her daytime sleep is not as deep as it was. You may find that your baby is more easily disturbed by household noises now. Encourage her to stay awake during the day by stimulating her with different toys and by playing and talking with her.

Immunization

At three months your baby will have the second round of immunizations for diphtheria, tetanus, and whooping cough (DPT), polio and Hib on the immunization programme.

Your baby is now using her whole body to show her feelings, and will start to recognize her favourite toys.

FOUR MONTHS

Your baby is developing rapidly. He is awake for much longer and during these waking periods will want to be sociable and will respond with delight to conversations with you and enjoy playing simple games.

You can encourage your baby's development by spending time responding to these early attempts at sociability. Make a point of showing your baby different objects and talk about them. Your baby will also enjoy seeing and talking to himself in a mirror. Place the mirror about 15-20 cm/6-8 in away so that he can keep his image in focus.

Motor development and learning progress at the same rate between four and five months. Hand and eye co-ordination is being learned and your baby may be able to reach out and grasp an object. He will try hard to learn how to sit because he will have discovered that sitting up gives him a different view of the world. At first he will need you to help him balance, but as his confidence grows he will learn to adjust his legs and to use his hands to keep himself upright.

Milestones

Your child may be able to:
- Lift his head up 90° when he is on his stomach.
- Raise himself up a little way, supported by the arms, when lying on his stomach.
- Laugh out loud.
- Hold his head steady when he is held upright.
- Roll over in one direction.
- Reach out for an object.

STARTING ON SOLIDS

Although babies can get all the nourishment they require from breast or formula milk during their first six months, you may want to start to introduce solids at around four months. A baby needs to be able to have control over his head before you begin to offer him solids. Even strained or puréed first foods should not be given until he can hold his head upright when he is sitting propped up. Chunkier foods

At four months your baby will try to sit up with your help.

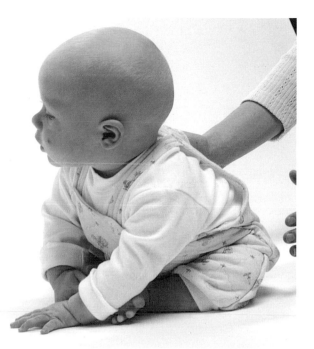

As your baby gains control over his head he will be able to hold it at different angles.

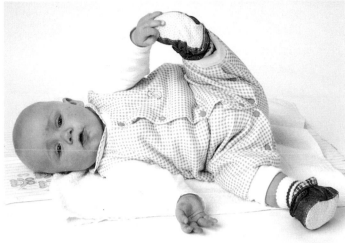

As he gets more active your baby will probably start to learn how to roll over in one direction. First, he will grab his foot with his hand and lift that leg up.

When your baby is lying flat on his stomach, he will now be able to raise his head up 90° and support himself more sturdily on his arms.

He'll then push down this leg, and helped by his bottom arm, roll his body over in one direction.

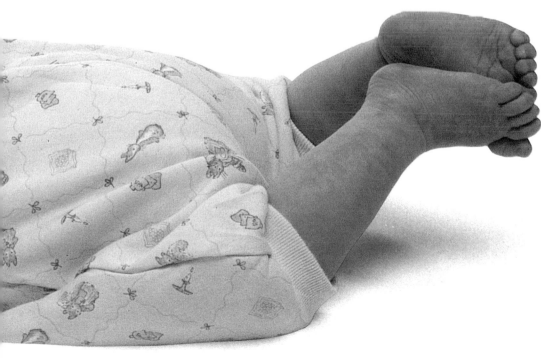

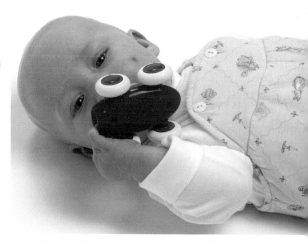

Your baby will now start to reach out for interesting toys and often try to put them in his mouth.

A young baby is fascinated by mirrors, but at distances she can only make out vague shapes.

If you place your baby 15–20 cm/6–8 in away from a mirror, she will be able to focus on her image and chat to herself.

that require chewing should not be introduced until your baby can sit up alone, which is not usually until about seven months.

First solids are little more than tasters that get a baby used to the idea of sucking from a spoon rather than from the breast or bottle. To be able to do this the tongue thrust reflex, which the baby was born with, must have disappeared. This is the reflex that causes the tongue to push any foreign matter out of the mouth and prevents very young babies from choking.

If the food offered is pushed straight back out of the mouth by the tongue and this happens several times, the reflex is still there and the baby is not ready for solids. To be able to eat from a spoon your baby also needs to be able to draw in his lower lip.

Another fairly obvious sign that your baby is ready for solids is if he shows any interest in the food that you are eating. If your baby watches intently while you eat and shows excitement or tries to grab your food, then he is probably telling you that he is now ready for more grown-up food himself. If you are unsure about when to start weaning your baby, remember to ask your doctor for advice.

THUMB SUCKING

Your baby will suck anything he can get into his mouth and now that he has some control over his hands, his fingers and thumbs will be preferred and he will suck them for pleasure and also for comfort. He may suck his whole hand, or one or two fingers, or he may prefer his thumb. This is quite normal and is not a sign of emotional distress, nor will it, at this age, damage the alignment of

permanent teeth. If your baby is breast-fed you need to make sure that he isn't sucking his thumb to compensate for suckling he is no longer getting at the breast; otherwise there is no harm if you let your child suck his thumb. Most children grow out of this habit naturally over the next year or two, although a child who uses sucking his thumb as reassurance to get to sleep may take a little longer to break the habit. This is nothing to worry about.

Immunization

At four months your baby will have the second immunizations for diphtheria, tetanus, whooping cough (DTP), Hib and polio.

You can now give some solids to your baby if she can hold her head upright and if food isn't rejected by her tongue.

Your baby will try to stand with help, but he shouldn't put too much weight on his legs.

FIVE MONTHS

Your baby's grasp of basic concepts is growing and she is thinking much faster. It is thought that a baby when she is first born will take between five and 10 minutes to get used to something new; by three months a baby may take between 30 seconds and two minutes and by six months she will take only 30 seconds.

Your baby will begin to learn about cause and effect by carrying out simple experiments, such as throwing a toy out of her pram. Initially she will believe that it has

Milestones

Your child may be able to:
• Hold her head steady when upright.
• Keep her head level with her body when pulled into the sitting position.
• Pay attention to a small object.
• Squeal with delight.
• Be able to say some vowel-consonant combinations such as "ah-coo".

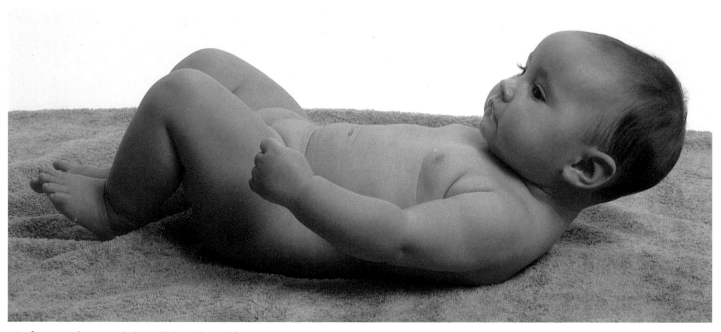

At five months, your baby will be able to lift her head up from a lying position and hold it steady.

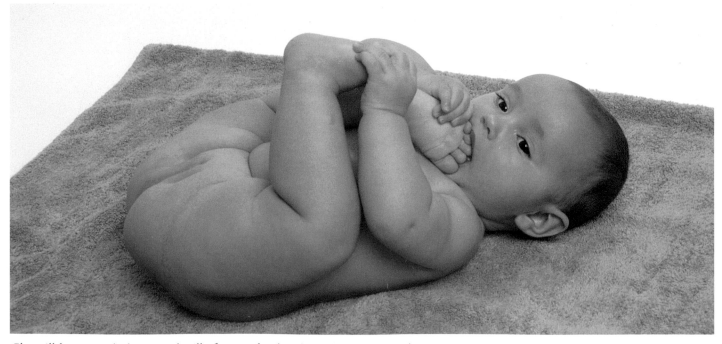

She will love to suck things, and will often put her hands or feet in her mouth.

Your baby's head movements are now getting much steadier as she gains more control.

vanished and won't understand where it has gone. If you pick up the toy and return it she will be both puzzled and delighted. She will do the trick again and again until she begins to realize that, by dropping the toy and getting it back, she is beginning to take control of her world by making things happen.

You can encourage your baby with her experiments by playing games such as peek-a-boo, or hiding an object that was in front of her and then making it reappear again. At this age your baby won't attempt to recover what you have hidden because she thinks that the object no longer exists because she can't see it.

It will be several months before she learns that this really isn't the case and starts looking for the hidden object herself.

TEETHING
There is no fixed time for your baby to start teething, but on average a baby's first tooth appears sometime

between now and seven months. Babies teethe differently, with some experiencing a lot of discomfort and others hardly seeming to notice their first teeth coming through. It is thought that tooth eruption follows hereditary patterns, so if you or your partner teethed especially early or late your baby may do the same.

Teething symptoms often precede the tooth itself by several weeks or even months, and vary from child to child. Drooling is often the first sign that teeth are on their way and this can start as early as 10 weeks. Excessive drooling can cause a dry skin rash or chapping on the chin and around the mouth, which should be treated with a mild skin cream. Biting is another indication of teething. Your baby may start chewing on anything she can get into her mouth as the counterpressure from chewing on a hard object helps relieve the pressure under the gums. Rubbing her gums with your finger may bring relief or you can give her something to chew on such as a chilled teething ring or a slice of carrot.

Delight your growing baby with different types of toys to keep her interested and fully stimulated.

Inflammation of the tender gum tissue often occurs when a tooth is coming through so your baby is likely to have red, sore gums before a tooth erupts. Ear pulling and cheek rubbing may also be a sign of teething as pain can travel along the nerve pathways to these areas. This is particularly common when the molars are coming through. If your child seems to be in pain you can give her the recommended dose of paracetamol. However, never attribute illnesses such as diarrhoea, fever, or earache to teething: if you are concerned seek medical advice.

Your baby will often prefer a simple toy like this rattle as it is easier for her to manage and play with.

SIX MONTHS

Your child is beginning to show a greater interest in what is going on around him. He will turn his head quickly to familiar voices and will examine things that interest him for longer periods.

THE BABY TAKES CONTROL

The baby is rapidly becoming more mobile and will probably be able to pull himself into the sitting position if both hands are held. When lying on his stomach, the baby may find that kicking will push him along, usually backwards at first. If he becomes frustrated because he can't get to where he wants to go, don't be too eager to help him. You can encourage him by placing a toy just out of reach, or by placing your hands against the soles of his feet so that when he kicks he has something to push against. If you pick him up and place him where he wants to go he will not learn how to achieve this for himself.

The baby's ability to reach and grasp is becoming more accurate and you can help him improve these skills by passing objects in such a way that he has to reach up or down or to the side for them. Toys strung across his cot or playpen will allow him to practise using these skills. Your baby will hold objects in the palm of his hands, and will be able to pass them from one hand to the other. You can encourage him by giving him two toys simultaneously, one in each hand, so that he has to reach out with both hands. If you offer him a rattle, shake it to make a noise as you hand it to him; he will reach for it immediately and then shake it deliberately to make the same noise.

Visually your baby is keenly aware of everything that is going on around him and will move his head and eyes eagerly in every direction to which his attention is attracted. He will follow what you are doing, even if you are busy on the other side of the room. His eyes now

Milestones

Your child may be able to:

• Laugh, chuckle, and squeal aloud and scream with annoyance.

• Use whole hand to grasp objects and can pass them from one hand to the other.

• Move his eyes in unison and turn his head and eyes towards something that attracts him.

• Play with his feet as well as his hands.

• Can manipulate small objects.

• Start to be wary of strangers.

Right and opposite: If you have a very active baby it is best not to put her in her high chair at meal times until her food is ready to eat or has cooled, as she will only get restless and may have a temper tantrum because she can't easily move around. A quieter baby will probably be quite happy to sit in her chair and play for a while with a stimulating toy that you have given her. If she is content to sit quietly and amuse herself until you can feed her, it will also give you peace of mind that she is safe and not getting into any other mischief as you prepare her food and drink.

move in unison so if your child appears to be cross-eyed (with an eye turned inward or outward all the time) he should see an eye specialist.

If your baby drops a toy within his field of vision he will watch until it reaches its resting place. Toys falling outside his visual field will be ignored or forgotten.

Your child is now very chatty and will vocalize tunefully both to himself and others in a singsong manner using vowel sounds and single and double syllables such as "a–a," "adah" and "er-leh." He laughs, chuckles, and squeals with delight when playing and will express anger or annoyance with loud screams.

INTELLIGENCE

Assessing a child's IQ (intelligence quotient) when he is very young is difficult, and the motor development tests that can be used to evaluate IQ in the first year do not usually correlate well with a child's IQ later on. Intelligence can be influenced by many factors, including stimulation, health and diet as well as social aspects such as poverty. Even trauma can play a part. At this stage in your child's development you can encourage his physical, social, and intellectual growth by raising him in a stimulating environment and spending time playing, reading, and talking to him.

It is hard to predict how fast your baby will develop, but she will be stimulated by your talking and playing with her.

Always buy toys that suit the age of your baby. This one has bendable projections that he can easily grasp.

Once you have helped your baby to sit up, she will often sit quite happily and watch you as you move around the room.

SEVEN MONTHS

At seven months your baby will be able to sit up and turn at the waist. She will also like to suck her thumb.

Learning to move from one place to another is a huge achievement for your baby and one which will give her a whole new perspective on the world. How this locomotion is achieved will vary from baby to baby. Some crawl on all fours, others creep by wriggling on their fronts, others roll their way from one place to another. Some push themselves backwards, which can be very frustrating for them. It is thought that the children who walk the earliest are those who have crawled first or those who have gone straight from sitting to standing. Bottom shufflers and creepers tend to walk a bit later. However, there is little to suggest that a crawler who becomes an early walker is any brighter than a creeper who walks a little later.

Your baby will be able to take some weight on her legs now and she may even be able to stand while you hold her in an upright position. Over the next couple of months she will probably learn to pull herself up from sitting, and then she will practise standing alone.

Your baby is developing a mind of her own and will often try to wriggle free when picked up or held.

DEXTERITY

Your baby may start to show a preference for using her right or left hand at this age. Offer her a toy held straight in front of her and see which hand she uses to reach for it. If your baby regularly uses the same hand she is beginning to show a preference, but this is by no means a final choice. Very often the hand she uses at seven months is not the same as the one she prefers at nine months

Milestones

Your child may be able to:

• Put weight on legs when upright.

• Sit with minimal support.

• Look for a dropped object.

• Babble combining vowels and consonants such as "ga-ga", "ma-ma" and "da-da".

• Feed herself with finger foods.

• Begin to crawl.

Your baby is now very much on the move and will be beginning to crawl everywhere quite quickly.

Your baby will hold toys in both hands with much more dexterity now. She will also still enjoy sucking them.

Try and talk to your baby as much as you can as he will reply with babble that mixes both vowels and consonants.

or a year. Once your baby is able to use two hands in a coordinated way, give her something which needs one hand to hold it and another to make it work – a pot with a lid that comes off is ideal – and see which hand she uses for which action. This will give you a better idea of whether your baby is likely to be left- or right-handed, although her final choice may not be made until she reaches two years of age.

You may notice that your baby no longer grasps things in the centre of her palm to hold them. She now uses her fingers and thumb so that her grip has become very much more refined. Now that she can operate her fingers and thumb independently, rather than using them as a rake, she can pick up an object as small as a raisin to examine it.

You can encourage the baby by allowing her to feed herself. Give her a bowl and spoon and let her get on with it. At first it is a good idea for you to have a spoon too, so that you can give her the occasional mouthful while she is still working out how to get the food from the bowl, onto the spoon and into her mouth. Finger foods will help your baby learn how to get food into her mouth using her fingers.

At around the time your baby starts to show hand preference her language also starts to become more fully developed and she will babble a lot more using both vowel sounds and consonants. Her cries also change to include both low- and high-pitched sounds and she will start to make different movements with her tongue and mouth.

As his hand movements improve, your baby will start to grasp toys, such as bricks, with his fingers and thumb.

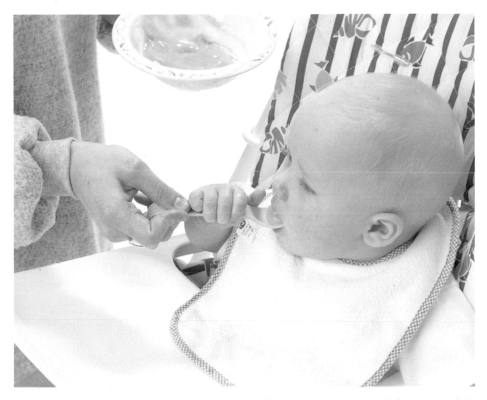

You can encourage your baby to eat solids by encouraging him to hold the spoon and feed himself.

EIGHT MONTHS

By eight months your baby will probably have started to be selective about the people with whom he is sociable. The outgoing friendliness of the earlier months may have been replaced by a certain wariness, especially of strangers. If you leave your baby with someone he doesn't know he may now burst into tears, whereas before he would have been perfectly happy, as long as he was being entertained and was warm and comfortable. This new-found wariness of strangers often occurs at about the same time that your baby is making a surge in his development. About a month after this, your baby may start to show distress, sometimes known as separation anxiety, when you leave the room. This distress at being separated from you or your partner will probably peak at around 15 months and then gradually subside.

If your baby does suffer from separation anxiety it can be misery for both of you. The best way of easing his distress is to leave him in a familiar environment with, if possible, a well-known person or relative.

Favourite and familiar toys can also be a source of comfort.

When you are leaving your baby to go out, try to leave quickly without making a fuss and keep your goodbyes down to a minimum.

As the bond grows stronger between you and your child, he will appreciate as much attention as you can give him.

Milestones

Your child may be able to:

• Stand up while holding onto something firmly.

• Get himself into a sitting position from his stomach.

• Pick up a small object with his hand such as a raisin.

• Turn round in the direction of a familiar voice.

• Move himself towards an out-of-reach toy.

DISCOVERING GENITALS

It is normal for your baby to start to show an interest in his genitals at around this age. This interest is an inevitable and healthy part of your baby's development in the same way that his fascination with his fingers and toes was earlier. There is no harm, either physical or psychological, in your baby handling his genitals and you should never make your child feel bad or think about punishing him because he is doing so.

A boy is capable of having an erection from before birth; this is simply the normal response to the touch of a sensitive organ. A baby girl has clitoral erections from a very young age too, although these are much less obvious.

INTRODUCING BOOKS

From eight months onwards, your baby's behaviour will become more flexible and he will begin to use his own initiative in a relationship. He will give you toys as well as taking them and may even start playing simple games with you. For the first time he will want to share his interest in an object with another person. This is a good time to introduce him to books which you can sit and read together. At first he will only be interested in the rhythm and sound of the words and the colour and pattern of the pictures in the book. By speaking slowly in a singsong manner, putting exaggerated emphasis in the right places, and encouraging your child to join in with simple sounds such as "moo" when he sees the picture of a cow, you will make reading a shared, enjoyable experience.

DEVELOPMENTAL CHECK

At between six and nine months your baby will be given another developmental check by your doctor

Your baby will happily respond to your games and will often try playful actions like grabbing your hair.

Left: As the grasping action is much more developed, your child will enjoy handling and playing with stacking toys. He may need guidance from you as to the order the shapes go in, and which colour should go next.

Opposite: A car or any toy with wheels is likely to be a particular source of interest for your baby. He may just want to sit and play with it, and only go after it if you join in and spend time pushing it back and forth to him.

or health visitor. She will be looking to see how your baby is developing and also checking that nothing has been missed in any previous health checks. Your baby's pelvis and legs will be examined to make sure there is no congenital dislocation of the hips. If your baby is a boy his testicles will be checked to make sure they are well down in the scrotum. A distraction test for hearing will be carried out. This involves making a noise for two seconds with something like a bell or rattle out of your baby's sight to see whether he turns towards the sound. His eyes will be checked to see that there is no sign of a potential squint. You will probably be asked if your baby has ever had any breathing problems such as wheezing, and his heart and lungs may be checked with a stethoscope. He may be weighed and his height measured and the circumference of his head checked.

If you are worried about any part of your child's development you should talk about your concerns now with your doctor. The health visitor or doctor will be able to help with any questions you may have and can also offer advice if you are experiencing problems with feeding your child or with his sleeping.

NINE MONTHS

A nine-month-old baby is capable of showing a wide range of emotions from happiness to fear, anger, and sadness and she will use these as a means of expressing feelings at any given moment. Your child needs you to be in tune with her feelings and to understand what she is trying to express, otherwise she will become frustrated and unhappy. She may begin to show signs of early independence, but she will still want the reassurance of knowing that you are nearby and ready to help out if required.

MOVEMENT

Your baby can now sit alone for 10-15 minutes at a time and will be able to lean forward to pick up a toy without falling over. She can also turn her body and will stretch out for something at her side. She will spend time manipulating a toy with her hands and is able to pass the toy from one hand to the other, turning it as she does so. She uses a pincer grasp, using her finger and thumb, to pick up small items. She will poke at things with a forefinger and may even start to point. You will notice that she still cannot put down a toy she is holding. She will still drop it or press it against a hard surface to release it. If she drops a toy she will look where it has fallen, even if it has completely disappeared from view.

Your child is now very active and she will begin to move herself

Your baby is now constantly on the move and will use her hands to help push her forward as she crawls along.

As she moves along she will be distracted if you call out her name, and might even topple over as her balance is still unsteady.

As she pushes forward with her arms, her legs will move back and forth to propel her along.

Milestones

Your child may be able to:

• Look for an object that she dropped out of view.

• Pull herself into a standing position.

• Pick up small objects using her finger and thumb.

• Enjoy games such as pat-a-cake.

• Wave goodbye.

• Cruise around the furniture.

across the floor either by crawling, or by shuffling or rolling if she can't yet crawl. She will try pulling herself to standing while holding onto something and may manage to hold herself upright for a few moments before sitting down with a bump. She won't be able to lower herself in a controlled way into a sitting position. If you hold her in a standing position she will probably make purposeful stepping movements with alternate feet as though she is practising walking.

ACTIVITY

You will notice that your child is becoming a lot more vocal now. She will shout for your attention, stop, listen for your response, and, if she doesn't get it, she will shout again. She will hold long conversations with you, babbling in a loud, tuneful way using strings of syllables such as "dad-da", "ma-ma", "aga-aga", over and over again. She not only uses this babble as a means of interpersonal communication to show friendliness or annoyance, but also as

After crawling for a while, your baby may try to push herself up, but will not be able to balance properly yet.

a way of amusing herself. She likes to practise imitating adult sounds, not just talking but also smacking her lips, coughing and making "brrr"-type noises.

By now your baby will be able to bite and chew her food well and she will be able to feed herself with some finger foods. She will probably try to grasp hold of the spoon as she is being fed. Let her have her own play spoon so that she can continue to practise feeding herself between the mouthfuls of food you are giving to her.

Your baby will probably enjoy games such as "peek-a-boo" and looking for something that you've half hidden while she watched. She will be delighted when she discovers the item and will show it to you with great glee. You may even be able to get her to look for something that you've completely hidden, but she won't necessarily be able to find it and this may cause her some distress and even annoyance.

If your baby seems at all worried by these first simple games you will need to encourage her to take part in them by responding to all her efforts with obvious surprise or

All toys will be held firmly now by your baby, who will use a pincer grasp with her finger and thumb.

Your baby's fascination with her toes will continue and she will often be found playing with them.

Right: As bonding with her father continues, your baby will enjoy being lifted up in the air and other games with him.

delight. She will be happy when you show her how much you enjoy her cleverness because she will enjoy your approval.

As your baby starts to become more confident, the games to play will become more adventurous. She will let you know when she is ready to progress to the next stage.

Below: Your baby will not play with an older brother at this stage, but she will be interested in toys he is showing her.

Standing up will be a problem unless there is a support nearby. If he lets go he will sit down with a bump.

TEN MONTHS

You will probably have discovered by now that your child has a sense of humour. At 10 months, your baby will not only enjoy playing games with you but will also rock with laughter at some of his own antics. For example, he will enjoy splashing in the bath and this will become even more fun if he gets you wet too. The more you protest the more he will enjoy splashing you. You may also find some of the things you do make your baby laugh uproariously. Appearing around a door saying "boo" can make him squeal with laughter and he will enjoy this game over and over again. Your baby may also enjoy teasing you in return by offering you a toy and then snatching it back before you can take it.

Traditional nursery rhymes and games can give your child endless fun. Try saying: "Round and round the garden, like a teddy bear, one step, two step, tickly under there!" as you run your fingers around his palm, then up his arm and end with a tickle. Another favourite is Humpty Dumpty. Build up to a climax at the point Humpty is going to fall off the wall and pretend to let

Milestones

Your child may be able to:
• Move around the furniture.
• Understand the word "no", but not necessarily obey it.
• Stand alone for a few seconds.
• Use the word "dada" to get his father's attention.
• Hold a feeder cup to drink from it.
• Roll a ball back to you.

Your child is now developing rapidly and will be trying to stand. He won't be able to do it on his own and will need your support.

He might try a few faltering steps, but can't easily manage these and will need to hold onto one of your hands as he moves forwards.

Supports, such as a chair, will be used by your child to pull himself up as he learns to stand.

your baby fall too. The baby has probably reached what is sometimes known as the joint-attention stage. This is when a child is able to concentrate on more than one thing at a time. You can encourage this by pointing out things while also giving your baby some information. For example, you can show your child a cat, then tell him that when a cat speaks it says "miaow". Later, when he sees a cat again, you can ask him what the cat says. This is a great way of sharing knowledge and making learning fun.

ESTABLISHING ROLES
Along with this sense of humour, new mobility, and the desire to share with you, comes a real talent for getting into trouble. Your baby's curiosity will lead him into all sorts of dangers and you will need to be constantly on your guard so that he isn't allowed to hurt himself. Your baby, on the other hand, may see thwarting your efforts at keeping

him out of mischief as a great way of getting a response from you. For the first time since your child was born you may begin to think about using some form of discipline.

Discipline doesn't mean rules and punishment, it means teaching the concept of right and wrong. It will be a long time before your child fully grasps the idea of what is involved, but by teaching him now, through your example and guidance, you will be helping him towards eventual self-control and showing him that he needs to have respect for other people.

It is important to remember that a baby cannot be bad because babies and toddlers do not know right from wrong. They learn about their world through experimentation, and by observing and testing adults. Introducing the concept of things being right or wrong at this early age is the first step to helping your child develop from a naturally self-centred baby to a much more sensitive and

caring child. The most effective discipline is neither uncompromisingly rigid nor too permissive. Either of these extremes can leave a child feeling unloved.

You need to set limits and standards that are fair and enforce them firmly, but lovingly. Never threaten to withdraw love from your child as this will badly effect his self-esteem and it is important that he knows he is loved even when you don't approve of his behaviour.

Don't smack your child. Smacking has been shown not to be an effective way to discipline a naughty child. It has many negative aspects including teaching the child violence and that using force is the best way of ending a dispute or getting what you want.

Opposite: A container with various slots for different shapes will keep a child amused as he tries to work out which one should go in the right hole.

A young baby will use a low stool for support as he moves around.

If a stool is at the right level, your baby may use it as a means of pulling himself up, and as a table to leave some of his toys there in easy reach.

ELEVEN MONTHS

Many babies speak their first word at around 11 months, although some speak as early as nine months and others don't say a word until well after a year. This is a remarkable achievement when you consider that not very long ago your child didn't even know how to smile. These first words take the longest to learn and you will need to be patient while you wait for your child to produce another new one. Sometimes these first words are learned as infrequently as one a month from now on, until your child has a vocabulary of around 10 words. After this the rate usually increases quickly, but this stage isn't reached until around 15 months of age.

DEVELOPING SPEECH
You can help your child to build up her vocabulary by saying the names of things in which she expresses an interest. By now she can probably point at items that she wants because she will have already discovered that pointing is an effective means of communicating with you. When you pick up the item and hand it to the child you probably tell her what

Milestones

Your child may be able to:
• Say the word "mama" to attract your attention.
• Stand on her own.
• Take her first steps.
• Respond to a simple command which isn't accompanied by gestures.
• Say her first word other than "mama" and "dada".

At 11 months your child will be much more responsive and will start reacting to simple questions and commands.

it is. For example, your child points at an apple, you pick up the apple and hand it to her saying something like: "You want this apple?" By doing this you are teaching your child new words; although she may not remember them straightaway, in time each word will become part of her vocabulary.

Don't worry if you are the only person who can understand your baby's first words. It is not unusual for others outside the family to be baffled by the way a baby speaks. It may well be two or three years before your child can be easily understood outside the immediate family. It is important not to keep correcting your child's pronunciation.

This will knock her confidence and she may become worried about trying to use new words. However, don't revert to using her wrongly pronounced words simply because they sound really cute. If you imitate her errors, the child will carry on using the incorrect words for much longer than she would otherwise have done.

MOBILITY

Your baby may have started to pull herself up onto her feet; she may even be walking by holding onto the furniture. Don't be tempted to rush out and buy shoes at the first sign of walking because the child doesn't need shoes yet, in fact they would

not be good for her feet at this stage. A child needs to wear shoes when she is walking confidently and her feet will need protection when she goes outside.

Learning to walk is a matter of trial and error. You can't really do anything to help your child apart from making sure that the area she is learning to walk in is as safe as possible. But even when you have removed all the obvious hazards in your child's path you need to stay close at hand to make sure that she doesn't hurt herself.

A child is bound to experience falls while mastering the art of walking and your reaction to these mishaps can colour your child's

ur developing baby will now start to share things and will happily hand you ʾs, such as a ball.

Even though she now has some teeth, your baby will still like the sensation of putting different objects in her mouth.

Right: Your baby will be particularly responsive playing games now. If you keep hiding a toy and then making it re-appear it will keep her happily amused for quite a while.

Below left and right: Your child will enjoy standing upright with some help from you. Provided she can hang onto something with one hand, she will eagerly pick up toys from the floor to show you, wave around or suck.

response to them as well. If you rush over in a panic every time she stumbles and demand to know if she is all right she may well shed more tears than she would if she'd really hurt herself. This over-reaction on your part may also make her lose her sense of adventure and make her afraid of attempting other normal physical development hurdles. By remaining calm and reacting with an "up you get, you're all right" sort of attitude, your child is likely to deal with minor tumbles in a matter-of-fact way.

Left: By pushing a baby walker, your baby can walk happily around the room. Keep an eye on her so that you can help if she gets stuck in a corner. It takes time for a child to learn how to walk backwards. Below: A child will place her favourite toys on a low-level table and play with them there. When she is bored she may just leave them and go off to do something else more interesting.

TWELVE MONTHS

You are the parent of a year-old child. One by one all the skills that will make your baby a self-dependent and integrated member of society are being perfected. You are both teacher and observer. And now the changes come very quickly indeed.

GROWING SKILLS

If your baby isn't actually walking he should be well on his way to doing so by the end of the first year. He will probably be able to pull himself to his feet and navigate by holding onto the furniture. He will certainly be crawling, bottom shuffling, or rolling, and he will be able to get around at quite some speed. He will be able to sit for long periods and can now get into the sitting position from lying flat.

Your baby's grasp is now more refined and he will be able to pick up small objects using the thumb and the tip of the index finger. He will drop and throw toys deliberately and enjoy watching them as they fall. If a toy rolls out of sight he may look for it. He uses both hands to hold toys, but he may start to show a preference for using one hand rather than the other. When your child wants to show you something he will point using his index finger. He's curious and will want to explore everything, so make sure that your home is a safe place. This doesn't mean restricting your baby to such an extent that he becomes frustrated. Try to compromise by leaving some safe cupboards for him to get into and locking the others.

When the baby is outside he will watch people, animals, or cars with prolonged, intent regard. He will be able to recognize familiar people or animals from around 6 m/20 ft and will probably greet them vocally with great enthusiasm. The child responds to his own name and can understand other words such as the

Milestones

Your child may be able to:
• Indicate what he wants in other ways instead of crying.
• Stand on his own.
• Walk a little way unaided.
• Wave goodbye to you, close relatives and friends.
• Say "mama" and "dada" with discrimination.
• Roll a ball back to you.

At 12 months your child will be able to let you know what he wants by pointing or reaching towards an object.

All children vary when they first start walking, but your child may well be taking his first few steps now, so you should give him every encouragement.

names of family members. He may be able to understand simple instructions such as "give it to Mummy", and he may even do as you ask.

You may find that your baby holds out his arm or leg when you ask him to while you are bathing or dressing him. You will see through his actions that he can understand much of what you say even though he can't yet express himself verbally. He babbles to himself and to you, making a lot of speech-type sounds and if he hasn't already said his first word then he soon will.

EATING HABITS

Your baby will be joining in family meals and will probably be eating a mashed-up version of whatever everyone else eats. He is still too young to eat spicy or seasoned food, so remove his portion before adding salt and pepper and other seasoning. He enjoys finger foods but will want to imitate others at mealtimes by using a spoon. It will be difficult for him to get food onto the spoon and then the spoon into his mouth, so he may well revert to using his fingers after a few attempts.

Your child will be able to drink from a feeder cup by himself and will probably be able to drink from an ordinary cup with your help, but he's still too young to manage this on his own. If you are weaning, or are about to wean your baby off his bottle or the breast, you may want to start giving him cows' milk as his main drink. This should only be introduced into your baby's diet after the age of one year and you should always give him whole, pasteurized milk. Skimmed milk has too much protein and sodium content for babies and should not be introduced into your child's diet before the age

of five. Semi-skimmed milk can be given from two years, but only if the child is eating a very varied and adequate diet.

Your baby may be reluctant to give up the bottle because it may be a source of emotional comfort, but it is recommended that a child stops drinking from a bottle at around a year because of the adverse effect it can have on his teeth. If you don't feel that he is ready to give up his bottle completely, try to limit the number of times he has a bottle each day. Encourage him to drink from a trainer cup at meal times and offer

him a bottle between meals and at bedtime. When you give a bottle during the day, fill it with water rather than juice or milk, because this will help reduce your child's interest in it. Insist that he drinks from it while sitting in an adult's lap and when he wants to get down take the bottle from him. Don't allow him to take his bottle to bed or to walk about with it. By restricting the use of a bottle like this you will limit the amount of potential harm it can do to his teeth.

Your baby may have as many as four or five teeth and you should

Toys such as a cuddly, soft panda will soon become a firm favourite with your child as he will enjoy its furry texture.

When your child has a favourite cuddly animal he will love to carry it around, hug and squeeze it, and may want to take it with him wherever he goes.

have been cleaning them from the time they appeared. These first teeth can be cleaned with a soft baby toothbrush and a pea-sized amount of children's toothpaste. If your baby is cutting teeth and is fretful, offer him a cold teething ring or a piece of raw carrot to chew on.

YOUR CHILD AND OTHERS
Even though he is confident and outgoing with you, your baby may still be wary of strangers. He may also suffer from shyness. This is an inherited trait which he will have got from either you or your partner, even though neither of you may appear to display the trait yourselves. Shyness can be modified, but it is rarely possible to eradicate it altogether. If you build up your child's confidence with praise and encouragement

this will help him to feel more comfortable with others and this may eventually help diminish any shyness.

It is possible that what you consider to be shyness is actually just a normal lack of sociability. At this age your child is not ready to make friends, and he probably won't be until he is at least three years old. Until then the social limit will probably be parallel play, which is when he plays side by side with another child. Don't try to force your child to play with others – pushing him may make him withdraw from social situations completely.

Don't expect a child to share his toys at this age. Right now the

only things that matter are his own needs and desires. Other children are seen as objects not people. If he displays aggressive behaviour towards other children, like biting or hitting, you need to respond immediately by removing him from the scene of the incident. Explain calmly why he shouldn't have behaved like that, then give him something to play with or point out a new object to distract him and change the subject. Of course he won't really understand what you are saying but, if you use this approach every time it happens, he will eventually understand that hitting and biting other people are just not acceptable behaviour.

Opposite: Although your child will be perfectly happy when being held by you, he may be shy and withdrawn with other people he doesn't know.

Below: Your baby will interact quite happily with his father and will keep experimenting with touch.

SIGHT AND VISION

Although your baby practised the blinking reflex by opening and closing her eyes while she was in the womb, the first time she actually uses her eyes for seeing is at the moment of birth. As soon as she is born she is capable of distinguishing objects and most colours; but she is only able to focus on items that are 20–30 cm/ 8–12 in away. These things will look slightly fuzzy and be lacking in definition and, since the images from the retinas of the eyes haven't merged yet, your baby's world will appear as if seen through two separate tunnels.

A newborn is very sensitive to bright lights and will blink and screw up her eyes if a light is shone in her face. Movement will attract a baby from birth and you may notice that yours actively seeks out moving objects. She will probably show a preference for an object which has a highly contrasting pattern rather than one which is just a solid block of colour. As your baby begins to control her eye movements she will start tracking moving objects, and it is then that her eyes will begin to start working together.

YOUR BABY'S WORLD

At first your face will be of more interest to your child than anything else. It is thought that a baby is born with a simple mental template of the human face and will actively search out and stare at any human face during the first couple of months. When she is first born, whether she is able to recognize you by your individual features is open to debate, but she will certainly know the general shape of your head and hairline and by two months will have started to recognize your features.

Your baby will soon become interested in other things and by six to eight weeks she will be concentrating on details, scanning faces and

A newborn baby's vision will be fairly limited and initially he will only be able to see a fuzzy image of you.

objects so that she can take in as much information as possible. At this age she may find it hard to disengage her attention when she is watching something and she may need you to distract her before she can remove her gaze. But by three to four months the pathways in the brain for voluntary action begin to take over and your baby starts to disengage her attention on her own.

By three months a baby can perceive colours fully, with all their different shades, and will be able to focus at different distances and to see things in 3D. From seven to eight months as

Your young baby will become fascinated by different objects and will become difficult to distract from whatever is capturing her attention.

Left: If your baby spots a colourful object ahead of her when she is crawling, she will go and investigate it.

As your baby's eyesight improves, he will intently watch everything that is going on around him (top and above).

Your baby's eyes will follow a moving object which is held within his range of vision.

she begins to interpret what she sees, your baby starts to realize that things don't necessarily cease to exist just because she can't see them anymore. A toy dropped over the edge of the high chair will be looked for; she will also enjoy playing "peek-a-boo" because she knows now that you will definitely reappear.

Learning the size and shape of things and understanding that something that looks small at a distance is in fact the same size close up takes some time for a baby to understand. She will also have to learn that a toy stays the same shape even when it appears

How you can help

• Give your baby plenty of stimulating things to look at.
• Hold an item within her range of vision and move it slowly in an arc so that she can follow it with her eyes.
• Play games like "peek-a-boo" and "hide-and-seek"with a toy or by hiding under a large cloth or blanket.
• Check that your child doesn't have a squint. If you are concerned, talk to your doctor.

different when looked at from the side, top, or bottom. It will take your baby around two years to have good vision and to be able to see as clearly as an adult does.

A SQUINT

Many babies are born with what may appear to be a slight squint and this often remains until they have learned to control the muscles around the eyes. It is quite difficult for a baby to hold both eyes in line with each other to focus on an object, and you may notice that when your baby stares at you one of her eyes wanders out of focus. A wandering eye usually rights itself by the time a baby reaches six months old, but you should always point it out to your doctor or health visitor as it may be necessary for your child's eyes to be checked thoroughly by a specialist.

A real squint is when the eyes never focus together on an object and, rather than moving together and then one wandering off, they are often out of alignment with each other. A squint needs to be treated from an early age so you must talk to your doctor as soon as you notice it in your child.

A brightly coloured mobile, moving in the breeze and suspended or held from above, will delight your child and keep him amused for a long time.

HEARING

During the last three months in the uterus a baby will have been hearing a variety of different noises. By the time a baby is born, he will already be familiar with his mother's voice, the beating of her heart, and the sound of the amniotic fluid in which he has been floating. His ability to hear at birth is almost as good as an adult's. His hearing threshold, however, is lower so your baby will be startled by loud, unfamiliar noises, although he will probably sleep happily through a constant loud sound such as a blaring television or loud music.

A very young baby will prefer to hear rhythmic noises that may not seem soothing to you: the noise of a washing machine or tumble dryer, the hum of the vacuum cleaner or hair dryer. These will probably reassure him and may even lull him to sleep, perhaps because he heard such sounds before birth and he finds

them both comforting and familiar.

Your own child will quickly associate you and your voice with comfort – it is thought that an infant of only a few days old can actually recognize his mother's voice. Your baby will respond to all the human voices he hears and will turn towards the sound of people talking and appear to listen intently. If he is being spoken to in the exaggerated, high-pitched tone, and rhythmic singsong manner, known as "motherese" that adults often instinctively adopt for babies, you will notice that your baby pays particular attention. He may even lose interest if the speaker reverts to a normal tone.

It is through hearing others speak that your baby will eventually learn to form the words which will make up early vocabulary. He will start to understand what is being said long before he can actually make the noises himself; if he has a hearing

defect this knowledge and the eventual ability to speak will be affected. As your baby gets older he will start looking for the source of the different sounds that he hears and will respond with obvious pleasure to familiar voices, words, and tunes.

HEARING TESTS

At your baby's first developmental check, at between six and eight weeks, your doctor will want to know whether you have any concerns about your baby's hearing and

How you can help

• When the baby is very young, try not to let him become startled by sudden noises which make him cry.
• Talk to your child, using "motherese", the high-pitched, singsong voice that babies find appealing.
• Introduce him to many different sounds from an early age.
• Let him sleep where he is happiest rather than insisting that he should be in a quiet room on his own.

From an early age your baby will respond to your voice and be interested in toys you are showing him.

He will turn towards any new or interesting noise that you make with a toy even if it is coming from behind him.

how he responds to your voice at home. You should mention if there is a close family history of hearing problems. If there is any concern, your baby can be referred to a hearing clinic.

At eight or nine months, your baby will have his next developmental check and this will include a screening test of your baby's hearing carried out by your health visitor. By now the response to sounds should be obvious, turning his head when you speak to him and responding to different noises of varying pitch and intensity. Both ears will be tested to identify anything previously missed.

If your child is deaf or partially deaf, his speech may not progress past the babbling stage and you may notice that he becomes quieter as he gets older. Any concerns about your child's hearing should be discussed with your doctor as soon as they occur.

Your baby will study your expression and listen intently to your voice before trying to imitate you.

SMELL, TASTE, TOUCH

SMELL

Newborn babies are very sensitive to smell and can remember certain smells almost from the moment they are born. They recognize their parents' natural smell and a breast-fed baby can distinguish the smell of her mother's milk from that of any other woman's just a few hours after birth. In fact, your baby will start sucking in her sleep if she smells your milk.

A bottle-fed baby will quickly learn to identify her own mother's smell and the smell of any other family members who also feed her. The smell of people who are familiar to her will help your baby distinguish between family members and people strange to her.

As your baby grows, certain smells will become associated with specific things, just as they do for adults. For example, food smells will suggest mealtimes and perhaps happy social occasions, while the smell of bath preparation and baby powder will become associated with bathtime and bed. Smells that your baby finds unpleasant will make her turn her head away even when she is only a few days old.

Your baby will use her sense of smell with her other senses to learn about the world around her.

From a young age, a baby has a highly developed sense of smell and she will delight in a sweet-smelling flower.

Taste is very important to a baby and she will experiment with the sensation of sucking her toys.

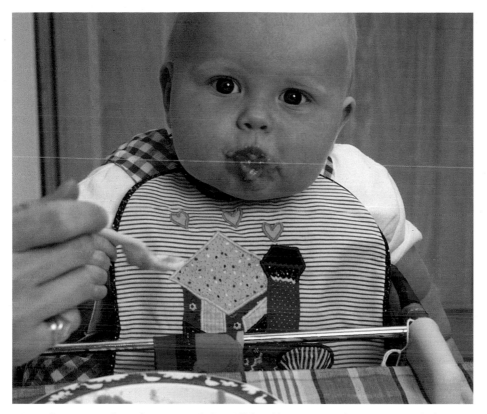

From the moment he is born, your baby will be able to react to bitter tastes and show a preference for sweet foods.

How you can help

- Spend time cuddling and talking to your baby so that she really gets to know you.
- Offer your child a wide variety of tastes once she is old enough to take solids, but avoid foods that are seasoned or spicy.
- Don't encourage your child to have a sweet tooth.
- Remember that a young baby cannot control her temperature as well as an older child, so you need to keep a constant check on her to make sure she isn't too cold or if she is becoming overheated.
- Your baby's skin is very sensitive so check that her clothes aren't tight or rubbing her skin.

TASTE

Smell and taste are intrinsically linked so it is no surprise that a baby is born with the ability to differentiate between tastes. From birth your baby's taste buds can detect sweet, sour, bitter, and salty. When offered any of these tastes she will give a definite and consistent reaction to each one. Her taste buds will become more refined with age, but even as a newborn baby she will show appreciation for sweet flavours and grimace when experiencing salty or bitter tastes.

All babies seem to be born with a preference for a sweeter taste, probably because breast milk is slightly sweet and it is important that she likes its flavour. This natural preference for sweet things won't harm your baby's teeth providing that you don't indulge her by giving her sweetened juice to drink, or adding sugar to her food when you start to wean her. When you start to introduce solids into your baby's diet it is better to encourage her to eat bland foods at first and then savoury foods and to keep sweet things to a minimum. Your baby will quickly develop her own tastes and you can help by giving her a varied diet once she is old enough to take solids.

By the time your child is around a year old she will use her experience of the different foods she has tried to help her distinguish between the more subtle flavours. For example, one brand of baked beans will taste slightly different to another and at a year old your child will be able to taste the difference.

TOUCH

Your baby uses touch immediately after birth. This provides her with a means of finding out about her new environment through the textures that her skin comes into contact with, like her clothes, your clothes, and skin. Your baby can also feel through her skin whether her environment is warm or cold, wet or dry. She feels pain and discomfort and, because a young baby has more sensitive skin than an adult, you need to treat her gently.

As she matures, your baby will use touch in different ways to help her learn. Touch-sensitive nerve endings are concentrated at the end of the fingertips and around the lips, and a young baby will use her hands and mouth for exploring new objects. Gradually, after a few weeks touch will also become associated with feelings and your baby will start to connect the feeling of your nipple in her mouth or your arms around her and associate them with warmth and security. One of the most important sensory experiences for your baby is through her tongue and mouth so that sucking is not only a means of obtaining nourishment, but is also

Your young baby will reach out and touch different objects, such as this furry panda, to get used to the different sensations.

a great source of comfort for her.

When you undress your baby you may notice that she becomes increasingly tense as you remove each layer of clothes and she may actually cry when you remove the garment nearest to her skin, usually her vest. This is not because you are being clumsy, but because she physically misses the feel of her clothes against her skin. She should stop crying as soon as you dress her again.

Between two and three months your child begins to use touch as a means of exploring and she will use her hands to hit out at things that are near her. By around five months she will have mastered hand and eye co-ordination and will learn by feeling and putting things in her mouth.

BONDING
Touch plays an important part in the main bonding process. This is the

formation of a close emotional relationship between you and your baby which will provide her with the love, comfort, and security that she wants. Although your baby is born with a deep-rooted psychological need to have a close interaction with you this doesn't always happen immediately. A child's bonding with her mother is often a gradual process which may not be fully completed until the baby is a few months old.

At a few months old a young baby will react to bright toys such as this octopus which has two different materials on the undersides of its legs. He will enjoy the feel of soft textures.

TALKING

Your child is born with the potential to learn to speak and a receptiveness to the influences that will help him communicate. A baby starts to learn about language while he is still in the womb, which is when he first begins to identify the voice of his mother. As a newborn he will prefer his mother's voice to any other because it will already be familiar and he will quickly associate it with warmth, comfort, and feeding. A

newborn baby's brain is tuned to pick out the texture, pattern, and rhythm of language and he will pay more attention to voices talking than any other sounds he hears. From the moment he is born your baby understands speech sounds in a way that allows him to segment the speech he hears into sound units.

Before he can speak fluently a baby has to go through distinct stages of development. In the beginning your baby's vocal skills will consist of cries and burps. The inability to speak in the early months does not actually hinder a baby's ability to become a talker. He uses this time to learn how to control his mouth and his tongue. You may notice that from a very early age your baby will move his mouth a lot, pushing his lips forwards and backwards in a kind of rhythm.

CONVERSATIONS
One of the skills your baby has to acquire before speech is the ability to interact with people. Your baby begins to learn about this process very early on and by three months he will already be using communicative gestures. Try raising your eyebrows to him and then watch as he imitates you. This is the first stage of learning about holding a conversation. These gestures will be accompanied by different noises as your baby begins to develop control over dozens of separate muscles which are involved in making speech sounds. When your baby coos and gurgles at you he is learning to coordinate tongue movements while taking air in. When you respond to these early noises you will instinctively use a high-pitched, rhythmic singsong tone, repeating words in such a way that you capture your baby's attention.

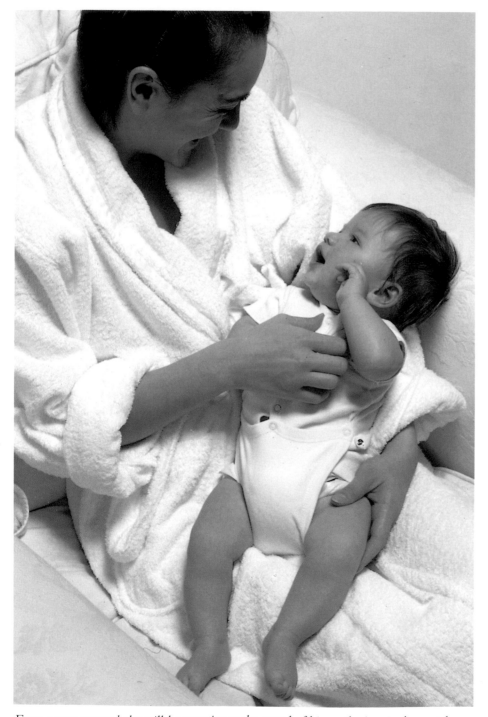

Even a very young baby will be receptive to the sound of his mother's voice because he will have heard it in the womb.

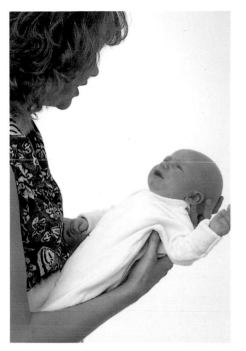

Chat to your baby when you hold him as he will find the sound of your voice soothing and comforting.

By around five or six months, your child will be concentrating on one-syllable words such as "ba" or "ma" which he will repeat over and over again, often when he is on his own. This use of early sounds is known as babbling, and is not yet being used as a form of communication. This is your baby's way of learning how to make new sounds. Soon after he has learned to babble you will notice that your baby starts to use his eyes to communicate with you and to direct your attention towards something that he wants. This communication is soon followed by what is called declarative pointing: pointing as a form of interacting, rather than just as a basic means of asking you to pass him

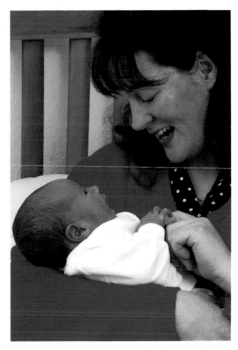

If you speak to your new baby in a high-pitched, singsong voice you will immediately get his attention.

Even at the young age of eight weeks your baby will respond to your voice and attempt to smile at you.

something he can't reach for himself.

After a month or two your baby's babbling will start to flow like speech, rising and falling as if he were holding a conversation. Although he is still not able to form words, he will understand simple words which are made clear, for example, "bottle" when you point to his feeding bottle. Understanding more than he is able to say will continue throughout baby- and toddlerhood until he can speak fluently.

FIRST WORDS
By the end of his first year your baby will probably produce his first word.

It may not seem recognizable as a word to you, but it will be a sound that he uses for one specific object, for example, "ine" for when he wants an orange. It is certainly no accident that "mama" and "dada" are often among the first recognizable words that a new baby says, because first words are simple and are associated with things that are special to a child.

Once speech has begun with your baby, he will continue to produce a handful of new words each month with the majority of this early communication being simple nouns or proper names.

How you can help
• Always respond to your baby's attempts at communicating with you.
• Don't be embarrassed to use high-pitched speech; it is the language your child likes best.
• Talk to your baby as you go about your daily routine and remember to speak clearly using simple words.
• Be consistent, using the same words for the same thing every time.
• Look at simple picture books with your baby. By telling him what is in each picture you will be increasing his understanding of words.

A mother can help her child learn to talk properly by repeating words and by pointing out objects and saying the word.

As your baby investigates colourful items, such as a yellow flower, you can talk to him about it, telling him which are the petals, leaves and stem.

SOCIAL BEHAVIOUR

A newborn baby doesn't appear very sociable to the outside world because she doesn't smile or respond verbally until some weeks after birth. But her parents' reactions to the baby's ordinary behaviour lead to the development of social mannerisms. For example, wind may cause your baby to appear to smile at an early age and you respond by smiling back. Your baby will eventually realize that this movement of her mouth makes you react in this way and so will use it deliberately in the future. It is this early, simple form of communication that is the basis for your child's social development.

All babies' early social learning comes from imitating the people with whom they have the most contact, generally their mother and father. A newborn of only a few hours can imitate some adult gestures such as poking her tongue out or yawning. This ability to imitate is one of the most important tools your baby has to help her learn about life.

Through imitation your baby will eventually start communicating. You will speak to her and she will respond with "coos" and will wriggle her body in delight. This first stage of conversation will eventually develop into the ability to talk and listen. These early conversations often start during feeding, because the rhythm of feeding initiates your baby into the basics of dialogue. A baby sucks in her mother's milk in bursts with pauses in between. It is during these pauses that her mother usually fills in the gap by talking happily to her.

IMITATION BECOMES CHOICE
Social interaction between you and your baby becomes increasingly intentional on her part during the first two months of life, with much of your baby's behaviour geared towards making you react. These early conversations and the ability to imitate are just two ways of getting you to respond; the other very effective way is crying. Initially, your baby's cries are a reflex to pain, hunger, or discomfort. But crying assures a baby of adult response, especially her mother's. Her cries will increase her mother's heart rate and, if breast-feeding, her mother will automatically start producing milk. Within a few weeks a baby will have learned to expect certain reactions to her crying, such as being fed or picked up.

At around six weeks your baby will learn to smile properly, another social skill which she will be able to use to her advantage. Although her

When young babies are placed together, they don't play with each other as they haven't yet learned how to interact. Instead they will just play on their own.

If you put two or three babies together in a playpen they will not play together as they haven't learned how to socialize.

first smiles are simply facial grimaces, your response will be such that she soon discovers that by using her facial muscles in this way she is guaranteed to get you to smile back. A baby will quickly learn to repeat an action if she gets a positive reaction. However, if she regards the response she receives as negative she is less likely to repeat the action.

By three months your baby will be able to show her enjoyment of people and surroundings. She will respond to friendly adults and will generally not mind who is with her as long as they are paying attention to her. Your baby will enjoy activities such as having a bath and often show pleasure when she realizes that bathtime has arrived. Feeding will be a great source of emotional pleasure and your baby will study your face unblinkingly while she feeds.

At around four months your baby will cry more deliberately. She will probably pause after crying to see if anyone is coming in response, before crying again. She has learned that crying brings attention and this new ability to manipulate is the beginning of some exciting discoveries.

CHANGING BEHAVIOUR PATTERNS
Somewhere after six months your child may change from a social, happy baby, who will go to anyone and reward complete strangers with smiles, to one who overnight has become wary of people she doesn't know. Your baby has reached the stage when she needs time and space to handle each new sight and sound; and a stranger may present her with too many new, unfamiliar things to be taken in at one time. This new wariness leads to what is known as stranger anxiety. It often manifests itself as loud protestations when your baby is about to be separated from you. She is at the stage of develop-

As your baby will feel safe with you, try to show her different toys and items to interest her and attract her attention.

ment when she is becoming increasingly sensitive to change and appears to be suddenly more dependent. She may try to avoid upsetting or stressful events by crying, clinging to you, or turning away from what is upsetting her. Towards the end of her first year she may start to use objects such as a favourite blanket, bottle, or thumb as a comforter.

Over the next six months your baby will probably show an increasing reticence with strangers but will be very responsive to people with whom she is familiar. She may become very clinging so that any separation from you is accompanied by real distress. This attachment may cause you problems, but it is in fact an important stage of development. Your baby now recognizes individuals as people and is beginning to develop selective, permanent relationships. She will use these relationships as a safe base from which to explore the world. Now that she is getting older, your baby will use her

A baby will sit with her brother because he is familiar. She will be interested in his toys but won't play with him.

developing vocal skills to create noise – this guarantees the attention that gives her the reassurance she needs. She may use mimicry to make you laugh and the more you show your appreciation the more she will repeat the antic which is amusing you. This is her first real control over her social environment.

By the time she is a year old, your child will probably have grasped the idea that she exists as an entity. She may even begin to use a word or

Your baby will sit quite happily on your knee, but may be wary of moving to his grandmother who is less familiar to him.

A baby will soon learn to recognize his older sister and will happily let her help him to stand up.

sound to describe herself as a means of expressing this. Her social skills, however, are still very limited and she will show little interest in anyone outside her immediate circle of well-known people. Other children hold very little appeal for your child at this age and are more likely to be treated as inanimate objects rather than playmates.

It will be another year or two before your child has enough social understanding to develop friendships with other toddlers.

How you can help

• Encourage your baby to imitate you by exaggerating your responses to her actions.

• Smile at your baby to let her know how pleased you are when she smiles at you.

• If she becomes wary of strangers don't force her to be sociable.

• When you have to leave your baby, say goodbye quickly; don't prolong the parting.

MOBILITY

All babies go through the same stages of mobility, but how fast they move from one to another varies considerably. Your baby may walk independently before he is a year old, or he may be content to shuffle along on his bottom or hands and knees until well after this. Your baby's mobility takes place in a set order, starting at his head and working down to his toes. He won't be able to sit upright or crawl until he can hold up his head, and he won't be able to walk until he can move his body along, either by crawling or doing a bottom shuffle.

Finally, your baby will learn to control his arms and legs before gaining control of his hands and feet. At each stage it will take time for the movements he has learned to progress from being awkward, rather clumsy and uncoordinated to the smooth, controlled movements he will ultimately achieve.

MAKING PROGRESS

A newborn baby has no control over his head, which will flop around if left unsupported. By about eight weeks, control of the head and neck begins and you may notice your baby practising lifting his head and holding it for a few seconds before letting it flop down again. At around three months most babies are able to hold their heads up steadily so that they can look around and examine the world about them.

The next stage in mobility comes when your baby starts to roll around, first from side to back and then, a few weeks later, from back to side. The way a baby rolls is highly individual and your baby will roll when he's ready and in his own way. Rolling is another way of practising control over his body and your baby will do it over and over again until he's mastered what to him is a new movement. The result of this

How you can help

• Hold your baby upright so he can bounce his legs up and down on your lap to help strengthen his muscles.
• Sitting a little way away from your baby, persuade him to come to you. Do this to encourage both crawling and walking.
• Once he can sit upright, you can help your baby learn to balance by placing toys slightly out of reach so he has to stretch out for them.
• To get your baby to twist around, place a toy behind him and then support him as he turns.
• Push-along toys will encourage your baby to crawl and walk.

movement will change your baby's view of the world and once he has discovered this, rolling becomes a new function: a means of getting closer to something that he wants. Your baby will have been using his legs to push with since he was born, although the first stepping movements he made as a newborn were a

All babies' first movements will be uncoordinated, but they soon learn a basic crawl and to sit upright unaided.

When your baby is placed on his stomach at a few months old he will attempt to crawl.

He will lift up his arms and legs in the swimming motion that is the prelude to crawling.

Before she's a year old, your baby will start to stand and balance holding onto a chair if you hold it steady for her.

She will grasp firmly onto the bottom part of the chair and start to pull herself up. Try to encourage her as much as possible.

As she straightens into an upright position, she will need support from the chair you are holding.

Now she is standing confidently, she will start to look around her to see what else is going on in the room.

As your baby starts to crawl, he will move towards interesting toys.   *When he is nearer the toys, he will probably reach out for them.*

reflex action. At around four months if you put your baby down on his abdomen, he will be able to lift his shoulders, arms, and legs off the floor and move them in a swimming-type motion, and by around five-and-a-half months your baby should be able to sit with some support, his back straight and shoulders braced. By around six months he will probably be able to support himself in a crawling position, although he won't be able to go anywhere just yet. By seven months he will be able to sit upright using his arms for support. Once he has done this he will quickly learn to sit unaided, and he will also enjoy standing and bouncing vigorously while you hold him.

By eight or nine months he will have learned to control his movements and he will be able to move his arms and legs in order to propel

By eight or nine months your baby will be able to crawl around on the floor.

himself either backwards or forwards. Once he has mastered this he will be off and it will only be a matter of time before he starts trying to stand up on his own. By about nine months he will be able to sit and reach in front, upwards, to the side and behind him without falling over.

As soon as he has learned to crawl at around nine months he will be ready to start pulling himself up into a standing position using you, or the furniture, for support. At this stage he will not have mastered sitting down so when he wants to sit he will simply let go and land down on the floor with a resounding bump. He probably won't be able to control his sitting movement until he is 11 to 12 months old.

Before he's a year old your baby

will start to navigate all around the furniture, taking little sideways steps. Once he can move around like this with some confidence he will let go with one hand. As soon as he is able to let go with his remaining hand, perhaps to cross a gap in the furniture, he will begin to get the confidence to walk about unaided.

Your baby's first steps on his own will be very wobbly and ungainly, with his feet placed wide apart to help him balance. But once he becomes more mobile his legs will straighten and he'll become steadier on his feet.

Your baby will try to stand with your help.

Lift him up supporting his arms.

Once up, he will need your hand to balance.

A baby walker can help a child to take her first steps and practise walking.

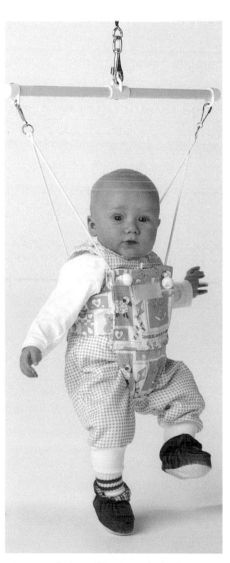

Once crawling your baby will go all over.

Other types of baby walker can be sat in and propelled along by your child's feet.

A young baby will enjoy a baby bouncer, but make sure it is firmly attached.

Your child's first steps are often wobbly and his movements may seem awkward.

PLAY

PLAY

Introduce your baby to games by teaching him nursery rhymes like "this little piggy went to market".

A baby is born with the potential to learn and play. She can see, hear, and feel. She is aware of her environment and will respond from birth to brightly coloured, moving objects and to sounds. She learns all the time and play is one of the ways in which she develops new skills, while toys are the play tools that she uses to stimulate herself at each stage of development. Toys don't have to be elaborate; your child will invent her own games and use everyday objects as toys when she is young. Watching you and trying to imitate your voice and facial expressions will provide hours of entertainment in the early months. Ultimately, the toy that a child enjoys and plays with most will give her the greatest learning experience, and in the first weeks of life this "toy" will be you.

Your child will change very rapidly during the first year so that a toy that entertains her at two months will not appeal to her when she is a year old. As she develops, your child will need different stimuli and the choice of toys for each stage of development should reflect these different needs. It is also very important that the toys you give a child are appropriate to this age. A toy designed for a younger child will be boring, while a toy for an older child may be too complicated and may even be dangerous if it contains small pieces on which a young baby could choke.

BIRTH TO THREE MONTHS

During the first few months, your baby is developing her basic senses – touch, sight, and sound. She needs

Your child will be fascinated by nursery rhymes that involve actions that use his hands.

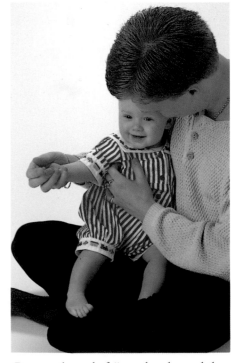

Because the end of "round and round the garden" includes tickling your baby, he will associate it with fun and ask for more.

As your child develops she will start to enjoy playing games with you such as "peek-a-boo"

As you teach her the game, she will enjoy "hiding" behind the chair and peeking out at you from behind the legs.

Games to play

• Gently bounce your baby up and down on your knee in rhythm to a nursery rhyme.

• Hold her palm open and play "round and round the garden" ending up with a tickle under her arm.

• Use her toes to play "this little piggy went to market".

• Take your baby as your partner and dance around the room with her in your arms.

You can buy your baby many expensive toys, but she'll still enjoy playing with simple kitchen utensils. Always make sure they have no sharp edges.

toys which will stimulate these senses and give experience of colours, textures, materials, and shapes. A good first toy is a mobile, hung where your baby can study it at leisure. It doesn't have to be expensive – one made from pictures cut from a magazine and suspended from a coat hanger will be just as effective as one you buy. Once your baby begins to wave her hands around and tries to swipe at things, she will enjoy toys that make a noise or that react to her actions, a rattle for example. This will give your child a sense of control as well as encouraging the development of manual skills and hand and eye co-ordination.

A newborn baby's hands are usually held closed in fists, but she will gradually relax them so that if you place an object in her open palm she will close her hand around it for a few seconds. The strong grasp reflex she was born with will have disappeared so that she will probably drop the object within a few seconds. By the

An activity centre is ideal for babies around nine months as they will love to push the buttons and manipulate all the different shapes and knobs.

age of two or three months she will try reaching out to touch things. These first grasping movements are important steps towards learning hand-eye co-ordination.

Once your baby is old enough to sit in a bouncing cradle she will be able to see more of the world around her and her hands will be free to explore. A toy fastened across the front of the cradle will encourage her to bring her hands forward to try and hit it to make it move. Once she has done this, she will want to do it again and again; gradually she sees that she is responsible for making this happen and her movements become more deliberate.

A newborn is acutely aware of sounds and will already have become familiar with your voice while in the womb. Talking and singing to your baby from the time she is born will encourage her to listen and help her develop her own speech later. As she gets older, hold her on your lap and try having a conversation with her. Say something, then wait until your baby makes a noise in response. Her response will be slow at first so allow her plenty of time. These conversations will help her learn about taking turns, listening, and copying – all essential parts of communication. Once your baby has got used to life

As she starts to move around, your baby will get pleasure from pushing a baby walker. She will also enjoy trying to put plastic shapes in the right holes on the walker.

outside the womb, she will find touch and the freedom to move her limbs exciting. Different textures will give her new sensations of touch, so offer her various things to feel that will give her experience of rough, soft, silky, or smooth textures. Bathing and changing times will provide an opportunity for your baby to explore touch and sensation. She will like the feeling of not being hampered by nappies and clothing and should enjoy the sensation of warm water next to her skin. Try tickling her gently, blowing raspberries on her abdomen, and kissing her toes when she is undressed.

THREE TO SIX MONTHS

As your baby grows and her movements become more controlled, she will reach out for things and take them in her hands. Her grip becomes stronger and she will be able to hold a wider variety of items. This means that she will start to experience the difference between things that are light and heavy, soft and hard. Her curiosity will be endless and every object will be a plaything. She may prefer to use her mouth rather than her hands to explore things at this age, so it is important to make sure that she can't get hold of anything which could do her any harm.

Your baby will probably play happily for short periods on her own, but she needs you to encourage her. When you play with your baby get her to do things for herself; allow her to use her hands and eyes to work out what she wants to do with the toy she is holding. It is better to give your child only a few selected items to play with at this age because she won't be able to concentrate on more than one thing at a time. A

stimulating, inviting environment is important for all creative play. Toys that are piled up in a jumble are not as inviting to a child as toys which are laid out for her in an attractive, inviting way.

SIX TO TWELVE MONTHS

Once your baby has learned to support herself sitting up and has started to make her first attempts at moving around, she will want toys that she can manipulate. This is the ideal time to give your child an activity centre with lots of different knobs and handles for her to twist and turn. By around seven or eight

months she will want to find out what things can do and will bang objects on the ground or table to find out if they make a noise or wave them in the air to see what happens. As her manipulative skills develop she will learn that she can use her hands and arms simultaneously and will start to bang things together. She will be able to reach out to you with both arms when she wants to be picked up. It takes a while longer for her to learn how to let go of items she is playing with, but you can encourage her by giving her an object, then holding out your hand and asking for it back. Once she's

A young baby will enjoy being read to from a simple board book and will be interested in touching the pages. She will soon learn how to recognize the book's pictures.

*Your child will often put different things
in her mouth to investigate them.*

can put things back into the container and will spend ages tipping things out and putting them back again. She will try doing this with different objects and may discover that some of them don't fit. As your child plays she will be learning about the nature of the objects, how they behave, and their relative size and shape.

Water play can be introduced now and your baby will enjoy filling and emptying plastic beakers while she is having her bath. Give her toys which have different sizes of holes in them so that she can spend time sprinkling or pouring the water from one container into another.

Once your baby has started to crawl, give her toys that roll and move when they are pushed along so that she can go after them. Later, as she starts taking her weight on her legs, you can encourage her and help her balance with sturdy push-along toys, such as a brick trolley. This will

got the hang of this game she will keep you busy for hours!

As she becomes more mobile, your baby will want to be into everything and her natural curiosity could lead her into danger, so you need to pay constant attention to safety. One of your baby's favourite pastimes will be emptying things out of containers. She will take things out of cupboards with just as much enjoyment as she will empty shapes out of a shape sorter. Once she has emptied a container she will want to examine the contents in great detail and will bang things together and may put them in her mouth before discarding them and moving on to the next object. When she has mastered this she will soon learn that she

A baby walker will help your child to walk and some double as an activity centre.

give her something to hold onto until she feels confident enough to let go and walk unaided.

BOOKS

It is never too early to introduce your baby to books. Start at an early age with brightly coloured rag books that your baby can chew as well as handle, or simple board books. At first she will enjoy these books as objects to be explored but, if you sit her on your knee and talk to her about the pictures in the book, she will soon learn to recognize them. Encourage her involvement by mak-ing the noises of any animals pictured in the books and then getting her to do the same.

Games to play

• "Pat-a-cake, pat-a-cake, baker's man" is a rhyme to which your baby will enjoy clapping. When you get to "prick it and pat it and mark it with ..." use your baby's own initial and then her name when you come to "put in the oven for ...".

• Blowing bubbles using either a made-up solution and a wand or washing-up liquid and your hands.

• "Peek-a-boo": use your hands to cover your face; then later hide and seek: hide objects under a soft cloth for your baby to find.

• Hold your baby's hands securely and rock her gently backwards and forward while singing "Row, row, row the boat ...".

• Sit your baby on your knee facing towards you and hold her firmly by the hands as you bounce her in time to "Humpty Dumpty". When you get to the big fall allow your baby to drop through your knees while hold-ing her firmly.

By just giving your baby one toy at a time to play with, she will be able to concentrate on it more fully.

USEFUL ADDRESSES

There is no need to feel alone during pregnancy or in the months after the birth.
The organizations mentioned below are happy to offer help and support to anyone who contacts them.
Remember to enclose an SAE when writing to them.

ANTE-NATAL AND BIRTH
Active Birth Centre, Bickerton House, 25 Bickerton Road, London N19 5JT.
Tel: 0171-561 9006

Association for Improvements in the Maternity Services (AIMS), 40 Kingswood Avenue, London NW6 6LS.
Tel: 0181-960 5585

Association of Radical Midwives (ARM), 62 Greetby Hill, Ormskirk, Lancs. L39 2DT.
Tel: 01695-572776

BLISS (Information for parents of special-care babies), 17-21 Emerald Street, London WC1N 3QL.
Tel: 0171-831 9393

British Pregnancy Advisory Service (BPAS), Austy Manor, Wootton Wawen, Solihull, West Midlands B95 6BX.
Helpline: 01564-793225

Foresight (The Association for the Promotion of Conceptual Care), 28 The Paddock, Godalming, Surrey GU7 1XD.
Tel/fax: 01483-427839. Contact at least four months prior to planned conception.

Foundation for the Study of Infant Deaths (Cot Death Research & Support), 14 Halkin Street, London SW1X 7DP.
Tel: 0171-235 0965
24-hour helpline: 0171-235 1721

Independent Midwives Association, Nightingale Cottage, Shamblehurst Lane, Botley, Hants. SO32 2BY.
(No phone number, but please send A5 SAE for register of independent midwives)

Maternity Alliance, 15 Britannia Street, London WC1X 9JN.

Tel: 0171-837 1265 (Mon, Tues, Thurs, Fri 9am–1pm. Wed 2pm–5pm)

The Miscarriage Association, c/o Clayton Hospital, Northgate, Wakefield, W. Yorks. WF1 3JS.
Tel: 01924 200799 (answerphone out of office hours)

National Childbirth Trust (NCT), Alexandra House, Oldham Terrace, London W3 6NH.
Tel: 0181-992 8637

Stillbirth and Neonatal Death Society (SANDS), 28 Portland Place, London W1N 4DE.
Tel: 0171-436 7940
Helpline: 0171-436 5881
(10am–5.30pm)

Toxoplasmosis Trust, 61-71 Collier Street, London N1 9BE.
Helpline: 0171-713 0599

WellBeing (Health Research Charity for Women and Babies), 27 Sussex Place, Regent's Park, London NW1 4SP.
Tel: 0171-262 5337

FAMILY LINKS
Gingerbread, 49 Wellington Street, London WC2E 7BN.
Tel: 0171-240 0953

Meet a Mum Association, 14 Willis Road, Croydon, Surrey CR0 2XX.
Tel: 0181-665 0357. Also post-natal depression and general advice.
Helpline: 0181-656 7318.

National Childminding Association 8 Masons Hill, Bromley, Kent BR2 9EY.
Tel: 0181-464 6164

National Council for One Parent Families, 255 Kentish Town Road, London NW5 2LX.
Tel: 0171-267 1361

Working for Childcare, 77 Holloway Road, London N7 8JZ.
Tel: 0171-700 0281

SPECIAL NEEDS
ASBAH (Association for Spina Bifida and Hydrocephalus), 42 Park Road, Peterborough PE1 2UQ.
Tel: 01733 555988

British Diabetic Association, 10 Queen Anne Street, London W1M 0BD.
Tel: 0171-323 1531

British Epilepsy Association, Anstey House, 40 Hanover Square, Leeds LS3 1BE.
Free helpline: 0800 309030

Cystic Fibrosis Trust, Alexandra House, 5 Blyth Road, Bromley, Kent BR1 3RS.
Tel: 0181-464 7211

Down's Syndrome Association, 155 Mitcham Road, London SW17 9PG. Tel: 0181-682 4001

Galactosaemia Support Group, 31 Cotysmore Road, Sutton Coldfield B75 6BJ.
Tel: 0121-378 5143

Mencap (Royal Society for Mentally Handicapped Children and Adults), 123 Golden Lane, London EC1Y 0RT.
Tel: 0171-454 0454

National Asthma Campaign,
Providence House, Providence Place,
London N1 0NT.
Tel: 0171-226 2260
Helpline: 0345 010203
(Mon to Fri 9am–9pm)

National Autistic Society,
276 Willesden Lane, London
NW2 5RB. Tel: 0181-451 1114

National Deaf Children's Society,
15 Dufferin Street, London EC1Y 8PD.
Tel: 0171-250 0123

National Eczema Society,
163 Eversholt Street, London
NW1 1BU.
Tel: 0171-388 4097

**Research Trust for Metabolic
Diseases in Children (RTMDC),**
Golden Gates Lodge, Weston Road,
Crewe CW1 1XN.
Tel: 01270 250221

**Royal National Institute for the
Blind (RNIB),** 224 Great Portland
Street, London W1N 6AA.
Tel: 0171-388 1266

Scope (formerly Spastics Society), 12
Park Crescent, London W1N 4EQ.
Tel: 0171-636 5020

SENSE (National Deaf-Blind and Rubella
Association), 11-13 Clifton Terrace,
Finsbury Park, London N4 3SR.
Tel: 0171-272 7774

Sickle Cell Society, 54 Station Road,
Harlesden, London NW10 4UA.
Tel: 0181-961 7795 (Mon to Fri
9am–5pm)

**Voluntary Council for Handicapped
Children**, 8 Wakley Street, London
EC1V 7QE.
Tel: 0171-843 6000

**FOR NEW PARENTS
Association of Breastfeeding
Mothers**, 26 Holmshaw Close, London

SE26 4TH.
Tel: 0181-778 4769

Association for Post-Natal Illness,
25 Jerdan Place, London SW6 1BE.
Tel: 0171-386 0868
(answerphone out of office hours)

Cry-sis, BM Cry-sis, London WC1N
3XX (Counsellors available between
9am–11pm)
Tel: 0171-404 5011

La Leche League of Great Britain,
PO Box BM 3424, London WC1N
3XX.
Tel: 0171-242 1278. Helps and supports
women who wish to breast-feed. (24-
hour counselling service)

**FAMILY WELFARE
Action for Sick Children**, Argyle
House, 29-31 Euston Road,
London NW1 2SD.
Tel: 0171-833 2041 (Mon to Fri
9am–5pm)

Children's Legal Centre,
The University of Essex, Wivenhoe
Park, Colchester, Essex CO4 3SQ.
Tel: 01206 873820

Citizen's Advice Bureau,
address and telephone number for
your nearest office in your local telephone book.

Compassionate Friends, 53 North
Street, Bristol BS3 1EN.
Helpline: 0117 953 9639 (Mon to Fri
9.30am - 5pm)

Contact-a-Family, 170 Tottenham
Court Road, London W1P OHA.
Tel: 0171-383 3555

Cruse (Bereavement Care),
Cruse House, 126 Sheen Road,
Richmond, Surrey TW9 1UR.
Bereavement line: 0181-332 7227
(Mon to Fri 9.30am–5pm)

Family Planning Association, 27-35
Mortimer Street, London W1N 7RJ.
Tel: 0171-636 7866

Family Welfare Association,
501-505 Kingsland Road, London
E8 4AU.
Tel: 0171-254 6251

**National Association for the Welfare
of Children in Hospital (NAWCH),**
Argyle House, 29-31 Euston Road,
London NW1 2SD.
Tel: 0171-833 2041

**National Childcare
Campaign/Daycare Trust**, 4 Wild
Court, London WC2B 4AU.
Tel: 0171-405 5617

**National Society for the Prevention
of Cruelty to Children (NSPCC),**
National Centre, 42 Curtain Road,
London EC2A 3NH.
Tel: 0800 800 500
(free 24-hour confidential helpline)

Relate (National Marriage Guidance),
Herbert Gray College, Little Church
Street, Rugby, Warks CV21 3AP, or
look in telephone directory under "R"
for Relate or "M" for Marriage Guidance.

SAFTA (Support after termination for
abnormality), 73-75 Charlotte Street,
London W1P 1LB.
Tel: 0171-631 0285

Samaritans,
Tel: 0345 909090 (24-hour confidential
helpline). For local number look in your
telephone directory.

Smokers' Quitline,
Tel: 0171-487 3000

**Twins and Multiple Births
Association (TAMBA)**, PO Box 30,
Little Sutton, South Wirral L66 1TH.
Tel: 0151-348 0020 (Mon to Fri
9am–1pm)

Vegetarian Society,
Parkdale, Dunham Road, Altrincham,
Cheshire WA14 4QG.
Tel: 0161 9280793

GLOSSARY OF PREGNANCY TERMS

ABORTION
The spontaneous or induced delivery of the fetus before the 28th week.

ABRUPTIO PLACENTAE
Part of the placenta peels away from the wall of the uterus in late pregnancy and often results in bleeding.

ALPHA-FETOPROTEIN (AFP)
A protein produced by the fetus which enters the mother's bloodstream. A very high level can indicate neural tube defects of the fetus such as Down's syndrome or spina bifida, but it can also mean that the woman is carrying more than one child.

AMNIOCENTESIS
A small amount of amniotic fluid is taken from the uterus through a needle inserted through the woman's abdomen and tested for chromosomal disorders such as Down's syndrome.

AMNIOTIC FLUID
The fluid surrounding the fetus in the uterus.

AMNIOTIC SAC
The bag of membranes which is filled with amniotic fluid in which the fetus floats during pregnancy.

ANAEMIA
A condition where the level of red corpuscles in the blood is abnormally low, which is treated with iron supplements.

ANALGESICS
Painkilling drugs which do not cause unconsciousness. The analgesics most commonly used during labour are Entonox (a mixture of nitrous oxide and oxygen, known as "gas and air"), pethidine and meptid.

ANTE-NATAL
Before birth.

APGAR SCORE
A simple test to assess the baby's condition after birth.

BEARING DOWN
The pushing movement made by the uterus during the second stage of labour.

BIRTH CANAL
See Vagina.

BLASTOCYST
The early stage of the developing embryo when it becomes a cluster of cells.

BRAXTON HICKS CONTRACTIONS
Contractions of the uterus which occur throughout pregnancy, but may not be felt until the last month or so. They feel like a painless, but sometimes uncomfortable, hardening across the stomach.

BREECH PRESENTATION
The position of a baby when he is bottom down rather than head down in the uterus.

CAESARIAN SECTION
Delivery of the baby through a cut in the abdomen and uterine walls.

CERVIX
The neck of the uterus or womb which is sealed with a plug of mucus during pregnancy. During labour, muscular contractions open up the cervix until it is about 10 cm/4 in wide so that the baby can pass through it into the vagina.

CHLOASMA
Slight discoloration of the skin, usually on the face, which occurs during pregnancy and disappears within weeks of the birth.

CHORIONIC VILLUS SAMPLING
A screening test for genetic handicap which can be done as early as 11 weeks. Cells are taken from the tissue that surrounds the fetus and are then analysed.

COLOSTRUM
A fluid that the breasts produce during pregnancy and immediately after the birth. It is full of nutrients and contains antibodies which will protect the baby from some infections.

CONCEPTION
The fertilization of the egg by the sperm and its implantation in the wall of the uterus.

CONGENITAL ABNORMALITIES
An abnormality or deformity that exists from birth. It is caused by a damaged gene or the effect of some diseases during pregnancy.

CONTRACTIONS
Regular tightening of the muscles of the uterus as they work to dilate the cervix and push the baby down the birth canal.

CROWNING
The moment when the crown of the baby's head appears in the vagina.

DILATION
The gradual opening of the cervix during labour.

DOPPLER
A method of using ultrasound vibrations to listen to the fetal heart.

ECTOPIC PREGNANCY
A pregnancy which develops outside the uterus, usually in the Fallopian tube.

EDD
Estimated date of delivery.

ELECTIVE INDUCTION
Induction done for convenience rather than for medical reasons.

ELECTRONIC FETAL MONITORING
The continuous monitoring of the fetal heart.

EMBRYO
The name of the developing organism in

pregnancy from about the 10th day after fertilization until the 12th week of pregnancy when it becomes known as a fetus.

ENGAGED
The baby's head is engaged when it drops down deep in the pelvic cavity so that the widest part is through the mother's pelvic brim. Another term for this is "lightening". Most babies are born head first and will have engaged before labour begins.

ENGORGEMENT
The breasts become congested with milk if long periods are left between feeds which results in painful engorgement.

ENTONOX
Gas and oxygen, a short-term analgesic, which can be inhaled during labour.

EPIDURAL
An anaesthetic which is injected into the fluid surrounding the spinal cord at the base of the spine to relieve pain but leave the mother fully conscious.

EPISIOTOMY
A small cut made in the perineum to enlarge the vagina if there is a risk of tearing when the baby's head is about to be born.

FALLOPIAN TUBES
Two narrow tubes about 10 cm/4 in long which lead from the ovaries to the uterus.

FETUS
The developing baby from the end of the embryonic stage at about the 12th week of pregnancy, until the date of delivery.

FH
Fetal heart.

FMF
Fetal movement felt.

FOLIC ACID
A form of vitamin B which is important for the healthy development of the embryo. A daily supplement of 0.4mg should be taken before becoming pregnant and then until the 12th week of pregnancy.

FONTANELLES
The soft spots between the unjoined sections of the skull of the baby.

FORCEPS
An instrument sometimes used to assist the baby out of the birth canal.

FOREMILK
The first breast milk the baby gets when he begins to suck which satisfies his thirst before the hind milk comes through.

FUNDUS
The top of the uterus.

GAS AND AIR
See Entonox.

GENETIC COUNSELLING
Advice on the detection and risk of recurrence of inherited disorders.

GESTATION
The length of time between conception and delivery (usually around 40 weeks).

GP UNIT
A special unit, usually in a hospital, where a pregnant woman gives birth under the care of her GP and midwife.

HAEMOGLOBIN (HB)
The pigment that gives blood its red colour and contains iron and stores oxygen.

HAEMORRHAGE
Excessive bleeding.

HAEMORRHOIDS (PILES)
A form of varicose veins around the anus.

HINDMILK
The calorie-rich breast milk that follows the foremilk during feed.

HORMONE
A chemical produced by the body to stimulate organs within the body, particularly those to do with growth and reproduction.

HUMAN CHORIONIC GONADOTROPHIN (HCG)
A hormone produced early in pregnancy by the developing placenta. Its presence in the urine is used to confirm pregnancy.

IMPLANTATION
The embedding of the fertilized egg in the wall of the uterus.

INCOMPETENT CERVIX
A weakened cervix that is unable to hold the fetus in the uterus for the full nine months. Sometimes a cause of late miscarriage or premature birth.

INDUCTION
The process of artificially starting off labour.

INTRAVENOUS DRIP
The infusion of fluids directly into the bloodstream through a fine tube into a vein.

JAUNDICE
Neonatal jaundice often occurs in newborn babies because of the inability of the liver to successfully break down an excess of red blood cells.

LABOUR
The process of childbirth.

LANUGO
A very fine covering of hair which appears all over the fetus during late pregnancy.

LIE
The position of the fetus in the uterus.

LIGHTENING
See Engaged.

LINEA NIGRA
A line of dark pigmentation which appears down the centre of the abdomen on some women during pregnancy.

LOCHIA
Post-natal vaginal discharge.

MECONIUM
The green matter passed from the baby's bowels during the first days after birth. Meconium in the amniotic fluid before delivery is usually a sign of fetal distress.

MISCARRIAGE
The loss of a baby before 24 weeks gestation.

MONITOR
Machine or instrument to measure the baby's heartbeat and breathing.

MOULDING
The shaping of the bones of the baby's skull as it passes through the birth canal.

MUCUS
A sticky secretion.

NAD
A medical term often used on medical records meaning "nothing abnormal detected".

NEURAL TUBE DEFECT
Development defect of the brain and/or spinal cord.

OBSTETRICIAN
Medical specialist in pregnancy and childbirth.

OEDEMA
Swelling caused by fluid retention.

OVARY
Female organ responsible for production of sex hormones and eggs (ova).

OVULATION
The production of a ripe egg by the ovary, usually on a monthly basis.

PALPATION
Manual examination of the uterus through the wall of the abdomen.

PELVIC FLOOR
The muscles which support the bladder and the uterus.

PERINATAL
Period from before delivery until seven days after the birth.

PERINEUM
The area between the opening of the vagina and the anus.

PETHIDINE
A drug given during labour for pain relief and relaxation.

PLACENTA
Also known as "afterbirth", this is the fetus's life-support system which is attached to one side of the wall of the uterus and to the baby by means of the umbilical cord. All the fetus's nourishment passes from the mother through the placenta while the fetus's waste products pass out through it.

PREMATURE OR PRETERM
A baby born before the 37th week.

PRESENTATION
The position of the fetus in the uterus before and during the delivery.

PRIMIGRAVIDA
A woman who is having her first baby.

PROSTAGLANDIN
A hormone which stimulates the onset of labour contractions.

QUICKENING
The first movements of the fetus in the uterus.

ROOTING
The baby's instinctive searching for the mother's nipple.

RUBELLA (GERMAN MEASLES)
A virus which can be dangerous if caught during the first three months of pregnancy.

SCAN
A way of screening the fetus in the uterus by bouncing high-frequency sound waves off it which build up a picture.

SHARED CARE
Ante-natal care shared between a GP and a hospital consultant.

SHOW
A vaginal discharge of blood-stained mucus that occurs before or during labour.

STILLBIRTH
The delivery of a baby who has already died in the uterus after 28 weeks of pregnancy.

STRETCH MARKS
Silvery lines that may appear where the skin has been stretched during pregnancy.

TERM
The end of pregnancy – around 40 weeks from the date of conception.

TERMINATION
An artificially induced abortion before the end of 28th week of pregnancy.

TOXOPLASMOSIS
A parasitic disease spread by cat faeces that can cause blindness in a baby.

TRIMESTER
Pregnancy is divided into three trimesters, each making up one third of pregnancy.

UMBILICAL CORD
The cord connecting the fetus to the placenta.

UTERUS (WOMB)
The hollow muscular organ in which the fertile egg becomes embedded.

VACUUM EXTRACTOR (VENTOUSE)
An instrument sometimes used to pull the baby out of the vagina.

VAGINA
The birth canal through which the baby makes its way from the uterus.

INDEX

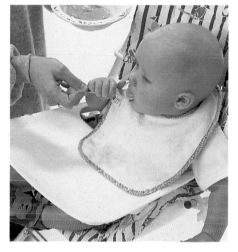